# BLUE SKIES, BLACK WINGS

# BLUE SKIES, BLACK WINGS

## African American Pioneers of Aviation

SAMUEL L. BROADNAX

Foreword by Alan M. Osur

Westport, Connecticut
London

Library of Congress Cataloging-in-Publication Data

Broadnax, Samuel L.
    Blue skies, black wings : African American pioneers of
aviation / Samuel L. Broadnax; foreword by Alan M. Osur.
        p. cm.
    Includes bibliographical references and index.
    ISBN 0–275–99195–4 (alk. paper)
    1. African American air pilots—Biography. 2. Air pilots—United States—Biography.
    3. Aeronautics—United States—History. 4. United States—Race relations.
    5. African Americans—History. I. Title.
    TL539.B75   2007
    629.13092′396073—dc22        2006037774

British Library Cataloguing in Publication Data is available.

Library of Congress Catalog Card Number: 2006037774
ISBN-10: 0–275–99195–4
ISBN-13: 978–0–275–99195–1

First published in 2007

Praeger Publishers, 88 Post Road West, Westport, CT 06881
An imprint of Greenwood Publishing Group, Inc.
www.praeger.com

Printed in the United States of America

∞™

The paper used in this book complies with the
Permanent Paper Standard issued by the National
Information Standards Organization (Z39.48-1984).

10 9 8 7 6 5 4 3 2 1

This book is dedicated to the Primary instructors at Tuskegee's Moton Field in World War II, the 41 African-American men who gave all they were allowed. These determined pilots were earlier denied entrance into the U.S. Army Air Corps. They turned that demeaning exclusion of No, upside down and added their exclamation to make "No"—ON! These persevering warriors physically and mentally trained as many black aviation cadets as possible to fill the positions in which they themselves had hoped to serve. The training by these highly skilled and committed airmen was superior.

This work is also dedicated to the thousands of specialists and technicians who maintained and serviced the many types of aircraft, trainers as well as combat, to keep our pilots in the air at home and abroad.

# Contents

# Foreword

Thirty years ago one could opine that the history of the Tuskegee Airmen and indeed the whole African-American experience during World War II was yet to be explored to its fullest. Today, numerous monographs have given us a solid picture of the endeavors, trials, tribulations, and triumphs of that experience. To complete this story, the monographs have been supplemented by a wide array of personal accounts that allow us to go beyond the facts and analysis to get a first hand account of what it was like to serve in the U.S. military during World War II.

Sam Broadnax adds to that literature by incorporating his own aviation experience from 1943 through 1945 with that of much of black aviation history through World War II. Born in Kansas and raised in California, he was exposed to the world of flight and took to it very quickly. Serving in the war was his obligation as a citizen, but Sam saw an opportunity to join the Army Air Forces and to become part of the Tuskegee experience.

Tuskegee, the Institute and the Air Base, was the pride of the black community, but Sam found out rather quickly that he would be serving against fascism while living and working within segregation. The ever-present segregation put additional strain on those going through the Tuskegee training, as if going through flight school did not contain enough stress.

Sam Broadnax's personal description weaves the story of blacks in aviation with what he saw and thus gives his account an important knowledge and familiarity of the topic, one that I appreciate and those of you reading this will also appreciate.

Dr. Alan M. Osur, Major, USAF (retired)

# Preface

The majority of America has long wrestled with the concept and belief that somehow the categorical racial differences exhibited by those of color firmly indicate a genetic inferiority. This flawed idea and misconception has been embraced and passed down through the centuries of this country's existence.

As aviation and the act of flying began generating strong interest in America blacks were summarily turned away or blocked from any aspirations of learning the then sophisticated art of flying. It did not matter that those persons were ready and able to pay for instructions. He or she was not wanted. Flying was considered such an excitingly new and dangerous adventure that only the very best could be granted the rights of admission. Certainly a lineage leading back to former slaves could not be considered the best. To even hint that the descendants of slaves would occupy the same spectacular air space would taint and tarnish a highly exclusive avenue that few could tread.

The official end of slavery in the United States came with the 1865 ratification of the Thirteenth Amendment. The passing of that historically important amendment freeing the thousands of enslaved humans did nothing to ameliorate or change the way they were regarded or treated. Most of those newly freed beings were illiterate because the useful tools of reading and writing had been forcefully withheld from them. Therefore the idea of lower intelligence bloomed, and the mark of inferiority was perpetuated and carried forward as a truth. The mere idea that the offspring of those unable to read or write might match the turns, the glides, and the soaring in the sky with those of known superiority was patently unthinkable.

Tempting offers of gold (cash) could not remove this barricade, a barrier of racial contempt. Much as in earlier feudal days when the male offspring of a cobbler or a miller could only look forward to those separate occupations so it was in America—the door to aviation was tightly shut for African-Americans. There was just too much glitter, too much sparkling prestige, and perceived power attached to flying to permit inferiors to bask in the same golden glory. Such farfetched thoughts would diminish and make a mockery of this newly found and budding realm.

This was the prevailing attitude of majority America toward its black citizens, a backward attitude of dedicated superiority.

Overlooked, however, was another mighty nation whose earlier and lengthy history had included tolerance with disregard to ancestry. France openly offered flying training to anyone who had the means of payment. France, at the time, was the only nation that offered a worldwide recognized license. It was through this open outlet that black Americans began to singly emerge with the coveted wings their own country jealously denied them. When the Army Air Corps excluded blacks from even the most subservient of roles it was not from the espoused belief that any admitted would fail to reach the high standards demanded by flying; it was just the opposite. It was the latent fear that they would succeed and in so doing forever dispel the promoted notions of racial inferiority. Still it required the intensity of thousands of Tuskegee Airmen to raise the torches and illuminate the truth.

# Abbreviations

| | |
|---|---|
| AAF | Army Air Forces |
| AF | Air Force |
| AR | Army Regulation |
| AWC | Army War College |
| AWOL | Absent Without Leave |
| CAA | Civil Aeronautics Authority |
| CO | Commanding Officer |
| CPTP | Civilian Pilot Training Program |
| CTD | College Training Detachment |
| EFTC | Eastern Flying Training Command |
| EO | Executive Order |
| ETO | European Theatre of Operations |
| FW-190 | Focke-Wolfe 190 (German fighter plane) |
| MAFB | Maxwell Air Force Base |
| ME-109 | Messerschmitt 109 (German fighter plane) |
| ME-262 | Messerschmitt 262 (German jet-powered fighter plane) |
| MOS | Military Occupational Specialty |
| MP | Military Police |
| MTO | Mediterranean Theatre of Operations |
| NAACP | National Association for the Advancement of Colored People |
| NASA | National Aeronautics and Space Administration |
| NCO | Noncommissioned Officer |
| OCS | Officer Candidate School |
| PL | Public Law |

PX          Post Exchange
SEACTC      Southeast Air Corps Training Command
TAAF        Tuskegee Army Air Field
TDY         Temporary Duty
WD          War Department
WPA         Works Progress Administration
WWI         World War I
WWII        World War II

# CHAPTER 1

# The Early Days

In the beginning, only carnivorous pterodactyls and some species of insects could perform the spectacular airborne feat of flying. Man's puny musculature and high body weight, obviously not designed for such levitated activity, prevented any imitations of other free flying creatures. This inability of man to lift himself from the ground or sail from the vantage point of a perch had nothing to do with skin color, stature, or geographical location. In other words he could not do it, whether at the North Pole or at the Equator. Weight lifters can hoist hundreds of pounds but not one can flap up one inch in sustained flight. They can pull heavy trucks and even trains but natural physical flight escapes man. All Homo sapien species began and remain groundbound without some kind of artificial assistance to do otherwise. Still, man's earliest recorded flight efforts arise in mythology in the writing of celebrated Latin poet Ovid who told of the daring aerial escape of Daedalus and his son Icarus. After designing the Labyrinth to contain the Minotaur, the half-man, half-bull monster, inventor-genius Daedalus incurred the wrath of King Minos for revealing how to get out of the endless maze. For that unforgivable infraction, Minos angrily threw Daedalus and his son Icarus into the Labyrinth. But the crafty genius quickly came up with a daring escape plan by devising wings of leather held in place by wax. The two, father and son, soared to freedom with ease but Icarus, as youngsters so often do, ignored his father's warning not to fly too high as the sun would melt the wax holding the feathers. As recorded, Icarus fell into the sea and drowned on the flight from Crete to Sicily.[1] It can also now be stated that Icarus became man's first flight fatality due to pilot error.

The Montgolfier brothers took to the air in a hot air balloon in June 1783, the first successful recorded attempt that was witnessed by a crowd of French spectators. Their flight lasted ten minutes and reached an altitude of approximately three thousand feet.[2] The man who came to be known as the master of the balloon, a less remembered Brazilian, Alberto Santos-Dumont, was the first to fly a controllable motorized balloon air craft around the Eiffel Tower in October 1901. A considerable controversy brewed about who was the first to fly a heavier than air aircraft. Santos-Dumont adherents say it was the little Brazilian in October 1905. They maintain that the widely accepted, 12-second historic jaunt by Orville and Wilber Wright in South Carolina in 1903, was undocumented and witnessed by only five persons. They point out that Santos-Dumont's flight was documented and witnessed by a thousand spectators. The Santos-Dumont side also quickly points out that the prestigious Smithsonian refused to accept the Wright Brothers' accomplishment for years. Santos-Dumont supporters say that all the other early, would-be fliers, including the famed Louis Bleriot, openly publicized their attempts, while that of the Wright Brothers was shrouded in secrecy.[3] Santos-Dumont would eventually design a helicopter which was never built.

The Wright Brothers unquestionably accomplished sustained flight in a motor driven aircraft and whether they or Santos-Dumont had first bragging rights seems unimportant at this late date. There is no argument that the early flying machines built by the Wright Brothers were better designed than the box-kite type craft flown by Santos-Dumont. The Wrights certainly had learned a great deal from Otto Lilienthal, the famed German aeronautical engineer. Lilienthal made more than 2,000 flights in gliders he designed, before a fatal injury on his last flight in 1896.[4]

This obsession and compulsion to take to the air using whatever means available can possibly be gleaned from the old expression "free as a bird." But there is also the heady exhilaration of having control over the power to bend earth's gravitational components and soar on high like the majestic eagle.

The "Experience" of Tuskegee began for me at about the age of six when my father and his friend drove out to an airfield, which must have been a wide, level portion of some farmer's unplanted pasture, on the outskirts of Topeka, Kansas. I must make note here to refer to Tuskegee as the "Experience" because there was another infamous program called the "Tuskegee Experiment" or more aptly called the "Tuskegee Study." (This was a U.S. Public Health Service study of 400 syphilis-infected illiterate black sharecroppers. The Health Service withheld all treatment of the men to study the effects of untreated syphilis in black men. The men were never informed that they were being used as human guinea pigs.)[5] I remember the airplane, a biplane painted either red or a rusty brown color, the first I can ever remember seeing. After talking with the pilot, my father returned and laughingly told his friend that the pilot had refused to take me up. My child's body was too small to stay under the safety belt. I remember the car almost as well as the airplane, because I do not recall being in one before. A big black touring sedan with a top and four doors; it was all open where there would normally have been windows in a modern vehicle. Spare tires rested on both fenders, each one covered with a shiny band. The friend and I waited in the car. I alone sat in the back seat while the conversation had taken place. The whole matter of going flying had all been my father's decision; I had not been asked or told why we were there.

Only in later life did I try to piece together the reasoning that took us to a land-wherever-you-can field for the purpose of my getting an aerial ride. I think it goes back to a previous event during a hot summer day in Kansas. I had followed a group of older boys to their favorite swimming hole. Seeing them strip down to their underwear and jump with laughter and wild abandon into the inviting coolness of that pool surrounded by shady green trees was all I needed. I had never swam before and had only faced that much water in the bath tub. In those days, as far as I knew, underclothes were of two types, the kind with a buttoned flap in the back and the other style that overlapped like a curtain. I jumped in and immediately went to the bottom. I remember seeing some grey fish swimming lazily along close to the bottom. That is my last recollection until I woke up being carried in a boy's arms near the front of our home. The group I had surreptitiously followed happened to be Boy Scouts and thankfully they had seen me plunge like a rock to the bottom. My father took me into the house after thanking my rescuer for saving me. Perhaps then, there was a glimmer that if I had enough gall to jump unhesitatingly into a deep pond without the faintest idea of how to swim, then the next daredevil act should be to fly. The exact truth shall forever be a mystery because my father never did explain why I alone was to go up in that red airplane. I should say now that my father, for as long as he lived, was always "Poppa," not "Dad," "Daddy," or "Father," but "Poppa."

There is no further distinct remembrance of airplanes until five years later when my father's ministerial assignment took us to Marysville, California. It must have been the sprouting of the earlier planted seed that sparked my interest in building model airplanes. They were not really designed to fly, those little ten-cent model kits, but I did not know that at the time. No matter how well I painstakingly constructed the little craft, none of them would fly even with the rubber band tightly wound to the dangerous point of the model collapsing. As a last resort I climbed atop the neighbor's garage roof and launched my handiwork from there, but to no avail; they still flew little better than rocks being dropped from the same height.

I painstakingly cut all the parts of those little kits from printed sheets of balsa wood using a razor blade. Usually that was fairly easy, except on one occasion; while attempting to build a model, two of my older brothers' friends came into the room to see my model building. In the process one of them stole some of the cut pieces while his coconspirator kept me engaged and looking the other way. Although I looked and searched, I never found the missing pieces and only months later realized what had happened and understood that I had not just carelessly lost those precious parts. I had been the innocent butt of a crank joke.

Not until I had grown proficient in model building, and over a span of months, having saved the monumental sum of ten dollars to purchase a real model gas engine, did the planes begin to fly. The first engine purchased in 1939, called a Phantom P-30, took two days and two very sore fingers on my right hand to run. I ended up with burned fin marks on my mouth when I had, with a sudden burst of elated joy, jubilance, and forgetfulness, kissed the hot engine after it had run all the gas-oil mixture from its tank. It did not matter that my cranking fingers were sore and my lips had first degree burns, I had a real running gas engine! Before too long, by taking in more yard work from the neighbors, I saved enough to buy three more engines, each one successively larger and more powerful than the last. I began to breathe, eat, think, and dream airplanes.

My father's final assignment took us to Oroville, California, where my adolescent pinfeathers began to sprout in a completely rural setting. Before long, I joined the Boy Scouts, Troop 29, the only Boy Scouts in that tiny farming community. Scouting taught me hiking, camping, and a host of useful skills such as recognizing poison oak and poison sumac. That is when I discovered that I had immunity to poison oak, my only symptoms being a slight tingling in the wrist area. But many of my troop mates required medical attention and those who made the serious mistake of scratching in the wrong places suffered miserably. At the heart of scouting, with the motto of "Be Prepared," was the earning of merit badges for advancement.

Oroville itself became a site of general learning that evolved in stages. A well-remembered example came from the simple olive tree, which abounds in that area. The idea of seeing gigantic black olives glistening so succulently on the tree, awaiting innocent fingers to pluck them for an expected tasty delight, brought a sudden and bitter awakening. No matter how dark and appealing this delicious fruit may be, it cannot be consumed without first being cured. Cherries, apples, figs, and plums are all as they appear. They are tasty and delicious straight from the tree, but not the olive; its attractiveness is heinously deceptive. It tantalizes and invites you to try it without a hint of the lurking bitter peril.

During this learning period, in the summer of 1940, daredevil acrobatic pilot Tex Rankin came to the outskirts of the town; Oroville's population at the time was around 9,000. If the flying bug had not already bitten me then, the infection became complete after watching Rankin go through his precision maneuvers. One of these daredevil moves included a slow roll close enough to the ground to pick up a mounded handkerchief, one with each wingtip, as he made a full roll in front of the crowd. Later, among other delights, he made smoke-outlined square loops.

Just after I entered high school, a carnival came to town and one of the shows featured a wingless airplane with an electric powered propeller suspended on a wishbone type affair that you could control to point straight up, spin around, and do almost everything a real airplane could do except that it remained suspended in that wishbone instead of having wings. Needless to say, I spent all of my carnival money on that one ride forgetting, the octopus, the Ferris wheel, or any other ride.

Some time after Pearl Harbor, I happened to notice in the *Pittsburgh Courier*, the newspaper that I sold, that a friend of the family, Herman Lawson, had graduated from Tuskegee, Alabama as a pursuit pilot and had joined the 99th Pursuit Squadron. The 99th was the first all-black U.S. military fighter group ever created. Now at age 17, I decided right then and there that I wanted to become not just a pilot but a pursuit pilot and help shoot down German ME-109s and FW-190s. In order to enlist, I had to take a bus from Oroville to the town of Chico, 20 miles away, which had an enlistment office in the post office and an Army Air Corps Field some six or seven miles out of town. The roundtrip bus fare left me with just 25 cents and no scheduled bus from town out to the airfield. Without a choice it meant putting shoe leather to the asphalt. Roller skates would have been a welcome alternative means of transportation that day.

Now in the middle of my junior year, I learned that aviation cadet candidates had to possess either a college degree or pass a written examination. The minimum qualification for pilots had been altered to allow entry into the examination category. I passed the exam but failed, in my excitement, to pass the physical because of high blood pressure. To allow me another chance, the good sergeant administering the physical had me lie down for 15 minutes to calm my excited nerves. The wait only served to cause my thoughts to go racing ahead like a runaway train. As a last resort the sergeant suggested I consult the family doctor. When I did, the doctor declared that there was nothing wrong with my blood pressure. After all, I participated in sports the year round, football, basketball, boxing, and track.

On the next trip to Chico I passed the physical with flying colors. The Base Adjutant, a Captain Howard, II, resplendent in his shiny brown boots and Sam Brown belt, asked me how I knew that the Air Corps was training colored men. I proudly pointed out that Lieutenant Herman Lawson, a family friend, had just graduated. Captain Howard smiled and wished me good luck. I had enlisted at the tender age of 17 with a notarized parental letter of consent.

Two months passed before I received a letter from the Army Air Corps telling me that I had been accepted as a candidate for Aviation Cadet and I would receive another notice some time after my eighteenth birthday telling me when and where to report for duty.

I turned 18 at the beginning of my senior year and our varsity football team had picked up where it stopped the previous year, beating every team we faced. As fate or providence would have it, in the middle of our game schedule, notice came to me to report to the Presidio of Monterey, on the central coast of California, for induction. I was sad at missing the final games but vivid thoughts of becoming a pursuit pilot jubilantly pushed all negative feelings far into the background. I was going to be a pursuit pilot! Little did I know then of the many obstacles, hurdles, hostilities, and bare, unconcealed hatred that would rip and tear me along the way.

Within three days I, with duffel bag, boarded a train headed for a processing center at Keesler Field in Biloxi, Mississippi and the beginning of what would be the most important phase of my entire young life, an abrupt and rude introduction to the treatment of blacks in the Deep South. Obviously, there was discrimination and prejudice in Marysville and in Oroville but in my youthful naiveté, I had neither seen nor felt it.

To understand the creation of a "Tuskegee Experience" necessitates going back in time, back to late August 1619, with the selling of the first black slaves near the crude wooden docks in Virginia, the first established colonial settlement of the young English-American colonies. Either John Rolfe, early tobacco grower and widower of the famed Indian princess Pocahontas, or Virginia governor George Yeardley, appears to have been the first purchaser of black slaves. The first recorder of Virginia, colonist Rolfe noted, "...came a Dutch man of war that sold us twenty negroes."[6] That Dutch man of war, named the White Lion, had pirated the slaves from a Portuguese slave ship, the Sao Joao Bautista, off the coast of Mexico. The captain of the Dutch ship had banded with the Treasurer, a ship out of Jamestown, to do a little profit-sharing pirating. The Treasurer, commanded by Daniel Elfrith, arrived at Jamestown a few days later with "30 odd" slaves to sell for rations but was turned down. Although there may be evidence indicating that this very first group of Africans was not forced by their owners into the slave role, they were certainly bought as slaves in exchange for food. It is recorded that some Africans did manage to eventually win their freedom as early as 1641. In fact one, who took the name of Anthony Johnson, became a prosperous farmer with 250 acres and owned slaves himself. Because of the paucity of early records, no exact date can be fixed for the beginning of slavery in America, but it remains quite clear that this first 1619 sale of Africans became the rough path that all too soon grew into a broad highway of slavery.

One fact that should be pointed out to those who insist that these first Africans were not slaves is that, five years later when the colonists counted noses, all the white indentured servants were listed by both first and last names, ages, and dates of arrival. The only entry for the Africans was a first name or none at all, that entry being "one woman" or "two negors."[7]

That was the same kind of notational record keeping used for merchandise or nonhuman cargo.

Early in the nineteenth century, the northern states stopped their practice of slavery, but for the South, the system of slavery lay at the very heart and foundation of its agricultural existence. In most slave states, if not all, it was forbidden and a felony to teach slaves either to read or write. Slave owners found it much easier to control their chattel property, which included slaves, if they kept that human property unlearned and docile. Whenever a rebellious slave surfaced, and a number did, cruel lessons could often be taught with whips, knotted ropes, pistols, and hangman's nooses as examples showing the rest what they had better not do. This outlines the very early and primitive lessons of teaching the black man "his place" in America. It also established the mental posture and attitude toward blacks that would continue long after they were freed.

For the owner, slaves served as little more than beasts of burden much as his horses and oxen, and he, or his overseer, drove them for the maximum output of his crops. Interest in the welfare of slaves revolved strictly around economics not humanitarianism, because, in the first place, they were regarded as only part human, except when some fetching female happened to catch the eye of the master.

Indeed, slavery goes far back to the time when tribes of early man fought and conquered each other. The earliest records indicate that as far back as ancient Greece and the Roman Empire, those who had been conquered and made slaves had certain rights and could, by payment, manumission, or other means, obtain freedom and status within both of those powerful societies. Islamic countries used slaves turned into eunuchs to guard the harems of sultans and others of high ranking. All nations who at some time dominated the high seas such as England, France, Spain, Portugal, and Belgium, conducted slavery. Except for Belgium, under King Leopold, and a growing United States, they all moved to abolish slavery beginning in the eighteenth century, for humanitarian and economic reasons.[8]

In America, the Emancipation Proclamation abolishing slavery in the southern states became effective January 1, 1863, more than 240 years after the buying, selling, and trading of human beings in the American colonies had begun. An official end to slavery came when 34 states ratified the Thirteenth Amendment on December 18, 1865. Ancient Greece, mighty Rome, and all the other slave trading empires, at some point, assimilated freed slaves, but America, founded by those seeking some form of freedom themselves, steadfastly refused such a naturally following act. Human partiality continues to be a major factor in American race relations today. It remained for noted Swedish sociologist Gunnar Myrdal to uncover the truth in his highly acclaimed study of the American race problem, "An American Dilemma." The study exposed the tacit falsehoods and the blatant lies perpetuated about Negroes and he underlined the reasons for them.

In his study, Dr. Myrdal concluded that the underlying basis for segregation arose from the fear of crossbreeding between blacks and whites, an idea completely intolerable, because, to whites, blacks were inferior and crossbreeding was a dire threat to white racial purity. Perhaps the most crucial factor pointed out by Dr. Myrdal's study is the physical appearance of the American Negro in relation to his white counterpart. The high profile conditions of skin color, hair texture, generally wider noses and thicker lips, all served to reinforce the illogically formed conclusions already fixed in the minds of white people. Because Negroes looked different they really must be different, since from slavery they had been classified as servile, culturally backward, and cursed with low intelligence.

In another aspect of exposing the inner working of the white man's thinking at the time, Myrdal stated that there was an inner feeling, a kind of "mystical feeling" that had no logical or scientific basis, of the Negro's inferiority. A mystical feeling deep within the white man's psyche held this thought as true. And again, Myrdal explained, "It becomes understandable and 'natural' on a deeper magical plane of reasoning that the Negro is believed to be stupid, immoral, diseased, lazy, incompetent, and *dangerous*-dangerous to the white man's virtue and social order."[9]

Early so-called scientific studies that purported to establish proof of the Negro's difference and inferiority to the white man carried over into the twentieth century. One of the most shameful efforts to deliberately create a false truth came to light in 1906. Robert B. Bean, a student of Professor Franklin P. Mall in Mall's Johns Hopkins laboratory, came up with a finding that the skulls of Negroes were smaller than white men's, and he found that the brains were less convoluted which meant less intelligence. After Bean published his findings, Mall himself repeated the same measurements on many of the same cadavers that Bean had used. Mall, professor of anatomy at John Hopkins from 1893 to 1917, found that Bean had not only fully distorted his measurements and his findings, he also had used such a small sample number as to be grossly inadequate.[10]

Thirty years later, following the 1936 Olympic Games, when sprinter Jesse Owens had run the heralded superiority of Aryanism out of the Berlin stadium, attempts were made to show that Negroes had a physical advantage as the reason for their athletic successes. It was put forth that Negroes had longer heel bones than whites and that gave them greater leverage and an increase in driving power. Dr. W. Montague Cobb investigated the facts and found Jesse Owens' calf muscle had a very long belly, thought to be a white characteristic, and that of Frank Wycoff, the white coholder of the 100-yard world record, correspondingly short, a so-called Negro characteristic.[11]

Owens was not the only Negro to bring home the gold from the 1936 Olympics. Although overshadowed by the cluster garnered by his teammate, Archie Williams took the gold medal in the 400 meters. He would also later become a flight instructor at Tuskegee. There for the whole world to see were the superior athletic accomplishments of two Negroes, considered inferior by the very country for which they competed. Ironically, those so-called inferior beings competed against the world's best and won. We know now that at the same time athletes from around the world competed against each other, massive preparations were underway for the world's mightiest conflict, World War Two (WWII). The achievements of Owens and Williams are presented here as a marker because of the precedents before and after their record-setting victories.

The ill-fated destiny of Germany began its calamitous journey when Adolph Hitler became chancellor on January 30, 1933, and then assumed the presidency with the death of Paul Von Hindenburg in August 1934. Hitler had a genocidal game plan whose linchpin, in the promotion of nationalism, was to blame all of Germany's woes on the Jews and he tactfully set out to destroy Germany's designated enemy, the Jews. While German military weapons were being field tested in the Spanish Civil War, the man with the funny mustache began making his first strategic moves.

England, France, and all the other nations, later to be called the Allies, stood by, doing nothing when, in 1938, Hitler's militant minions annexed Austria. In fact, England, France, Italy, and Germany signed the Munich Agreement in September of the same year. These allies failed to move even after Hitler continued his early gambit for world domination by next annexing Czechoslovakia in March 1939 and then announcing what he planned to do after that.

Not until September 1, 1939, when German troops smashed Poland with the world's first blitzkrieg in a matter of three weeks did England and France declare war on Germany under a pledge of support to Poland. France, relying on its unfinished and so-called impregnable concrete Maginot Line fortification, suffered the same fate as Poland. Hitler then turned his attention to England. In the meantime, to keep his backsides—the Eastern front—secure, Hitler signed a treaty with Stalin of Russia and handed over a nice slice of Poland as bait while he readied the next mastermind move.

All through 1938 and up until December 7, 1941, the United States had hidden behind a series of Neutrality agreements while at the same time sending materials and supplies to open allied countries. Only after the bombing of Peal Harbor did the United States declare war on Japan and its axis mates. All along it had never really been a matter of "if" but only one of "when" the United States would be forced to enter the soon-to-be global conflict. To that end, President Franklin Delano Roosevelt had envisioned an air force of 50,000 planes and to fuel that dream with men, the Civilian Pilot Training Program (CPTP) was enacted in June 1939 to create a pool of pilots for those thousands of airplanes.

From its inception, the Air Corps moved straight to center stage as the Army's newest and most elite division. They wanted only the cream of the cream in this most aristocratic unit. Featuring the trailing white silk scarf draped around the neck, highly polished boots, and the long-stemmed Prince Albert pipe, the Air Corps stood out as the ultimate branch of the Army. This was the day of the magnificent men in their flying machines, the period that promoted the spectacular aura of soaring on high with the eagles and the seeming thought of invincibility created by one of man's most daring endeavors.

This high aura and this elitist attitude, prompted the commanding officers of the Air Corps to see that no Negroes were admitted in any capacity. It must be remembered that those in command were themselves brought up in a society that then held Negroes in contemptuous low esteem. To support its stand of exclusion, the Air Corps drew heavily upon the findings of the Army War College (AWC), especially two of the ten or so studies produced between 1925 and 1937. One typical study of the AWC, taken from the memo of 1925, contained a report titled "The Use of Negro Manpower in War." This study began with a statement that regarded the Negro as a subspecies of the human family. It further espoused that Negro men instinctively believed they were inferior to white men. Blacks were considered fair laborers but inferior as technicians and fighters. The study also stated that if any blacks scored well on any particular intelligence test, it only happened because those who did so had a heavy strain of white blood.

The 1925 report further concluded that blacks were deeply superstitious and filled with a common abundance of moral and character weaknesses. "Petty thieving, lying and promiscuity are much more common among negroes than among whites."[12] And then a bottom-line bombshell, "In physical courage it must be admitted that the American negro falls well back of the white man and possibly behind all other races."[13]

The AWC did admit that the Negro was indeed a citizen of the United States and entitled to all the obligations of citizenship, but it remained convinced that no Negro officer should ever command a white officer, because it believed Negro officers lacked courage and the mental capacity to command.

The officers and researchers who put those horrendous AWC studies together attempted yet another contrived source to bolster and sustain false conclusions. They used the results of intelligence testing performed by civilian psychologists in the effort to create for the War Department the tools to classify military personnel based on their scores. These tests did not include adjustments for such variables that could influence scores such as educational opportunity, economic differences, and other individual background factors.[14] However, even here the compilers ignored differences when they did not fit the goal toward which they worked. In front of them, in black and white, test figures showed that Negroes from the North scored higher than Negroes from the South. The compilers purposely tried to ignore these figures, because also in front of them results showed that

Table 1
Test Results of Black and White Soldiers, Army Results, 1918

| Southern Whites | | Northern Blacks | |
| --- | --- | --- | --- |
| Mississippi | 41.25 | Pennsylvania | 42.00 |
| Kentucky | 41.50 | New York | 45.00 |
| Arkansas | 41.55 | Illinois | 47.35 |
| Georgia | 42.12 | Ohio | 49.50 |

*Source:* R. M. Yerkes, "Psychological Examining in the US Army," *National Academy of Sciences*, Vol. 15 (1921).

Negroes from the North also outscored whites from the South. Now the statisticians found themselves in a show and tell situation. The scores from all the testing could not be eagerly shown without doctoring, because then it would indeed be difficult to keep the Negro in "his place." The simplest approach would have been not to present the figures at all. That would have kept the slate clean and avoided any trip ups or probing questions. Actually, in the stumbling efforts to keep the lid on and the truth in darkness, an opposite effect was created. According to Col. Noel Parrish, the final base commander of Tuskegee Army Air Field, "... their distribution in a rather conservative pamphlet caused such a frenzied effort to suppress the pamphlet that the figures were widely discussed."[15]

Like the deliberate falsifying that had been done by Robert Bean in his efforts to cast Negroes as very low forms of Homo sapiens, the AWC also seemingly did everything possible to discredit Negroes so that their only use in a war effort would be in performing menial tasks and common labor.

Obviously the War Department focused its efforts on a directed result, an outcome that it wanted and that meant the figures obtained from the Army's own testing during and after World War I (WWI) had to be either suppressed or ignored.

Besides the AWC studies, another influential factor weighed heavily in War Department and Air Corps thinking—the fact that racial problems were a product of every day living, and it was common American thought at that time which promoted a belief in the inferiority of blacks. But since the military itself consisted of those from this every day living and every day thought, the military would certainly not take the responsibility to correct the social wrongs of American society. In reality, the military believed it should steadfastly maintain and enforce what the civilian majority held to be absolute truth.

American society had created and nurtured the belief of superiority for one and inferiority for the other, and the War Department merely followed the dictates of American practices. Federal Judge William Hastie, the first black federal judge, repeatedly called for an end to segregation. Yet, near the end of 1941, an officer of the War Department's Adjutant General's Office said, in part, in a speech, "The Army is not a sociological laboratory; to be effective it must be organized and trained according to principles which will insure success. Experiments to meet the wishes and demands of the champions of every race and creed for the solution of their problems are a danger to efficiency, discipline and morale and would result in ultimate defeat."[16]

The War Department had previously issued its official statement on segregation. "The policy of the War Department is not to intermingle colored and white personnel in the same regimental organization. This policy has proven satisfactory over a long period of years and to make changes would produce situations destructive to morale and detrimental to the preparation for national defense."[17] So in this manner, the darling, and the youngest of the Army branches, upheld its policy of segregation by isolation and exclusion until political pressures became irrepressibly great.

It should be noted that the AWC purposely ignored the fact of courageous black men who had posted superior records in fighting in earlier battles and wars for other countries. The first of these outstanding men was Sosthene H. Mortenol born November 29, 1859, in Guadeloupe, a French possession. Following Mortenol's Polytechnic graduation, he was appointed ship Lieutenant in 1889; in 1904, he became Captain of a frigate; in 1912, he was made vessel Captain. In 1915, Mortenol commanded the air defenses for Paris. He retired in 1917, but following a ministry decision he kept his post and remained active until 1919. Too old to fly during WWI, Mortenol's leadership and valor brought him membership in the prestigious Legion of Honor.[18] There are no questions about the color of the many subordinate officers and enlisted men under his command and there is no question about his ability to lead them.

The second black man, Eugene Jacques Bullard, born in Columbus, Georgia in 1894, was the son of a freed slave. Bullard was 10 years old when his father forcefully fled the South with five other children to escape the Ku Klux Klan after defending himself against the abuses of a white boss. At that tender age, Bullard became a drifter and as he later wrote in his journal, his sole ambition was to get to France where his father had told him blacks were treated as equals. Bullard stowed away on a German cargo ship and sometime later arrived in Paris. When he turned 20, Bullard enlisted in the Foreign Legion and fought in the battle of Somme and Champagne in 1915, and in the battle of Verdun in 1916. In this last battle he was hit in the legs by shrapnel and lost most of his front teeth. While convalescing, Bullard began to dream of becoming a pursuit pilot and of flying high, high above the slimy mud, the blood, and the pestilence of stench-prone trenches.

Still in the hospital, Bullard requested a transfer which was shortly granted and allowed him to attend the legendary French Flying School. In May 1917, Bullard began flying his blue Spad S VII with the famous air combat group headed by Felix Brocard. Bullard soon gained the admiration of his fellow

French fliers and officially received credit for shooting down two Fokker triplanes, the very best of the enemy aircraft.[19] On the side of his Spad, Bullard had painted "all blood runs red."[20]

America entered the war in April 1917, and the elite U.S. Army Air Corps brought its insidious prejudice and racism with it. Toward the end of 1917, the American Army invited all American pilots flying in the Lafayette Flying Corps and other French units to join the ranks of the U.S. Army Air Corps with the offer to promote all who did. Bullard recounted in his journal that he and the other Americans traveled to Paris for their physicals. Five young uniformed American doctors examined Bullard. They asked him a lot of questions even though he could see that his military records lay open in front of them. One of the first questions asked was how he had learned to fly. Bullard informed them that he had been flying for months and had been in a number of air battles.

After returning to his squadron he watched and waited as one after another of his American comrades was called to the American flying units, and Bullard, who had a "feeling," never received that call. To compound indignity with humiliation, the Americans pressured the French commanders to keep their Negroes "in their place." This resulting negative racial pressure soon prevented Bullard from flying or even associating with his fellow pilots. He became an outcast.

Bullard, however, did fight for France again, at the beginning of WWII, by enlisting in the French underground and acting as a spy for the Free French. Eventually he was forced to flee Paris just ahead of the dreaded Gestapo. He made his way to Spain where the American Ambassador gave him a passport and helped him get passage to New York.

In 1954, Bullard was chosen to relight the flame at the Tomb of the Unknown Soldier in Paris. He returned to the United States and back to his job as an elevator operator in the RCA Building in New York City. Bullard died in October, 1961, in Harlem, the victim of cancer. By his last wishes, he was buried with honors in the uniform of a French Legionnaire in a plot of the Federation of French War Veterans in Flushing, New York. The single flag draped over his coffin was the tri-color of France.

An entry in Bullard's official record states that he was decorated 15 times for his services during the two wars, including the Croix de Guerre with Star. The entry continued, "The racism which prevailed in the American Air Corps prevented him from serving his country, even in wartime. It is also easy to imagine what an asset this man would have been to the American Army had he been allowed to serve his country." The summary of his record concluded with, "Eugene Bullard, who was American, was the first and only black pursuit pilot to fight within the ranks of the French Air Corps long before the United States declared war."[21]

Many other blacks were flying or had been flying years before the United States was finally forced from behind its shield of neutrality with the bombing of Pearl Harbor in December 1941. The first black person to be licensed to fly in the U.S. was a woman, Bessie Coleman or "Queen Bess", as she was popularly called. While working in a beauty parlor on the South Side of Chicago, Coleman had a dream of learning to fly and of opening a flying school. Although she repeatedly applied, no school in the country would accept her as a student. Eventually, with financial help from friends, Coleman set sail for France where she received her pilot's license in 1921, from the famed Fédération Aéronautique Internationale, the only organization that then licensed pilots worldwide. She obtained her license two years before the famed Amelia Earhart began her flying career.

Coleman returned to the United States with that very coveted license, but it did not take long to discover that no money could be made by a black pilot unless you were booked up with a barnstorming air show. Again, Coleman was thwarted; she had not taken aerobatics, so once more the ugly specter of prejudice appeared, and no school in the country would teach her. This meant back to France and aerobatics school, where for the second time, not the color of her skin but the color of her money brought the training she sought.

Coleman became as skilled in generating publicity as she did in flying. For the next five years she toured the country with flying shows, she spoke to churches and before other groups to promote the idea of flight for black people. Coleman not only flew but also made parachute jumps to provide additional thrills for her audiences. On April 30, 1926, she was killed while making an aerial appraisal of the race track in Jacksonville, Florida, before a scheduled performance and jump on the following Sunday. After asking William Willis, the white pilot who had ferried Coleman's plane, an old Army Air Corps (Curtis)JN-4 from Texas, to take the controls, she apparently unfastened her safety belt to get a better look which, because of her height, she could not do with the belt fastened. Witnesses say the plane went into a spin, flipped over at 500 feet and she was thrown out to her death. Wills never regained control and was also killed in the resulting crash. Thus Queen Bess, who had planned to open a flying school for blacks that very year, was tragically prevented from realizing the rest of her sought after dream.[22]

At that time the only other black licensed to fly in the United States was Hubert Fauntleroy Julian, a swashbuckling pilot from Trinidad. Julian had appeared in many air shows along with Queen Bess but he had expanded his prowess in many other directions. He could have headed the Ethiopian air force in that country's fight against Italy, but Emperor Haile Selassie became so infuriated with Julian's antics that he demoted him. It is recorded that Julian became so angry that Hermann Goering, the Reichmarshal of the vaunted German Luftwaffe (air force), had once written that Negroes were baboons that he had challenged Goering to an aerial dogfight to the death. Known as the "Black Eagle," Julian was reputed to have been a mercenary, a gunrunner, a stunt pilot, and a diplomat, or whatever else the situation required.[23]

Another renowned black pilot who, though not considered as flamboyant as Julian, nevertheless had considerable skills both mechanical and as a pilot. John C. Robinson was the very first black man to graduate from a white flying school in the United States. Robinson completed his studies at Tuskegee Institute in Alabama in 1924, and after opening an auto repair shop on the South Side of Chicago he tried many times to enter flying schools in the Chicago area. It was always the same answer; no Negroes were accepted for flying training. But Robinson was one of those staunch individuals who refused to take "No" as a final answer. At the Curtis-Wright Aeronautical School he took a job as a janitor, and in his spare moments he would seize opportunities to tinker with motors and machines as would be done by school instructors.

Robinson's abilities did not go unnoticed and when a new chief administrator was hired for the flying school, Robinson reapplied and was accepted. In 1931, the "Brown Condor," as he would be called later, became an instructor at Curtis-Wright for the more than two dozen black students that he had convinced to learn to fly. When Ethiopian and Italian border patrols clashed in 1934, Robinson began to pay great attention to the stage settings being arranged for WWII. Robinson offered his services to Ethiopia as a pilot, but Emperor Haile Selassie, despite badly needing that kind of technical assistance, demurred, initially, because of the bad taste the swashbuckling Julian had created. Once that hurdle had been crossed, Robinson was commissioned a Colonel and later put in command of the antiquated 25-plane air force. Because the planes were so obsolete in comparison with those of the Italian air force, Robinson's efforts were limited to flying communications missions in an unarmed plane between the fighting on the front lines and the capital at Addis Ababa.

When Emperor Selassie was forced into exile, Robinson fled back to the United States. He later returned to Ethiopia at the end of WWII only to be killed in the crash of a training plane he was flying in 1954.[24]

There was yet another black pilot who emerged in a later scenario of flying and fighting for a foreign country. James Lincoln Holt Peck, born in Stoops Ferry, Pennsylvania, learned to fly at a Curtis-Wright school in West Mifflin, Pennsylvania in 1931. Reportedly, Peck proved an excellent student, but the Federal Flight Examiner stated that he would fail him because he did not believe Negroes should be allowed to fly. The owner of the flight school urged Peck to transfer to the Cleveland Institute of Aeronautics in Ohio, where he would be judged on his flying ability, and he arranged for the transfer. After receiving his pilot's certificate and spending as much time in the air as his funds would allow, Peck tried first to enter the U.S. Army Air Corps and then the U.S. Navy Air Service. Both summarily turned him down because of his color.

In August 1937, Peck enlisted as a Loyalist in the Spanish Civil War to fight for the Spanish government in the Republican Air Force. In the four months that he flew as a pursuit pilot, flying several different types of Russian-made planes, such as the I-16 Mosca, Peck shot down five enemy planes and was credited with half of another kill.[25] As military historians know, the Spanish Civil War was a testing and proving ground for Germany's soon-to-be-used military hardware then being supplied to the rebel forces of Francisco Franco. The superiority of numbers and materials gave the insurgent Franco a dictator's victory over the Loyalists. It would have given the United States something even more valuable, an experienced combat pilot who had gone up against airplanes that might be used by the Luftwaffe two years later.

The U.S. Army Air Corps did not want even a lowly black orderly to shine the boots of its officers, so without question, it would not want a *black* pilot, even one with recent combat experience. When Peck returned to the United States, reporters asked him whether he agreed with the strong statements made by aviation hero Charles Lindbergh that Germany had a fighter aircraft, the Bfw-109, that was superior. Contrary to reports that he had gone to Washington to try to warn the Air Corps that the Curtis P-40, the best U.S. fighter at that time, could not match the German fighter, Peck said that was all distorted. He said, "I told the interviewers that I hadn't heard Lindbergh's statement. But I said after knowing guys who've been up against the Bfw-109 it damn well is!" Peck said he had faced and shot down two Heinkel 51s but had never crossed swords with any 109s. And that was just as well.

Peck ended up in the Merchant Marine as a lieutenant in charge of antiaircraft gunnery between 1941 and 1945. He unhesitatingly stated that he was not even sure flying was the major part of his life. "My contribution was in aerospace. I was with TRW for eleven years and General Dynamics for eight. I was the first black guy to be employed at Cape Canaveral in 1959 in an engineering capacity. I couldn't stay at the Satellite Motel; I had to stay at the bachelor officer's quarters at Patrick Air Force Base. I didn't mind that at all considering what I accomplished." While Peck acknowledged that flying in the Spanish Civil War and becoming an ace was certainly a major first, his greatest achievements came outside the flying game.[26]

# CHAPTER 2

# Breaking the Barrier

Although Eugene Bullard became the first and only black man to fly as a pursuit pilot during WWI, he was not the first to fly. Charles Wesley Peters of Pittsburgh, Pennsylvania has been identified as the first black man to pilot a heavier-than-air craft in 1911, as well as the first black man to design and build an airplane. He began by building kites and gliders and other flying devices in his spare time. He built a glider which he flew in 1906, just three years following the Wright Brothers' historic flight. Peters then reworked an automobile engine and converted it to fit his own designed airplane. He made numerous 12-minute flights in it and charged admission to the curious to see his airplane up close. When it burned, he built another one and took it to the Fifth Annual Georgia State Negro Fair, in Macon, Georgia. A 1911 newspaper (the Savannah Tribune) account stated that Peters held out for some $3,500 more as a cash advance than had been originally agreed upon.[1] Oddly, the state of Pennsylvania and France seem to have been the only early cradles that allowed blacks the opportunity to learn the art and skill of flying, and despite the many prevailing obstacles and opposition in the United States, they did just that.

Western Pennsylvania, like a protective hot house, produced numerous other air-minded blacks who yearned for the upper reaches of space. In 1920, Charles Vincent Proctor of Hollidaysburg became stricken while watching Wilbur Stultz and friends build race cars in a nearby garage. Stultz, who would later become Amelia Earhart's pilot, gave Proctor his first flying lesson. Genuinely committed to flying, Proctor's advance was many times stymied by the lack of funds and the jobs to generate more than living

expenses. Abram P. Jackson earned his private pilot's license from the old
Fairview Airport, west of Erie, and later became a ground school instructor at
Tuskegee. Mayer Field was both the learning and teaching site for Joseph
D. Ellison, Charles Asa Ross, as well as for other early pilots such as Jake
Lytle, Bill and Bob Foley, Bill Welch, and George Allen. The Foleys, Lytle, and
Welch gave flight instructions at Mayer while Allen instructed at Latrobe
Airport. Holding a commercial and instructor's ratings brought Allen fame as
an excellent flyer and a host of flying jobs in Western Pennsylvania that ranged
from carrying cargo to carrying passengers. The outbreak of the WWII took
Allen to Tuskegee as one of its key instructors. Lawrence E. Anderson, Jr.'s,
piloting fame rivaled Allen's at Greensburg's Airport, where he earned all the
pilot ratings from private to instructor. Despite many hours of flying, the Air
Corps used a subterfuge to deny him entry through the racial barriers still
sturdily in place. With bushels of flying hours under his belt, Anderson
remained a ground school instructor at Tuskegee through the end of the war.

The list of black Pennsylvanians taking to the air is lengthy, helped in the
1940s, by the Civilian Pilot Training Program (CPTP). James T. Wiley joined
the all-black 99th and in June 1944, the mayor of Pittsburgh gave him the key
to the city for his exploits. Marshall Fields, William Edwards, and Mary
Parker finished the program with Parker punctuating her achievement by
becoming the first black female pilot to solo in a seaplane from the Kanawha
River in 1941. Art Barnes, a Pittsburgh native, learned to fly as a result of
his after-school job, refueling seaplanes at a base on the Allegheny River.
Two brothers who owned five seaplanes there taught him while he still
attended high school in 1934.[2]

There were many other blacks who had mastered the air, and, then baton-
like, passed their enthusiasm on to others. While accomplishments of the
black aviators mentioned previously are intentionally not chronological,
it would be grossly unfair to continue without recognizing a number of
others whose aerial exploits were widely known prior to the start of WWII.

Thomas C. Allen and James Herman Banning were the first blacks to
make a transcontinental flight across the United States in 1932, in a publicity
effort to promote an air show. The trip from Dycer Airport in California to
Valley Stream Airport in New York took 19 days with numerous stops for
repairs and fund raising. Banning, who was the first black pilot to be licensed
in the United States, did the flying and Allen was his mechanic. Banning was
killed in a plane crash in 1933 at Camp Kearney, California, but he was not
at the controls because blacks were not permitted to fly in that location.[3]
Charles Alfred "Chief" Anderson and Dr. Albert E. Forsythe made goodwill
flights in 1934 to the West Indies and Central and South America in the
"Spirit of Booker T. Washington." They were the first blacks to complete the
round trip transcontinental flight from Atlantic City to Los Angeles in 1933.
Following that flight, the two then flew up to Canada for their second long
distance junket.[4] The team of Anderson and Forsythe, as much as anyone,

brought worldwide recognition to the abilities and undeniable aviation skills of black pilots. Chief Anderson was the first black to receive a commercial pilot's license in the United States. Only after being forced to buy his own airplane did Anderson find a flight instructor willing to teach him the art of flying near his home town of Bryn Mawr, Pennsylvania.[5] He later became the chief of flying operations at Tuskegee Institute for the CPTP as well as the Primary training phase under the Army Air Corps. William J. Powell, an early black pilot, opened the Los Angeles branch of the Bessie Coleman Aero Club in 1929, and in 1931 the club sponsored the first all-black air show in the United States. In 1938, Grover C. Nash became the first black pilot to fly an airmail route during National Airmail Week. Nash flew an intrastate route between Chicago and Charleston, Illinois.[6]

Willa B. Brown became the first black woman to obtain a commercial license and working with her husband, Cornelius R. Coffey, operated the Coffey School of Aeronautics in Chicago beginning in the mid-1930s. She also became the first black woman to be a commissioned officer in the Civil Air Patrol. Coffey had the distinction of becoming the first black certified aircraft mechanic in 1932. He was finally admitted to the Curtis-Wright School of Aeronautics after a threatened lawsuit in 1929. Coffey, still flying at the age of 89, also became the first president of the National Airmen's Association of America.

Dorothy Darby, another black woman, was not only an excellent pilot but billed herself as the only professional female parachutist in the country. Parachute jumping in the 1930s was truly a daredevil act. In a jump during an exhibition in 1932, at Curtis Field in Chicago, Darby broke both legs and suffered internal injuries. She recovered to continue flying and parachuting, then made a spectacular jump again three years later over the training camp of heavyweight champion Joe Louis.[7] There were numerous black-sponsored air shows during the 1930s, air shows to thrill and hold the mostly black spectators riveted in awe and the price of admission was 35 cents. Performing at many of them was Willie Jones, nicknamed "Suicide" because he would delay opening his chute until he was only 800 feet from the ground.

Although her name is not mentioned as often as Coleman, Brown, or Darby, Janet Waterford Bragg, a registered nurse, received her pilot's license in the mid-1930s and bought the first airplane for the Challenger Air Pilot's Association which was founded by John C. Robinson. Bragg continued to fly for more than 40 years, and at one point owned three airplanes in the Chicago area. The Challenger Air Pilot's Association was Chicago's first black flying club, and because blacks were summarily excluded from all established airports in the Chicago area, the club built its own airstrip and hangar in the all-black township of Robbins, Illinois in 1933. Los Angeles has the distinction of being the first area in the country to feature black aviation. Led by William J. Powell, the Bessie Coleman Aero Club was formed in 1929, to spark an interest in aviation and the idea of flying among blacks. Powell published the book "Black Wings" in 1934, which urged black men and women to "fill the air with black wings." Ahead of his time, Powell called on black youth to reach for the skies by becoming not only pilots but aircraft designers and leaders in the business end of aviation as well. An early pilot himself, Powell also founded a club called Craftsmen of Black Wings to train aviation mechanics and pilots under a federal educational program in Los Angeles and in New York. Powell envisioned thousands of skilled jobs for blacks in the blossoming field of aviation as well as a drop in prejudice when it was shown that blacks could fly, build, and service airplanes.[8]

Then there was the critical flight of Chauncey E. Spencer and Dale L. White in May 1939 from Chicago to Washington, D.C. Spencer and White had made many other flights around the country to promote black events and Spencer had made parachute jumps at air shows. This particular flight may have been the catalyst that cracked open the door to the soon-to-be-enacted CPTP to blacks. After meeting with civil rights leader Edgar G. Brown, Spencer and White had a chance meeting with then senator, Harry S. Truman, who, after seeing the plane they had made the flight in, expressed amazement that their trip had been successful at all. He was further surprised when told that blacks had not been considered for enrollment in the CPTP.[9] It is strongly believed that Truman's behind-the-scenes maneuvering and political clout were instrumental in keeping the door of government-sponsored aviation open to blacks.

Besides Truman, President Franklin Roosevelt entered the picture to become a major player, as he looked for an unprecedented third term in office. In addition, the fair-minded First Lady, Eleanor Roosevelt, provided a very important third factor. They acted separately and, just by chance, in concert, together providing the right amount of pressure at just the right time, to give blacks the timely opportunity to spread their wings in the military skies of America. So glossy and refined was the image of actually leaving the ground, of commanding a winged vehicle to rise into the clouds, of soaring higher than the majestic eagle that common American thought precluded the descendants of slaves daring to ever achieve this special calling reserved for the select few. But the day of awakening lay ahead. The disbelievers and the denigrators would be force-fed with the indisputable facts of accomplishment.

In November 1940, in a last ditch attempt to shore up the sagging support of black voters, President Roosevelt promoted Colonel Benjamin O. Davis, Sr. to Brigadier General, the first black to ever achieve that rank. In addition, the president appointed Federal Judge William Hastie as Civilian Aide to the Secretary of War and Major Campbell C. Johnson received appointment as Executive Assistant to the Director of Selective Service. These appointments produced many inches of newspaper space and headlines beginning the Saturday before election day.[10] Roosevelt's strategy worked and black voters flocked to him rather than to Republican candidate Wendell Willkie. Strangely though, instead of causing a lessening of pressure from black leaders and the black press, these new appointments served only to stir up an increase in demands on the White House, the War Department, and ultimately, the Army Air Corps.

When the National Association for the Advancement of Colored People (NAACP) demanded that blacks be used in at least some of its service units, the Air Corps responded that it only accepted men with mechanical and technical experience or at least men who had those capabilities. Since blacks did not then project this overall image of technical excellence or learning, there could be no place for them in the Air Corps.

The publicity of black men flying and showing mechanical skills prior to WWII was a matter of record, ignored and disallowed, but nevertheless fact. So, the generally affirmed mental attitude of black inferiority had not only to be kept intact but reinforced. However, to do that required the deliberate exclusion of reported events, falsification of facts, and the perpetuation of a cultivated hatred. Despite being purposely held back and denied educational opportunities for more than two centuries, blacks would demonstrate an inimitable ability to quickly catch up when permitted to do so.

The indisputable reality that blacks could fly, were flying, and had in fact, been flying for years only makes larger the shame of the contrived negative evaluations of their abilities and capabilities. The concept of superiority-inferiority had become so deeply ingrained and genuinely believed that the deliberate use of falsehood was needed to turn aside the strong surge of truth. These were not mistakes; the hypocrisy, a studied effort, worked very well until subjected to the acid test. General Henry H. (Hap) Arnold, Chief of the Army Air Corps, stood firmly adamant in his stand of excluding blacks because he could foresee the absolute unsavory situation of having black officers on the same base as white enlisted men, a hopeless and dangerous powder keg combination to his way of thinking. In addition, Army Regulation 95-60 (AR 95-60) specifically required that the commanding officer of all posts be white.

The low regard held of the military capabilities of Negroes was voiced by Secretary of War, Henry L. Stimson, in his diary based on the flawed AWC findings. He wrote that Negroes could not become good officers because "leadership was not yet embedded in the Negro race." Stimson further jotted, "...making black officers would bring disaster" and he also predicted that Negroes would fail as pilots. Next, General Arnold stated that "Negro pilots...would result in having Negro officers serving over white enlisted men" which would be "an impossible social problem."[11]

To preserve this special flavor of white America's bottom-of-the-pit regard for Negroes, at the time, and it was from this broad pool of America that War Department heads, top military leaders of all branches of service and political leaders came, more slanted findings were used by the AWC. The 1925 Memorandum signed by AWC Commandant, Major General H. E. Ely, concluded that Negro men themselves believed they were inferior to white men and that they were naturally subservient and lacked initiative and resourcefulness. The memo additionally stated that Negroes inherently possessed "mental, moral, physical and other psychological characteristics" which made it impossible for them to "associate socially with any except the lowest of Whites."[12]

The War Department relied heavily upon the doctrine of "separate-but-equal," a rigid racial policy bolstered by the 1896 ruling of the U.S. Supreme Court in Plessy versus Ferguson. That ruling held, in so many words, that segregation was not discrimination as long as the facilities and training were equal.[13] In fact, only in 1954 did the high court finally move to strike down its "separate-but-equal" doctrine.

What the AWC and the War Department studiously ignored was the fact that Negroes had been involved in every battle in which the United States had ever been engaged. There was first Crispus Attucks, one of the leaders in the mob opposing the British and one of the first to be killed in the 1770 Boston massacre when the British Redcoats fired into the crowd. This led to the beginning of the Revolutionary War.

An interesting historical note is that in 1763 the population of the American colonies numbered 2,000,000, with one quarter of that total being German and Scots-Irish and one fifth being Negro. Twenty-seven years later, in 1790, at the first census, the total population was 3,929,214 of which 757,208 were Negro. Most of these were slaves but some, such as Attucks, were not.[14]

During the years of the Civil War, and after, between 1863 and 1898, black soldiers earned 38 Medals of Honor with more than 37,000 being killed during the Civil War alone. Not mentioned in any of the AWC findings was the fact that a black gunner's mate fired the first salvo from the ill-fated battleship Maine in Havana harbor in 1898. Not mentioned was the all-black 9th and 10th Cavalry that charged up San Juan Hill with Teddy Roosevelt's Rough Riders in the Spanish-American War that followed in Cuba. Also ignored was the U.S. Navy record indicating that as many as 20 black seamen are still buried in a watery grave, having gone down with the ironclad Tecumseh warship in Mobile Bay during the Civil War.[15]

Black soldiers and sailors had compiled enviable military records of bravery and heroism fighting for America, and yet after WWI some of these same decorated men faced such intense racial hatred that some were even lynched while still in their uniforms.

To anyone, such as Dr. Myrdal, examining these facts objectively, it would seem a strange paradox indeed to see black Americans clamoring, rallying, and fighting for the patriotic right to fight for a country that fully despised them. Even stranger, this dynamic drive by blacks to fight an enemy overseas who was preaching and practicing, with furtive genocide, the same type of hatred they were experiencing in America, the land of the free.

"An American Dilemma," pointed out the galling contradictions that Negroes had to bitterly swallow. Based on the American Creed, the essential dignity of the individual was stressed in the United States. Along with liberty, equality, justice, and a fair opportunity for everyone, was the inalienable right to think, act, and talk under the influence of high national and Christian precepts with a devotion to the idea of human brotherhood and the Golden Rule.[16] In American society and in the U.S. military, blacks were shown, told, and made to "stay in their place." Ironically, at the same time, blacks were ready to fight and give up their lives on some foreign soil for principles that they could not fully realize and enjoy at home.

One can only wonder in sheer puzzlement how the AWC, with its in-depth studies and intelligent minds, could be so far from the truth in its conclusions regarding the Negro. After all, General Ely, commandant of AWC, stated that the conclusions were the result of several years of study by the faculty and student body. Again, a shrewdly observant Myrdal found the reason. "In our study we encounter whole systems of firmly entrenched popular belief concerning the Negro and his relations to the large society, which are bluntly false and which can only be understood when we remember the opportunistic ad hoc purpose they serve."[17]

In other words the AWC seemed to go out of its way to produce and use doctored facts and contrived falsehoods to achieve the results it needed to keep the Negro "in his place." Bean's cranial size of Negroes is quoted in the study, without refutation, as further proof of the Negro's inferiority. That "place", however, would be severely tested and challenged as WWII began to spread. We should mention here that during WWII, white Americans adopted the "V" for victory in the fight against the Axis powers while black Americans created the double "V" as a signal for victory against fascism abroad and victory against racism at home.

As late as August 1941, President Roosevelt and Britain's Prime Minister, Winston Churchill, held their first meeting at sea to draw up the Atlantic Charter, the framework of what the allies would attempt to do. The United States had already abandoned its Neutrality Act in November 1940, at the height of the Battle for Britain, but despite heavily increasing the supplies to Britain and providing convoys for the supply ships, it continued to maintain a semi-formal neutral position until Pearl Harbor. Even before the sneak attack on Pearl, there was really no doubt about the United States entering the war—it was only a matter of time before it happened.[18]

Planning for what was considered an eventuality, Congress enacted Public Law 18 (PL 18) April 3, 1939, which provided for a large-scale expansion of the Air Corps. One section of PL 18 called for civilian contracts for primary flying training and at least one school was to be designated for the training of blacks. PL 18 did not explicitly state it but blacks falsely assumed that completion of this primary training would put them into the Air Corps for basic training, the next flying stage following primary training.

Two other hard-hitting pieces of legislation soon sprang up to hammer and chisel at the buttresses of exclusion by the Air Corps. On June 27, 1939, the CPTP was established to create a pool of civilian pilots that could be called up in the event of war. Again, blacks were excluded until Senator Harry Truman, black leaders, and the black press turned up the heat on the White House and the War Department. Finally, in November 1940, Congress added sections to the Selective Training and Service Act that specified that there was to be no discrimination because of race or color.

Despite the provisions of PL 18, the Air Corps continued to stonewall the intent and purpose of those provisions in violation until 1941, saying that although one school was to be designated for blacks it was not specifically stated that any of them had to be trained.[19]

Some three months after the CPTP began, in 1939, an enterprising and well-connected director of trade and technical studies at West Virginia State College won Civil Aeronautics Authority (CAA) approval of CPTP for the first of six black institutions that were to qualify. The others were Delaware State, Hampton Institute, Howard University, North Carolina A&T, and lastly Tuskegee Institute. Strangely, not only was Tuskegee the last to be approved it also required a special trip to Washington, some special politicking on the part of G. L. Washington, Director of Mechanical Industries at Tuskegee, and some special concessions by the CAA. The initial application by Tuskegee had been turned down.[20]

Two black noncollege schools also qualified, both in the Chicago area; the Coffey School of Aeronautics and the North Suburban Flying School at Glenview, Illinois were allowed into the program. There were also a few Northern and Western schools that permitted blacks to receive CPTP training.

G. L. Washington mentions in his writings that in making his pitch to Leslie A. Walker, Chief of the Vocational Section of Private Flying Development, he ended with the "type of approach I would make to a southern white man for a favor . . . "[21] During their conference, Washington found out that Walker came from Notasulga, Alabama, a name that would crop up again. One of the stipulations for CPTP approval was that the flying school must be within a 10-mile radius from the university or college. The municipal airport at Montgomery, Alabama was 40 miles from Tuskegee and that distance later became a major obstacle, a financial millstone around the neck. Obviously a special mileage concession was made for Tuskegee from the very beginning and the big question, still unanswered, was why?

We take note here that, according to the U.S. Bureau of the Census, as of January 1939, there were a total of 125 Negro aviators licensed in the United States. Of that, 12 were student pilots and 82 held amateur licenses. There were only 4 with commercial pilot ratings and there were 3 of 4 others with limited commercial ratings that were current. Of the remaining 23 private licenses issued, 5 had expired.

In its application, Tuskegee listed Joseph W. Allen, a white commercial pilot who operated the Alabama Air Service, as the instructor of flying training. Allen, with the exception of one other instructor, Don S. Porter, ran a one-man operation and was apparently eager to secure a contract under the CPTP. G. L. Washington listed William Curtis and Joseph Fuller from Tuskegee's own Mechanical Industries School as ground school instructors. But some intuitive or gut feeling of Washington caused him to contact two professors from the all-white Alabama Polytechnic Institute (now Auburn University) at Auburn, Alabama, Robert G. Pitts and Bloomfield M. Cornell. After having Curtis and Fuller approved by CAA, Washington then substituted Pitts and Cornell as ground school instructors. Pitts had recently completed his Master's degree in Aeronautical Engineering at California's Institute of Technology and was a certified aviation mechanic, while Bloomfield had graduated from the U.S. Naval Academy and had served as a naval aviator before he retired.

The change that Washington made proved as prophetic as well as meritorious, for when the CAA Examiner had finished his testing of the first class of 20 students, not only did they pass, their average scores were the highest of any school in the country. Two of the twenty were females and two others were alternates. This first class was not formed without having to overcome one major obstacle, that of getting parental permissions. A number of parents were concerned about safety and others believed that enrolling in the program meant their youngsters would be joining some branch of the military. For the very first time, CPTP at Tuskegee rated an unprecedented full page in a southern daily's Sunday edition. The writer reported, " . . . because of trees, slope of field and other obstacles, every landing for these colored boys is a spot landing . . . ."[22]

At the same time, Washington hurriedly initiated efforts to move the flying operations to the Tuskegee vicinity inasmuch as Colonel John C. Robinson and Chief Alfred Anderson had earlier landed and taken off from institute property. It had already become glaringly clear that the 80-mile round trip to Montgomery would cause a collapse of Tuskegee's CPTP involvement. Washington dashed off a letter to CAA figure, Leslie Walker, telling him that the reason for the CAA's initial thumbs down on Tuskegee was correct for distance. The cost was running three times higher than the government's payment to the institute. The government was paying approximately 300 dollars per student to cover the expenses of ground school and flight training. Washington also stated, "We were late with the program and it will be impossible to finish flight (training on time) when this academic year closes."[23]

Washington speculates in his writings that if Kennedy Field, located across the highway from the institute, had not been approved by the

Regional CAA office, the schedule for completion of flying training would have been greatly exceeded. He further added that trying to continue ferrying the students 40 miles instead of 10 would most likely have ended CPTP classes. That extra mileage burden would have allowed the CAA to pull the program for the same valid reasons it was hesitant in approving Tuskegee for participation in the first place. The impending development forced Washington to scramble for a site closer to the institute. The ideal site, Kennedy Field, was practically across the road from the institute. Three white pilots, including Stanley Kennedy, had built Kennedy Field for their personal use and when approached, readily agreed to sublease it to the institute. Permission also had to be obtained from the owner of the land, John Connor. Since the field would not be approved by the CAA until it was upgraded and inspected, Kennedy and his flying friends would greatly benefit from the upgrade because they would also continue to be able to use the field. Improvement of the site to CAA standards was conducted by the institute's aviation students volunteering their time and efforts to cut trees, level high spots, fill pot holes, and build runway markers.

Not only did G. L. Washington lean on Walker for that change, he also put in a bid for advanced CPTP training which he had been alerted would soon be announced. The proposal of May 20, 1940, was actually signed by Dr. Frederick Patterson, President of Tuskegee Institute and sent to Grove Webster, Chief of the Private Flying Division of CAA. Once more Washington led the institute out on a tenuously thin limb because the only nearby acceptable landing field belonged to all-white Alabama Polytechnic (API). The institute's leased Kennedy Field was much too small to accommodate the larger airplanes that would be required for the advanced training.

Reasoning that a slice of bread can be buttered on either side, Washington hurriedly enlisted Professor Cornell, who was already one of those teaching Tuskegee's ground school subjects, to approach Polytechnic's President L. N. Duncan for using their field. Duncan resisted such a move until his elderly secretary chided him on the fact that they had been attending many affairs at Tuskegee for years and it was not right that now Tuskegee's students could not use their airfield. It ended up with API's aviation students themselves being given a vote in the matter and they unanimously voting for approval. API, also conducting a CPTP program, did not gain approval for secondary training until spring of 1941.[24]

In the meantime, President Patterson had made a trip to Washington and had met with and convinced Chief Anderson to leave Howard University and head Tuskegee's rapidly growing flying activities. Anderson readily agreed but all secondary training instructors were required to take a refresher course in acrobatics, which Anderson did in Chicago, with the institute writing the check. On Dr. Patterson's Washington trip, he had also met with Grove Webster, CAA honcho, and CAA chief, Robert H. Hinckley, the latter in regard to a grant to build a new airfield.

Five weeks after making the pitch for secondary training, G. L. Washington received a call on June 27, 1940, from Atlanta CAA regional head, Edward Nilson, who told him that Chicago was in the midst of making a strong bid for the secondary training. It was understood that all Negroes selected by CAA-Washington for secondary training would attend the one site chosen. It appears that CAA-Washington's selection of that one site hinged on Nilson's recommendation which, in turn, came after G. L. Washington's correct answer to two key questions. One, would the Institute of Tuskegee improve Kennedy Field, and two, would Tuskegee handle the flight training itself rather than contract it out. Washington answered in the affirmative to both questions and on July 1, 1940, CAA announced that Tuskegee Institute would be the base for advanced CPTP training.

Understandably, G. L. Washington personally felt that Chicago's School of Aeronautics, operated by Willa Brown, should have been the logical place for the advanced training center, Washington reasoned that aside from the ground school staff, Tuskegee had no supporting equipment that could match Chicago's; Tuskegee had no flight equipment, no flight personnel, and no suitable airfield for the advanced training. What apparently outweighed all of these negatives was Tuskegee's reputation of "accommodation" with State and Federal Governments; the goodwill of key people in the South and North whose opinions were consequential; the widespread publicity from the recent ground school tests; and perhaps most importantly, its eagerness to become a compliant partner in a segregated project.

With its feet now firmly being held to the fire, the War Department, in October 1940, announced that blacks were being trained as pilots, mechanics, and technicians. But the falsehood of that proffered statement was quickly sniffed out by the *Pittsburgh Courier* when it noted that all black pilot training was being done by civilian institutions and not the War Department. Pressure continued to mount and just one day after Howard University student Yancy Williams filed a suit against the War Department for admission into the Air Corps, the pressure gauge blew sky-high. On January 16, 1941, the War Department finally announced the formation of the 99th Pursuit Squadron, an all-black unit. Further, the announcement stated that Tuskegee, Alabama, would be the training site.

About two weeks before the announcement, Dr. Patterson and G. L. Washington had been called to Maxwell Field, Alabama, for a hurried conference with Brigadier General Walter R. Weaver, commanding general of the Southeastern Air Corps Training Center. They were told that Chicago was making such a strong and well-organized bid for the new airfield that General Weaver urged Patterson and Washington to go to Washington, DC in person. To that end, he sent Captain James Ellison from his own staff to assist them in the desperate fight. The trio met with the War Department and with Alabama's congressmen; and with attitudes being what they were at the time, these meetings would be behind the force that changed the logical course of coming events.

Again, there is this feeling or hint of cloakroom politicking, of deals being made in the best interests of certain parties and of decisions hatched to steer a particular course. This feeling was borne out by the comments of Tuskegee Army Air Field (TAAF) historian, Major Edward C. Ambler, Jr., "It has always been understood by the writer (Ambler) that there was a large amount of political influence in the background of a good many of the events that have happened at the Tuskegee Army Air Field. However, as would be expected, it is very unusual that we ever find a written reference to this influence."[25]

Major Ambler then pointed to one source of pressure or influence in quoting a paragraph of a letter from the Southeast Air Corps Training Command Headquarters at Maxwell Field to Division Engineering, South Atlantic Division; Richmond, Virginia. It stated, "The project at Tuskegee is considered by the War Department as No. 1 priority due to political pressure that was being brought to bear upon the White House and War Department to provide pilot training for colored applicants. For this reason training must be initiated on schedule regardless of cost."[26] This apparently points out one of those very rare instances of a written reference that the good major mentioned earlier as being very hard to find.

Director G. L. Washington states in his notes that during the January meeting with General Weaver at Maxwell Field, Dr. Patterson requested that Captain Benjamin O. Davis, Jr. be transferred from his station at Ft. Riley, Kansas to Tuskegee to take flight training with the first group of cadets. The objective of that move would be to have Davis as eventual commander of the 99th Pursuit Squadron. That request was immediately agreed to.

Although Tuskegee was the last school to be approved for CPTP, it became the first school in the nation to receive the new Waco YPT-14 trainer, a plane comparable to the primary trainers used by the Air Corps. Chief Anderson flew Tuskegee's new plane down from Chicago on the same day that he finished his refresher aerobatics course. According to Washington, when Anderson buzzed the campus, faculty, students, government hospital personnel, and residents of Greenwood, the black district off campus of Tuskegee, rushed, forewarned, to Kennedy Field to greet him by the time the plane landed.

Flight instruction for secondary CPTP training began on July 29, 1940, at Auburn's approved Works Progress Administration (WPA)-constructed field since Tuskegee did not have one then. Of course, there was great interest by the aviation students of the all-white school, since API had not yet been approved, and also by the local white and rural residents. Washington notes that there were many expressions of surprise and astonishment made by the spectators watching the takeoffs and landings of the

Tuskegee students such as, "Did you see that nigger land that plane!" Regardless of those types of comments Washington believed that there was a certain amount of goodwill present because the Waco was tied down in the open each night and it would have been easy to set it afire or otherwise damage it.

Once more G. L. Washington, the super planner, began to worry about the future. The students were traveling about 20 miles for their training at Auburn but a bigger concern began to grow—what would happen when Auburn received its own approval for secondary training? There loomed the danger of conflicting flight schedules and the daily use of the API field. Chief Anderson was already flying seven days a week, including the Fourth of July. The CAA had, with some motive of reasoning, bent over backward to make concessions on behalf of Tuskegee from the beginning. For example, Tuskegee was the only university or college of the 400 in the nation to be flight training it students. Standard practice had the school to conduct only the ground school portion and a private commercial school to do the flight training.

The CAA requirements for the fall 1940 secondary session, scheduled one flight instructor for every five students which meant that another instructor besides Chief Anderson would be necessary. Anderson recommended Lewis A. Jackson who, at the time, was instructing students at Willa Brown's school in Chicago. After a number of exchanges of correspondence, Jackson joined the Tuskegee staff. At this point a second Waco was ordered so as to have one plane for each instructor, and two more Piper Cubs were purchased so that apprentice instructors could teach trainees in the elementary courses. The quota of students for the fall secondary session began with 11, 10 regular and 1 alternate.

Aviation training at Tuskegee began to mushroom, and mastermind G. L. Washington promptly hired the aforementioned George W. Allen of Pennsylvania but then realizing that the well of licensed commercial black pilots was nearly dry, Washington decided that they would have to integrate their staff. He placed an advertisement in a New York newspaper and secured the services of commercial pilot Joseph Camilleri and combination mechanic-commercial pilot Frank Rosenberg.

At the end of spring 1940, director Washington had an unexpected visitor at his office—none other than Grove Webster, the Chief of CAA's Division of Private Flying Development. Webster abruptly asked him how Tuskegee would like to have an airfield all of its own. Just as quickly Washington responded, without trying to conceal his jubilation, "Yes," with a capital "Y." Washington remembers having a feeling that Webster was clearly acting for some "higher authority," most likely the Air Corps. The two men talked, then looked over a site that had been earlier selected by the Alabama Aviation Commission, and then Webster departed without further explanation.[27]

A major roadblock had to be first overcome, the tough issue of acquiring the estimated $400,000 needed to construct a first-class field suitable for the secondary training. President Patterson had seemingly run out of financing sources when the Julius Rosenwald Fund decided to hold its annual meeting at the institute. On the board of trustees sat First Lady Eleanor Roosevelt whose considerable influence had a direct bearing on the Fund's eventual decision to loan $175,000 to help finance construction of the field. First Lady Eleanor visited Kennedy Field and over the protest of her Secret Service bodyguards had Chief Anderson give her an aerial tour of the campus and the surrounding areas.[28] What the First Lady dramatically accomplished and publicly showed was the unquestioned confidence in entrusting her personal safety to the skill of a black pilot, a skill that certainly contradicted what the military had been heartily promoting.

Because the Selective Service Act would bring a staggering number of black inductees into the Army, in proportion to the population, Army officials began pressuring the Air Corps to take its fair share of this influx of men and reduce the distribution burden on the ground force units. For the first time since its inception, the Air Corps forcibly began to rapidly formulate plans to utilize black troops within its ranks. One of the ways conceived involved the formation of so-called Aviation Squadrons of 250 men, each at air bases throughout the South.

These Squadrons were nothing more than work or labor battalions where the men did pick-and-shovel work, road repair, and yard mainte-nance, nothing of a technical nature.[29] However, no relief or escape could avoid the relentless pressure being exerted on the War Department with regard to pilot training, pressure that then passed directly on to the Air Corps.

On November 8, 1940, General Weaver was instructed by the Training and Operations Division of the Air Corps in Washington, DC to submit a general plan for the establishment of a (colored) pursuit squadron at Tuskegee. General Weaver sent back his plan the first week of December 1940, which called for 4 weeks of basic military, 10 weeks of basic flying training, 10 weeks of advanced flying training, and 6 weeks of tactical orga-nization. All supervision would be under 11 white officers and 15 white noncommissioned officers, until a sufficient number of Negro officers could be trained to replace them.[30]

Earlier, near the end of November 1940, as part of General Weaver's plan, a group of Air Corps officers from Maxwell Field Alabama, headed by Major Lucius S. Smith, met with Dr. Patterson and G. L. Washington at Tuskegee to secure their assistance in finding a site suitable for training black military pilots. The search for an airfield went on for days with aerial photographs taken of each area under consideration. The search finally centered on Ft. Davis, a little village some 14 miles south of Tuskegee.

The white town leaders of Tuskegee had already indicated in no uncertain terms that they definitely did not want a black-operated airbase in their midst.[31] Five weeks later Washington, DC wired General Weaver that the Tuskegee project had been approved and funding would come as soon as possible.

On February 14, 1941, a site board of five officers, led by Major Mark M. Boatner and which included Major James A. Ellison, was appointed by the Secretary of War to officially survey the Ft. Davis area. This action came after the War Department and the Air Corps had formulated a plan for an all-black air unit. Their reasoning apparently hinged on the supposition that such a plan would quell the constant and annoying loud rumblings in Washington. At the same time it would put to the test the belief that Negroes would be unable to absorb the rigorous and precise training necessary to master the complicated intricacies and sophistication of modern combat aircraft.

The immediate effect of the announced plan divided the country's blacks into two distinct camps, those who hailed an all-black unit as a major breakthrough and those who saw it as just another continuation of segregation. Typical of the strong feelings on both sides was the plight of Dr. William Pickens, Director of Branches for the National Association for the Advancement of Colored People (NAACP). The NAACP had declared a policy against "any segregation" whatsoever in all armed services.

On the other side, Dr. Patterson, in an interview, stated in part, "...Squadrons now training at Tuskegee...are giving colored men a foothold in the Air Corps and will in time lead to mixed air units." Judge William Hastie felt so strongly that he eventually resigned his position as Civilian Aide to the Secretary of War in protest on January 31, 1943.[32] In fact, Judge Hastie's opposition prior to his resignation was so strong that it caused the War Department to hold up the announcement of its plans to move ahead even after Dr. Patterson had promised absolute cooperation with the Air Corp.

The Air Corps clearly moved very quickly, probably beginning in early January 1940, in developing a strategy to reduce the amount of heat it was taking. But exposure of the subterfuge it had attempted in falsely announcing the training of black pilots, mechanics, and technicians left only one course open, to initiate real plans for the training but on terms the Air Corps would dictate.

Part of the report by, the official site board indicates very clearly the direction of Air Corps thinking when it gave the okay to Ft. Davis. "The close proximity of Tuskegee Institute makes this site ideal for the training of Negroes, since that Institute furnishes many precepts and examples in conduct and attitude. It is a center of Negro learning and culture, and it has temporary accommodations for Negro personnel.

Further, it is an Institute whose leaders exert great influence in the affairs of the Negro race."

"Tuskegee (the town) is predominantly white, while Tuskegee Institute is naturally entirely a Negro community. This condition would assist largely in handling the problem of segregation."[33]

While these scenes were being played out, other important actors wanted to climb on stage. Willa Brown and the Coffey Flying School, battling and aided by Congressman Arthur Mitchell, attempted to have the secondary training portion shifted to Chicago. TAAF Historical Officer Ambler opined that the selection of Tuskegee came because of Chicago's heavy aerial traffic and the better weather in Alabama. He also felt the choice came because of the cooperative attitudes displayed by Dr. Patterson and G. L. Washington. Major Ambler's opinions regarding better weather and less aerial traffic fly in the face of the official board's remarks in its report that Alabama would, in fact, be nicely isolated from Northern agitators and other trouble makers who could otherwise come to the quick aid and assistance of black pilots if the need should arise. Ambler further states in his report that he found no written record at Tuskegee to indicate why it was picked over the more logical Chicago area.

But all the maneuvering to get Ft. Davis quickly set in concrete after its selection went for naught because on April 10, 1941, the District Engineer turned thumbs down on Ft. Davis. Ft. Davis had bad soil. General Weaver immediately requested authority to find either another site or enough funds to take care of the poor soil conditions at Ft. Davis. The response from Washington, DC to General Weaver was to take whatever action necessary in finding a new site. The cost of bringing Ft. Davis up to grade would have cost about $700,000 and caused a delay in the project of some six months.

On April 28, 1941, Weaver appointed a new site board and instructed it not only to find a site in the Tuskegee area but to have the results of that selection reported directly to the War Department in just four days.[34]

Now, more strange circumstances float to the surface. Could it have been military pressure, a political threat, a monetary inducement, or some combination of all three that caused the white leaders of the town of Tuskegee to suddenly change their previous adamant position against a black airfield in their midst? There is nothing to be found in the records. G. L. Washington theorizes that when the town leaders heard of Ft. Davis and of the economic potential coming from the military base it was enough to cause the change of heart. However, those same leaders surely must have considered those same economic factors earlier but still did not want a base of armed Negroes so dangerously close to them. The full truth will probably never be known because those responsible for bringing about the change did not put it in writing and their lips have since been forever silenced by time.

By now German panzer units had smashed their way across Europe, and the Luftwaffe was sending wave after wave of Stukka dive bombers and Heinkel heavy bombers to soften up a surprised Poland. At the same time, the peaceful and verdant Alabama countryside encompassing the 1,647.20 acres destined to become Tuskegee's Army Air Field languished quietly under a lush cover of trees and plots of cotton. The trees, mainly the tall and stately southern long leaf pine, shared space with sturdy oak, gum, and yellow poplar; the pine and oak would be harvested commercially. The gently rolling hills, comprising most of the acreage, acquired by the War Department was owned by eight different individuals including the predominantly black County of Macon.

In December 1940, Air Corps Headquarters in Washington advised the Southeast Training Center that it would not establish a Primary flying school for Negro cadets, as would be the usual case for white cadets. It planned instead to utilize the graduates of Tuskegee's secondary training and place them directly into the Basic phase. Later, this changed under the influence of Major Ellison who forcefully suggested that for a fair chance, the Negro cadets should have the identical training given to white cadets.

Once the final go ahead for training black military pilots had been given, General Weaver decided to have all the specialists and support personnel trained at Tuskegee. This time Major Lucius Smith of his own staff objected saying that to afford the best training for this operation, all of the training should be done at bases already established. Correct reasoning prevailed and Chanute Field, Illinois was chosen to begin the training of the technicians. A directive issued stated that all colored personnel, except pilots, were to be trained at Chanute and held there until they were needed at Tuskegee.

Just before the War Department issued its grand announcement of the all-black 99th Pursuit Squadron, and the location of its training, Grove Webster made another special trip to Tuskegee on behalf of Air Corps Headquarters in Washington. Dr. Patterson was asked if he would mind letting Chicago have the Primary training contract since Tuskegee was getting the lion's share, the new airfield. Patterson's answer was a firm, No![35] There would be no sharing of the pie as an appeasement to Chicago.

The next step was to let out the contracts for building the Tuskegee Army Air Field Base. The firm of black architect Hilyard R. Robinson of Washington, DC was awarded the contract for drafting the design of TAAF. We make note here that Robinson's firm had never before designed an airfield or an airport of any kind. The construction phase was given to the black company of McKissack and McKissack of Nashville, Tennessee. Another point worthy of note is that McKissack's company did not have the heavy earthmoving equipment necessary to do the grading work required. To make up for that lack, McKissack formed an association with a white contractor who specialized in earthwork. This association was carried forward even though Archie A. Alexander, the black president of the construction company, Alexander and Repass, the same company that had built most of Moton Field, the field that became Tuskegee's secondary training site, that had experience, and the equipment, had even pleaded with McKissack for an alliance. The turn down remained in place even after Alexander, whose integrated company was from Des Moines, Iowa, had appealed to the War Department with the help of his congressman.[36] Construction on Tuskegee's Air Base began on July 12, 1941, with the clearing of timber. At the same time, the technicians training at Chanute were just a month into their courses.

# CHAPTER 3

# Training Begins

The 99th Pursuit Squadron was officially activated at Chanute Field on March 22, 1941, the activation being made about a month before Robert Wilson arrived. Wilson, born in Meridian, Mississippi, had been studying aeronautical engineering at the Illinois Institute of Technology in Chicago when he got word that Negroes were being allowed into the Army Air Corps. He remembers that 16 black students traveled down to the courthouse in Chicago to take the entrance examination and that only 2 of them passed—he, along with Charles Bowman, who had attended Fresno State College in California. The two men achieved the highest scores that had been attained on the entrance exam.

Wilson had been working his way through school after having attended Shurtheleff College in Alton, Illinois two years earlier. His early thoughts had centered on becoming an athletic coach. After the second year, Wilson decided that he did not want to become involved in sports as a coach and he moved to Chicago. In the Windy City, he had a chance meeting with John C. Robinson, one of the early pioneers, who convinced him that aviation was the absolute ultimate and he encouraged Wilson to enroll at the Institute. When Wilson and Bowman arrived at Chanute, Wilson recalled, "They told us that it would take about eight months before we could get into the cadet training." Because of their high scores Wilson and Bowman became the only two to be trained as instrument technicians. Even though they were all segregated, Wilson said, "Others in our group considered us somewhat elite and so they started calling us the nickname of Cuties from Chanute."

   The technical training lasted from April 1941 to October 1941. Then the entire group shipped out to Maxwell Field, Alabama on November 5, 1941. They ended up at Maxwell because Tuskegee's base was still far from ready. At Maxwell, Wilson recalled, "The white officers tried to get us technically trained men to do menial jobs on the post just like the aviation squadron labor battalions who were already there. They tried to assign us to clean latrines and barracks building that we weren't living in and we just flat refused to do that." As a result of their refusal, the Post Commander put the entire group on restriction. Military Police (MPs) patrolled their area but only two at a time so Wilson and some of the other men would wait until the MPs walked far enough out of sight allowing a few to slip out and go wherever they wished. Wilson recalled that they happened to have a colleague in the group whose real name was Major Whitmore. The men finally persuaded him to be party to a scheme that would benefit all of them. Wilson said, "Whitmore called the main gate and identified himself as Major Whitmore and he ordered the MPs to lift the restriction on the men scheduled to transfer to Tuskegee. Well, we were able to leave the base on buses without trouble for two whole days of freedom before the Post Commander got wind of it." A very angry Commander immediately tried his utter best to find the Major Whitmore who had countermanded his order because he intended to court martial him. The countermanding Major was never found.

   According to Wilson, the black aviation squadron on the base was assigned to their unit and the men in it were quite willing to clean barracks until some of the technically trained leaders convinced them not to do any more of such menial work. Finally, the time arrived for the technicians group to leave for Tuskegee—that knowledge alone caused morale to soar because the men believed they would be dealt with fairly despite having to live in tents and endure torrential rains and a glue-like sticky muck called mud.

   On their arrival at Tuskegee, Wilson became the single remaining lead person for instrument training because his bosom buddy Bowman had decided to transfer to Officer Candidate School (OCS) to enter the tank corps. For the very first class of aviation cadets at Tuskegee, Wilson was the one and only instrument instructor, but he soon trained other personnel to help out with that phase of the training. At first he reported directly to Lt Colonel Noel Parrish, then head of base operations. When Parrish moved up to headquarters, a white captain became Wilson's immediate superior and that soon led to a serious problem. Just before the captain went on Temporary Duty (TDY) Wilson was told he could get or order whatever he needed. In the words of Wilson, in the good captain's absence, a promotion list came through. Wilson filled it out, including his own name, and in ignorance signed the order for Captain Johnson. The list was turned over to Colonel Parrish who accepted it without looking at it but by the time Wilson had reached his office he had an urgent call to immediately report back to headquarters.

Colonel Parrish knew that Captain Johnson was TDY and could not understand how he could have signed the promotion orders. After Wilson explained that he had signed it, according to what he thought the Captain would have wanted, "Parrish let me know in no uncertain terms that no one signs another's name without putting 'for' and the signer's own signature." For that grievous error Wilson said, "I was 'busted' from staff sergeant down to buck private. And it took several changes of orders before I was able to regain my original rank again."

Months later, on the day Wilson was to transfer to Lockbourne Air Base in Ohio, he happened to pass by Post Headquarters. Colonel Parrish came out in shirtsleeves to personally tell him how much he appreciated the good work he had done despite the demotion and urged him to stay with the Air Force. Wilson later took the cadet examination again but after passing it he refused to accept it because of the treatment he had seen given to blacks. At this point Wilson decided to accept a promotion to Warrant Officer because of his training at Chanute and the Chicago Institute. While at Tuskegee, he had finished the instrument pilot instructor's school at Bryan Air Base, Texas, and had received his pilot's wings after 70 hours of training in an AT-10 twin-engine trainer.

Wilson recalled only one serious racial problem at Tuskegee. While in charge of link training, someone sent a white staff sergeant over to his office. The staff sergeant informed him that from now on he, the staff, would be in charge and they would immediately get the place straightened up as it should be. Wilson exploded. He yelled at the "staff" to "get the...outta here"! Wilson then made a quick beeline for headquarters and had a consultation with Colonel Parrish. The "staff" was immediately transferred elsewhere. Wilson swears that none of the hundreds of cadets that he trained ever tossed their cookies in any of the link trainers but he freely admits that some did come out with severe cases of vertigo.[1]

Fred McLaurin was among the same group of men called up with Robert Wilson to Chanute. A native of Jackson, Mississippi, McLaurin was working in a Civilian Conservation Corps (CCC) camp in Illinois when he spotted a notice on the bulletin board that said Negroes could enlist in the U.S. Army Air Corps. He volunteered but failed the physical at Chanute because he weighed only 110 pounds and the minimum was 118 pounds. The physical was the same as that given to pilot applicants. Now out of the CCC and not in the Air Corps, McLaurin returned to Mississippi only to be drafted 6 months later. While taking his basic training, another directive came out asking specifically for trainees as aircraft mechanics. Again, McLaurin volunteered and this time ended up in a group of 300 men that was sent to Lincoln, Nebraska for training at mechanics school.

The school was segregated with all black trainees taking classes during specific shifts, 24 hours around the clock. He recalled that, "The white trainees lived close by the classrooms while the black students were quartered way out in the boondocks in facilities that were adequate but very old and poor by comparison." McLaurin had married just before being drafted and he had permission to live off base for a brief period that lasted less than a month. "Only six black families lived in Lincoln at the time and black troops were not allowed in town because they couldn't stay over-night." Luckily for McLaurin, his wife and two children managed to rent a room from the mother of the local black barber. But it soon turned out that poor transportation to the base and some very harsh weather convinced Mrs. McLaurin to take the kids and flee back to Mississippi.

On the base, McLaurin's rebellious nature served to keep him in almost continuous hot water. He developed some kind of a rash, went to the hospital and was put in one of the end beds in the 20-bed ward. The next morning a white enlisted man brought him a mop and bucket and said, "Boy, you're gonna mop this here barracks." McLaurin flatly refused saying there was just no way he would do any mopping as sick as he felt. Within the hour, orderlies came to put up a curtain of sheets around his bed isolating him from the rest of the ward for the remainder of his stay. The doctor later told him that the rash was caused by the heat buildup at the top of the hangar while he worked on engines.

McLaurin complained to his commanding officer about the isolation treatment with the sheets and the Major told him that they thought he had some sort of contagion. McLaurin said, "That contagion stuff only came up after I refused to put my hands on that mop handle."

McLaurin also remembered that Hubert Julian, the flamboyant one men-tioned earlier, roomed in the same barracks and took the same training although Julian was not in the military. He believes it was because of Julian's presence and his notoriety that they were accorded somewhat better treat-ment than those in some of the other barracks. Julian had accumulated reams of newspaper accounts of his aerial daredevil deeds, and he was not in the least reluctant to show off his press-worthy accomplishments at the drop of a hat.

At the end of eight months all 300 men graduated and boarded a troop train for Tuskegee. They arrived on the very night the 99th Pursuit Squadron was finally shipping out for its point of debarkation in New York. When McLaurin's wife first arrived at Tuskegee from Mississippi, she was stuck in the little box of a train station at Chehaw for six hours because the sheriff refused to help her or even call the base for someone to know that she was there. Once again luck selected McLaurin in helping him find quarters for his family not too far from the base. But that luck became both, a plus and a minus because it sorely tempted him to flirt with disaster again by sneaking off the base every night. He remembered one night that while John "Mr. Death" Whitehead, then a cadet, was making night landings, the MPs spotted a shadowy someone dashing across one of the runways. McLaurin, though short in stature, was very fleet afoot and eluded the frantic hunt for the unauthorized person seen scampering quickly across the runway. McLaurin maintains that, "Growing up in the South helped me by not having to make any major adjustments to the humiliating demands of segregation like that faced by the other guys who were brought up in the North."[2]

George W. Porter was another Southerner who entered the Army and received his basic training at Fort Francis near Warren, Wyoming in late 1942. In December of the same year, Porter, a native of Slidell, Louisiana, was selected as a Tuskegee Airman candidate and sent to the same aircraft and engine mechanics school in Nebraska in the same class as McLaurin. At Tuskegee, Porter became a crew chief on the P-40 fighter and the AT-10 twin-engine trainer. He quickly rose in rank to master sergeant and suddenly encountered his first real personnel problem.

When for some unexplained reason a white technical sergeant was put in charge of Porter's duties, he began to take extended three-day passes and was finally called to face the officer in charge of maintenance, a Major. The tech sergeant had listed Porter as being Absent Without Leave (AWOL) and the Major was frankly puzzled because his record up to then had been just perfect! The write up simply stated that Porter had not reported for work. Under questioning, Porter said he had been on leave with a three-day pass. The Major responded that he could not have a three-day pass without permission. To that Porter inquired, "Sir, you are a Major. Do you have to get permission from the Captain down on the maintenance line to go on leave?" "Hell no!" the Major exploded, "I'm a Major." Porter quickly said, "Well, sir, I'm a master sergeant and they told me to get permission from a tech sergeant."

A check of the Charge of Quarters (CQ) showed that he had, in fact, properly signed out and back in on each occasion. The Major grumbled loudly suggesting that what he was doing must be illegal but Porter held his ground by asking again, if he, as a master sergeant, had to take orders from a tech sergeant, a full rank below him. "In order to save some face the Major, the tech sergeant and a line chief tried to assign every misfit and eight ball on the flight line to me. I guess they were hoping to make things real hard on me. But I had an answer for them in a hurry." An enterprising Porter brought out a brand new deck of cards and took all of those misfits over to the Non-commissioned Officers Club and treated them to a big "beer bust." During the course of beer guzzling, Porter detailed just how he wanted the men to act, clean shaven, haircuts, have clean fatigues, and on the flight line at 7 am sharp. He explained to them logically, "If we can drink all these suds together we can damn well work together." From that time on his crews topped the list.

Porter recalled that he and the other top mechanics at Tuskegee during the early days had to master four different kinds of inline engines that were used in the P-40. In those early days, transition to the P40 from the AT-6 trainer was conducted at TAAF and in order for all the pilots to get in their flying time in the limited number of aircraft available, each plane's engine was kept running for consecutive missions. It so happened that one of the flaws of the P-40, once the nation's top fighter, was its proclivity to overheat on the ground with the engine idling. The mechanics had to come up with a solution. Porter said they solved the heating problem by shooting water into the oil cooler with a hose while the pilots were changing places. Early on, Porter said, "It was the crew chiefs that did all the work; whenever we had any major problems the crew chiefs all working together helped each other overcome those problems, no matter what they were."[3]

Porter retired in 1965 as a senior master sergeant who had worked on, flew in, or managed 20 different types of aircraft in the 23 years he spent on active military duty.

Luther Pugh grew up in Philadelphia, Pennsylvania, but his birthplace was Orangeburg, South Carolina. Soon after the Japanese had bombed Pearl Harbor, Pugh enlisted in the Signal Corps and was called up in June 1942. He trained at Ft. Monmouth, New Jersey and his finish there created a major mix-up, a real snafu! They transferred Pugh to a signal company in New Orleans, Louisiana but when he arrived, the all-white company refused to take him assigning him instead to a quartermaster company. Since he was not even a quartermaster trainee, all Pugh had to do was lie around and take life easy. The major drawback, he recalled was, "For two months I couldn't draw any pay because somehow my papers had become lost." Being broke forced him to borrow money from whoever would lend it to him. But eventually that led to having a couple of friends who would hide if they saw him before he saw them.

Finally, they did send Pugh to Tuskegee where his lost papers miraculously and mysteriously reappeared allowing him to collect his back pay. Pugh's recollections of Tuskegee are not very fond; in fact, he came very close to saying that he hated his tour there. He remembered waiting on the weekends at the bus stop to see how many white patrons got on the bus he wanted to take, counting to see if there was any room left for Negroes. The all-white town of Tuskegee lay just blocks from the campus of Tuskegee Institute and Pugh recalled, "You had to either be at the bus station or on the campus by 10 o'clock at night; if you were caught in town after that you were in serious trouble." This was generally the case throughout the South; blacks had to be off the streets or in the Negro sections of town at the time of curfew, usually a few hours after sundown. Punishment for violators varied from jailing to beatings and other forms of verbal or physical abuse as example setters.

Pugh recalled an incident in which he was in a little "joint" for Negroes when a white deputy sheriff came in to search a civilian and then took a knife away from the offender. In attempting to break the knife blade the deputy cut his hand and then callously proceeded to bloody up Pugh's clean uniform when he patted him down. From that time on he said, "I stayed on the base to make certain I kept out of trouble because I couldn't handle the humiliating racial practices of the South."[4]

These men were typical of the thousands who came from every section of the country, from every city, town, and hamlet. Each was anxious and eager to join the war—efforts that would band them together to smite the evil dictatorial forces that were already in motion, threatening to overwhelm the free world. There were college graduates with high degrees, there were world class athletes, and there were those not so well educated and those not so athletically gifted. But the common denominator for all of these men was the willingness to make the supreme sacrifice for freedom. They were staunchly ready to support a cause that not one of them could then fully realize, the cause of freedom, first class freedom under the very flag where they stood poised ready and willing to fight.

Heavy seasonal rains alternately slowed and then stopped construction on the acreage that was gradually becoming Tuskegee Army Air Field. Graded roads to and from construction sites on the base were, in most cases, impassable except for four-wheeled vehicles. Nevertheless, the first truckloads of military personnel, the first of their kind, the bare skeleton that would soon fill out, become a part of history, arrived on November 8, 1941. Among this group were six aviation cadets, including Captain Benjamin O. Davis, Jr., of Class 42-C. Of this group, all would graduate except one cadet, Frederick H. Moore, Jr., from the Basic and Advanced phases of training.

When this historic first black pilot training class began their Primary training, there were a total of thirteen cadets. Listed alphabetically they were: John C. Anderson, an all-American athlete from Toledo, University; Charles D. Brown, a college graduate from Abbeville, South Carolina; Theodore Brown from New York City with an MA from Northwestern University; Marion Carter, a college graduate from Chicago; Lemuel R. Custis from Hartford, Connecticut with a degree from Howard University; Captain Benjamin O. Davis, Jr. a West Point graduate; Charles DeBow from Indianapolis a graduate of Hampton Institute; Frederick H. Moore, a graduate of Tuskegee Institute from Sommerville, New Jersey; Ullysses S. Pannell from Regan, Texas with a degree in agriculture; George S. "Spanky" Roberts, a native of Fairmont, West Virginia and a graduate of West Virginia State; Mac Ross also a West Virginia State grad from Dayton, Ohio; William Slade, a college graduate from Raleigh, North Carolina, and Roderick Williams from Chicago a graduate from the University of Illinois.[5]

When the cadets arrived at Tuskegee, only one of the six runways (North-South) could be used in a graded but unpaved condition. The others were still in various stages of completion as were two enlisted men's barracks and the warehouses for Signal, Ordnance, and the Quartermaster Corps. The foundation for the administration building itself was curing prior to accepting its structure.

To give an inkling of the intense pressure on Washington, Major Ellison, as Project Officer, in his report of August 13, 1941, to the Commanding General, Southeast Air Corps Training Center, stated that the project would not be completed until January 31, 1942, instead of the expected November 8, 1941 date. This report did not make minor ripples; it made monstrous waves. As stated earlier, the immediate answer from General Weaver, because of intense political pressure on the White House and the War Department, was to order the start of pilot training for colored candidates to begin on schedule regardless of the cost.

On November 8, 1941, the day the men arrived, everything was on a makeshift basis, tents were used for communication, cadet ready room, parachute room, and supply and maintenance. Actually, the cadets and all enlisted personnel were quartered in a tent camp that became a wet, muddy, and soggy mess when heavier rains hit in December. The tent camp was appropriately named Camp Hazard, locally in honor of Post Executive Officer, Captain John T. Hazard. Major Ellison became the first Post Commander effective July 23, 1941, although at the time the post was little more than a mucky quagmire sprinkled with tents.

Prior to November 10, 1941, all security on the base had been performed by white civilian personnel hired by the Corps of Engineers. But on the above date and again on November 24, 1941, 31 black enlisted men were placed on special duty with the MPs. The official report says that when the white civilians were replaced by black military personnel, some of the civilians called on Post Commander Ellison and loudly protested being replaced by Negroes. They then made threats against their replacements as well as against those responsible for making the changes. This provides yet another indication of the prevailing hostile and dangerous attitude of the white community that surrounded the base.

In those early days, just before and following Pearl Harbor, officers and enlisted personnel kept the training at Tuskegee going on in the face of almost insufferable conditions. The enlisted men and the cadets were quartered in tents two miles from the flight line, the repair hangar was a tent, the men ate in a crude Hawaiian style mess hall tent, and ground school was conducted in a tent and one of the unfinished barracks. Drinking water was hauled in by truck from the town of Tuskegee and all the heating was provided by grossly inadequate little portable "Sibly" stoves. For a further description of what conditions were like at the time, there is the statement of historian Ambler, who at the time was Post Intelligence Officer. Ambler stated that after finally obtaining a desk, following two weeks of haggling and begging, he made an office in the orderly room of an unfinished barracks that was unheated. During the rainy days, of which there were many, he walked the mile from the barracks to Post Headquarters because it was impossible to get a vehicle through the muck and mire.[6]

Even before he was named the first Post Commander of Tuskegee Army Air Field, Major James Ellison intended making Tuskegee a first class operation, like any other base. When black MPs stopped white civilians at the base entrance and refused them entry without proper identification the protests and threats from local white Tuskegee officials reached a new high. But Ellison acted quickly and with high-ranking military dispatch in standing behind his men who were carrying out their assigned duties.

Major Ellison, like his colleague Major Lucius Smith, had taken a lot of censure and guff from fellow officers because of their conscientious and dedicated work on the Tuskegee project. Their fellow officers made behind the hand statements that would have probably delighted Hitler and Goebbels to the highest. Ellison often vocally stated that his ambition would be to fly across the country with a Negro squadron just to prove that it could be done.[7]

The original plan was not to have a conventional Primary flying training stage at all, as was customary. The men were to report directly from secondary CPTP training to Basic training. Again, Ellison and Smith went to bat. They argued that the men would be handicapped if they were not trained properly in the fundamentals of flying, and if they were not given equal training then they could not be judged with equal standards. Once more General Weaver was convinced and the search spread for a suitable Primary training site. It turned up on the Notasulga Road near Tuskegee Institute. Notasulga was the name earlier mentioned on G. L. Washington's politicking trip to the nation's capital to elicit and curry favors for Tuskegee as it fought for a chunk of the CPTP aviation pie. The final chosen site would be called Moton Field.

Major Ellison's solid resolve to stand firm against the loud, ominous threats of the hostile surrounding white community ultimately would become the cause of his being relieved of command in January 1942. The transfer made him extremely upset at not being allowed to finish the project in which he had so much faith, the project that would later be called the Tuskegee Experience.

The banner headlines that announced the formation of the first black combat squadron in the young history of the Air Corps drew thunderous opposition from those who were pushing hardest for it. The NAACP in its magazine, "The Crisis," said, the segregated squadron was " ... by no means the answer to the demand of colored people for full integration into all branches of the armed services ... " and it stated in conclusion that the group "can be forced to accept it, but we can never agree to it."[8]

That same announcement triggered long and frequent protests by Judge William Hastie. He fired off a stream of memos calling the "in concrete" segregation plans a serious mistake and he demanded an end to them. But General George C. Marshall, Chief of Staff, viewed Hastie's demands as trying to force the Army into solving a complex social problem, one that had hung around the country's neck like an Albatross, since slavery. Not only did Hastie's pleas go unheeded, Secretary of War Stimson and Assistant Secretary of War John J. McCloy kept Hastie in the dark on the very things he had been appointed to look into. A special committee headed by McCloy on Special Troop Policies was created, but it quietly excluded Hastie.[9]

Judge Hastie astutely raised the question of training only a pursuit squadron when medium and heavy bomber pilots were also in great demand. He reasoned that the real issue was strictly one of race. Bombers carried crews of five to nine men as opposed to a single pilot in a fighter craft. Bombers flew much greater distances and a flight of three medium bombers piloted and manned by blacks would cause no end of problems and troubles in landing at a white base. There would be the black officers giving orders to white enlisted personnel and the basic problems of quartering the crews, crews that could total up to fifteen or more, and the problem of where they would sleep and where they would eat? In addition, fighter pilot training was presumed more exacting and could certainly lead to quick expulsion for those lacking all the proper qualities. There were high hopes that failure in this more exacting training would bring an early end to the relentless pressure on Washington. The thinking by Air Corps strategists was that once it became openly known that blacks could not fly combat fighter craft it would then be a simple matter to close the segregated base, a base buried in isolation in the Deep South. This expected and anticipated failure would allow the Air Corps to go on with its war efforts without missing a beat.

It did not take Hastie very long after his appointment, to see that War Department and Army Air Corps decision-makers were playing a cat and mouse game with him. Plans were concocted and decisions made without consulting or even notifying his office. His ideas and opinions were either discounted or just plainly ignored. But the final straw for Hastie came when he learned from a newspaper the plans to make Jefferson Barracks in Missouri a black base and establish a black OCS there. Hastie became so infuriated that he quickly turned in his resignation on January 16, 1943, along with five scathing pages of deficiencies, primarily directed at the Air Corps. He complained that although thousands of weather officers were needed, less than 10 blacks could be "accommodated." The rest were summarily turned down. He stated that fully qualified black pilots were not being accepted even as service pilots and that black medical officers were receiving their training by correspondence instead of being admitted to the School of Aviation Medicine at Randolph Field in Texas. Service pilots were those who performed noncombat functions such as ferrying aircraft and supplies. He further pointed out that Tuskegee itself was tightly segregated with separate dining and restrooms, Post Exchange (PX) facilities; black MPs were forbidden loaded side arms and the officer's accommodations were Jim Crow instituted.

Judge Hastie was replaced by Truman Gibson, one of Hastie's former aides, but with his resignation, like the ram's horn sounding to the Walls of Jericho, the Air Corps' previously impregnable wall of segregation began to crumble. Chief of the Air Staff Major General George Stratemeyer, quickly took personal control and immediately began making changes. He ordered the Director of Individual Training to make certain that no Air Corps training school or facility had segregated training. But even here there was a catch—Tuskegee would be the one unique exception! Stratemeyer told the Commanding General of the Technical Training Command that there were to be no colored schools operated on a segregated basis. He further ordered that black officer candidates at the Miami OCS be given equal treatment; that they "go to the same classes, to the same drills, and eat in mess halls the same as Whites."[10] Stratemeyer then notified the Air Surgeon that there would be admittance for Negroes at the School of Aviation Medicine at Randolph Field. The massive uprooting of longstanding practices did not stop there; an order went out that the segregationist policies being practiced at Tuskegee Air Base itself be ended. By this time Colonel Noel Parrish had become the final Commander of TAAF and he immediately began to institute the policies to put black officers in administrative positions and, for the first time, brought dignity to the black military personnel at the base.

It was Colonel Parrish's immediate predecessor, Colonel Frederick von Kimble, who had acted quickly to placate the irate white townspeople by making Tuskegee Air Base as Jim Crow as the town. The word Jim Crow was coined from a white minstrel show performer who, around 1830, blackened his face to sing and dance ludicrously to demean blacks in the South. The term was later applied to the many state and local laws enacted to legally enforce segregation in the South. After two black airmen had visited the white section of the base PX and had refused to leave until ordered to do so by an officer, Kimble had "Black" and "White" signs placed over all the base facilities. Not only did this act create a segregated base within a segregated community, but it also caused the morale on the base to snapp into a steep nosedive. Kimble even complained to his headquarters that all other bases should follow the War Department's policy of segregation so when black personnel went to other bases, primarily in the North, the practices everywhere would be the same. He wanted the stated policy at all bases to pattern itself after the policy of the surrounding community. Oddly enough, Kimble was born in Oregon, a region not primarily known then for heavy racial intolerance.

Nevertheless, Colonel Kimble, who had taken over command of TAAF from Major Ellison in January 1942, would himself be removed from his command in December of the same year. Colonel Noel Parrish received this duty after serving as commanding officer of the 66th Army Air Corps Training Detachment, which was the Primary Flying School stationed at Tuskegee Institute and included Moton Field, the primary flying field.

Unlike Kimble, Parrish was a southerner, born and raised in Kentucky. He had entered the army as a private in the 11$^{th}$ Cavalry on July 30, 1930. He was appointed flying cadet on July 1, 1931, at March Field, California and completed Primary training before joining the Basic phase at the newly constructed Randolph Field in Texas. He finished his advanced training at Kelly Field, Texas in July 1932. Graduating as an attack pilot, he served one year of active duty with the 13$^{th}$ Attack Squadron at Ft. Crocker at Galveston, Texas. Parrish then enlisted as a private in the Air Corps at Chanute Field, Illinois in September 1933, and transferred to the 1$^{st}$ Provisional Transport Squadron in February 1934, where he stayed flying transports. In July 1935, he received his commission as a Second Lieutenant in the regular army. Assigned to the 13$^{th}$ Attack Squadron once more, he spent the next three years at Barksdale Field in Shreveport, Louisiana.

There would be still other transfers for Parrish; this time he returned to Randolph Field as a flight instructor of primary students. At the beginning of the CPTP he was sent to the Chicago School of Aeronautics where he stayed until being transferred to Tuskegee in May 1941. He became Director of Training of the Tuskegee Primary Flying School in December 1941.[11]

A good portion of Parrish's greatness evolved because he refused to believe in or practice hearsay, and dug into problems and issues for the truth and once armed with that he stayed on a course of right against wrong. His sharp sense of justice and fairness is loudly voiced in his dissertation at the AWC. "An Army Officer . . . who allows his judgment of fact to be influenced by his personal preferences is therefore prejudiced and to the extent of his prejudice, his judgments are unreliable and dangerous. An officer whose conduct is dominated by personal likes and dislikes, rather than by his concern for the welfare and efficiency of the entire group for which he is responsible is violating trust."[12] Without the astute leadership of Colonel Parrish, there is little doubt the grudging opportunity to train black military pilots would have failed and failed miserably, as it was hoped and predicted by many. Parrish noted in his dissertation that because he had spent more time early in the training plan, flying with black pilots than anyone else, he was repeatedly asked, "How do Negroes fly?" That same question was asked by military men, of all grades, as well as politicians in the upper levels of government. Parrish said that few were ever satisfied with or were able to comprehend his only possible answer. "Negroes fly very much like everyone else flies."[13] To have known Parrish would have been to have known the very faint sly smile that would have accompanied that statement.

As a career military man, Colonel Parrish became a well-polished statesman and a firm buffer against the seething hostilities surrounding the Tuskegee Air Base. He became the staunch military bulwark of equal treatment and justice for all the men under his command. Because of his innate ability to isolate the true causes of many problems bristling hostilities were kept at a safe distance and potentially explosive situations were defused and rendered harmless.

Repeatedly in his dissertation Parrish exposes the super ridiculous postures of attitudes held by, especially, Southern white men about all black men. He relates that those thoughts held that all black men were exactly alike in all things, and they were regarded as a group, clones of not very bright child-like ancestors. And because of this limited mentality they could only succeed in the white world if they were led by the superior white. In another section, Parrish chides the misplaced and faulty double standards applied to skin color. There was a good-will tour of officers from Latin America that stopped over in Montgomery, Alabama, so the staff officers from Maxwell Air Base staged a big party for them. The affair was held in the Jefferson Davis Hotel and college coeds from Huntington College were brought in to help with the entertainment. It was said that the girls were very much attracted to the Haitian officers who were dark, handsome, and spoke with a delightful French accent. At the same time, Parrish observed, Haitian pilots were being trained at Tuskegee because of their color, many darker than many of the native African-American cadets. But the height of this inane senselessness was that the Air Corps top brass at Maxwell had arranged for a big interracial party for foreign officers many of whom were dark complexioned but on the other hand there was this monstrous Negro problem. A comparable simile from the old saw of being able to open the throat and swallow the goat but hopelessly gagging on a single black, troublesome gnat.

Parrish also ripped into the criticisms that, at times, came to him from visiting officers or officials complaining of seeing a white woman walking with a black man on base. In fact he would have to explain that the woman happened to be a black woman of very fair skin. Then he would show the complaining visitor some white employees who were darker than some of the other black personnel on the base. It was almost a game of charades because after that the nonsense of trying to identify race by skin color led to derisive confusion.

# CHAPTER 4

# The Selection Process

By early 1943, the crush of young black men vying for the chance to become military pilots in the Army Air Corps had swelled to such a volume that Tuskegee could no longer physically accommodate such numbers. Now the military brass frantically searched for a staging area where large numbers of these eager young men could be lopped off by screening and testing. The area selected was Keesler Field in Biloxi, Mississippi, the perfect Gulf of Mexico site, isolated and in the Deep South. Besides for the screening, the base also served as a basic training camp, drilling, marching, firing weapons, and learning the Army way in a category called the Pre-Aviation Cadet Candidate. Keesler would also become a third site used for training black mechanics.

After reporting to the Presidio of Monterey on November 17, 1943, Keesler Field became my home six days later until February 1944. Home at Keesler, for the first three weeks, turned out to be a huge green tent with a floor of sand and no stove for heating. That unforgettable stay was marked by snow falling in the Gulf of Mexico for the first time in 25 years. I never really got to know any of my tent mates because two weeks later I would be all alone in that big green icebox sleeping in all the clothing I had been issued in order to stay warm at night. My tent mates had been eliminated quietly, almost surreptitiously, one by one. Every couple of days one of the beds would be empty with no warning or explanation other than a rolled up mattress on a bare cot.

Keesler Field was where the neophytes, those innocent believers in free chocolate cake and fresh apple pie in the military, learned a very basic constant, never volunteer for anything! When truck drivers were asked for, only the unsuspecting recruits like me raised innocent trusting hands for the promptly issued wheelbarrow, broom, and shovel to keep the streets and gutters cleaned of everything larger than a grain of sand.

Several tents had been pitched in the icy white sand between barracks buildings to house the overflow of cadet candidates. But it took another week of living alone inside the green monster before being moved to another tent with three new roommates and a stove but with nothing provided to burn in it. Each of us scrounged up all the paper and scraps of wood possible, but on a well-policed base such as Keesler, wood of any kind, in scrap form, just did not exist. Desperation helped us to discover the availability of the wooden fencing between our tent and the adjacent aircraft runway. We began breaking off pieces of the bottom portions of the latticework of the fence leaving the total piece shorter but the upper ends untouched. That became our major source of fuel. Fortunately, we moved after two weeks to the warm confines of the nearest barracks across the street. What we did not realize at the time was that the now available room created in the barracks came as result of other eager young applicants being eliminated.

Barracks life was vastly more comfortable and superior compared to the monster tents but now we had a sergeant telling and showing us how to make the beds, assigning us to latrine duty and getting us up in the still darkness of the mornings. The two-storey barracks was open upstairs and downstairs with only the sergeant privileged to have private quarters, a room near the entrance. Rows of beds lined the unfinished pine walls in head to foot manner such that either the head or foot of each bed stood near the center aisle. Friendships formed quickly under these circumstances and all the tricks and pranks that could be played with bedding on friends and scapegoats were revealed. Cracker crumbs, walnut shells, short sheeting, and even hiding bedding and mattress on the roof so the hapless victim had to sleep on the bare hard springs for the night was fair game. As a rule, the same individuals were made the butts of these pranks over and over. The potential victim always had to make certain, first of all, that he had bedding then he had to carefully check for all kinds of things, such as frogs, that could be waiting for him in his bed.

There were three primary barracks for those lucky or fortunate enough to be still in the running of being processed at Keesler, processed being another term for being evaluated. There were physical tests for reaction times, coordination, dexterity, depth of sight judgment, as well as psychological evaluations. Besides marching and drilling, Squadron 707, which occupied the barracks on the corner, took its turn in rotation, a half squadron at a time, of doing kitchen police (KP) with the other two squadrons.

KP proved much more than a real learning experience, for, along with cleaning huge pots and pans, scrubbing floors on hands and knees with a brush and a block-like brick of extra strong GI soap, opportunities allowed pilfering extra goodies like apples from the kitchen and pies from the pantry. We also had experts who knew the specialized art of giving a hot foot, not the comedy movie kind but the second degree burn go-to-the-hospital kind. They reserved this treatment for goldbricks (fellows who skillfully avoided all work) and in 707 there were two such characters. Both tempted fate once too often by sleeping on a mess hall bench while the rest of us scrubbed the floors. The art of this operation required a small lump of shoe polish packed between the side and sole of the shoe and inserting two match heads into the polish and lighting the ends of the matches. When the small initial flame reached the match head buried in the flammable shoe polish it flared up and became almost blowtorch hot. Both goldbricks ended up in the hospital and when they returned neither again made the mistake of sleeping or trying to sleep while the rest of the group worked.

There was absolutely no way to completely avoid working on the base and it soon became clear that some jobs were much better than others. It did not take long to feel that the best duty was theater detail because when the six-man crew finished cleaning, sweeping up popcorn, and picking up candy wrappers, work was done for the day plus the movie could be attended for free. There was no balcony and the seating was divided down the middle from entrance to front row by a rope. White on one side, colored on the other. While we cleaned, the rope did not exist—both sides were treated equally. The way the segregation scheme worked was that whoever sat on one side or the other first caused the other race to take the opposite side of the rope. And you only found out on which side to sit on after entering and peering into the darkness to see who was sitting where. At times we made a game of it by making certain to arrive first and arbitrarily picking a seat, but it meant nothing because both sides were identical in every way.

For Christmas dinner, we received the full spread of turkey with all of its trimmings, as we had for Thanksgiving. But this time it was different because a classmate whose last name was Brown and the shortest man in the squadron somehow, in broad daylight, managed to steal a whole roasted turkey. He used the turkey for snacks and stored the unfinished portion in two large brown paper bags on the roof of the barracks. The low temperatures allowed him to finish it before spoilage and I do not recall that he shared any of his booty with anyone. Of course they missed the turkey but our cunning food thief was never caught and the rest of us grudgingly admired him for his brazenness and greedy appetite for being such a small fellow.

Sometime in January 1944, the whole squadron was driven out to the firing range where we learned to fire the carbine, the 45 caliber machinegun and the 45 caliber sidearm. On the second trip we were scored on accuracy with all three weapons. I recall receiving a score of 285 out of a possible 300 and earned the proud title of sharpshooter. After the firing range we bivouacked where up to four men could put their quarter tent sections together forming one big unit or the loner could sleep under his own little quarter section. We had to crawl through the grass on our bellies cradling a heavy rifle that we would probably never fire in battle. The tall green pointed strands of the grass grew so high that you could not be seen as long as you crawled. That went quite well until one of the men suddenly jumped up and yelled, "Snake!" He slammed the butt of his rifle down where his face had been and then gingerly poked around in the grass using the barrel like a stick. The sergeant hurried over, looked at the spot and began to laugh, "Just a little grass snake," he said. Sure enough the tail section of a greenish colored snake, the size of a garter snake, still wiggled, the head part had vanished through the grass and would, the sarge said, live to grow another tail. The sarge then, in a very loud voice, firmly warned us that in the future, no matter what came under our noses, not to stand up because we would likely get our butts shot off.

The large group, 707, was called a squadron but that was broken up into smaller groups of men called flights, while in the infantry they would have been called squads. It was from this smaller element that we learned the rudiments of falling in fixing your position in relation to the man on each side of you, and if you were not in the front row, the distance between you and the men in front of you. All this was necessary for the practice of close order drilling, the following of commands given by the sergeant or his designate. We finally learned how to perform an "about face" without falling over and how to begin marching together with each man starting off on the correct foot. Of course, the sergeant would, at times, have fun with so many green recruits by giving us quick commands that early on had us bumping into each other or having some of us turning in the wrong directions. At length we did begin to shape up. We did begin to take pride in being able to follow with exactness and pride the sharp orders barked out by the leader. We developed the idea that we could look good in marching if we tried and that became an objective to be achieved.

The men in 707 came from all over the country, the East, the West, the North, and the South. We were there to be sifted out, to be tried, and tested. We were all young eager beavers anxious to become pilots in the U.S. Army Air Corps. I do not think any of us was fully aware of the turmoil, the explosiveness of the admitted fact that the Air Corps did not want us solely because of our color. We were unaware of the hard skirmishes, the battles, the racial humiliations, and the bitter turn downs that had preceded us. We had not suffered the pains inflicted upon those who, already at the time, were offering their lives for freedom. We would be given our own hurdles to clear and our own battles to win by achievement. Most of that still lay ahead. For the present we struggled to learn the basics of military life and soldiering. Being in the air as a pilot was a different element. Being on the ground, where most of our time would be spent, meant having to learn how to do that the Army way. Keesler was, in fact, that basic learning place but it acted also as a flow control valve. This fact was established by having to use tents pitched between the barracks to house more men than the base was prepared to handle normally. The spigot could be opened or closed to allow a specified number to move on to the next level. I had arrived alone and I would later move out, not in a group with three or four others but singly. Most of the men in 707, I would never see again.

Payday soon arrived and for the first time in ages I managed to have more than 50 cents in my pocket. Everyone in squadron 707 made ready to go into Biloxi for the first contact with civilians in more than a month. It had rained heavily during the night and the streets were soaking wet. Our transportation, a grey-colored, low-slung, semi-trailer had four windows and wooden seats inside. The driver stopped after he crossed the railroad tracks that marked the boundary of the Negro section in the town of Biloxi. My very first step from the bus was into a large mud puddle. There were a couple of bars or "joints" all on one side of one street. They sold and supplied something called a "setup," a big bowl of ice, lemon slices, and bottles of Coca Cola. You purchased whisky from individuals out on the street before entering the bar and brought your purchases inside in brown paper bags. That was my first and last trip into town for the rest of my stay at Keesler Field.

Much later, I learned that Keesler also served as a processing center for white Pre-Aviation Cadets, though we had no contact with each other. It also became a training center for black bombardiers and other aviation technicians of both races. One mid-February afternoon, they summoned me to the orderly room and told me to pack up my gear; I was being sent to Tuskegee. It was another of those glad-sad moments as it had been leaving school during football season. I had formed some good friendships at Keesler and now that was being severed. Of the 60 men that were in 707, I could only recall seeing 4 later. Fortunately, one had been one of those close friends. Once more I boarded a train with only my trusty duffel bag as company. The ride to Chehaw became one of stop and go, stops to pick up the metal milk cans left in the little wooden waiting sheds it seemed every five miles. The sheds were little more than open benches with roofs, sort of early day bus stops. Chehaw, the train station of Tuskegee, was a little bigger and at least the waiting room had a door. With a short ride into Tuskegee, I checked into a College Training Detachment (CTD) dormitory on the campus of Tuskegee Institute. The CTD was another control valve designed to slow the burgeoning numbers swamping the Tuskegee Air Base. The CTD program endeavored to cram a year's worth of college level Math, Physics, English, and other courses into 6 months. Military style order was kept and drill instructions were given regularly by student officers. Called TAC officers, these students wore little round silver buttons on their caps to distinguish them from the rest of us. I recall the physics professor as being short, rotund, and having a gold watch chain looped through the vest of his dark suit. This professor stands out more than the others because we nicknamed him "square root" as a result of his physical shape but also because this particular professor had an 11-year-old son who could work the physics problems as well or better than the rest of us. Since the son seemed an exact miniature of his father in stature and in brainpower, he was aptly named "cube root."

For the first time in months, another enticing factor reemerged. Lots and lots of pretty girls strolled about on campus and even though Institute officials firmly discouraged the dating of female students and military personnel, some of it took place. Aside from actual dating we talked to one another, compliments of the phone system that linked all the dormitories. We would pick up the phone and dial one of the female dorms and just talk to whoever picked up the other end. Sometimes the person on the other end would follow the dictates of authority and hang up, but other times a lengthy conversation would ensue. Take out the drilling and early morning reveille and we could have been on any college campus with its ivy-covered brick buildings and tree lined streets. There was even a soda parlor two blocks away from our dorm quarters that had a large plate glass window. It allowed us cadet types to stroll by and take a quick peek; if any pretty girls happened to be there, we could saunter in to buy a soda and hope to strike up a conversation. Greenwood defined the black section of the town of Tuskegee, separate and distinct from the Institute itself, but darkness marked the curfew hour for being either on the campus proper or within the boundaries of Greenwood.

The biggest attraction during the CTD tour was the 10 hours of orientation flying time we received in Piper Cubs at a cleared opening called Kennedy Field among the tall pine trees surrounding the field. It was enough to make you giddy, this physical act of actually flying in a real airplane, getting off of the ground. All the instructors were black and all were smartly dressed in forest green uniforms with matching caps. Kennedy had only one grassy runway and a little wooden operations building. For those of us who had never flown before those 10 hours became the consummation of everything that was good, the sweetest supernal nectar and ambrosia for the mind and the spirit. Students sat in the back seat of the little yellow fabric-covered planes, instructors in front. My instructor would turn his cap around backwards and put his feet up in relaxed fashion over the instrument panel as if the panel was a desk on the ground while he instructed me.

A few students did not take to the air with the greatest of ease. For those who could not contain their food we called it "feeding the buzzards" and if you fed the buzzards, besides cleaning the plane, you contributed 25 cents to the buzzard kitty, a Mason jar on the waiting room table. But that quarter fine did not compare to the jibes and good natured razzing dished out to those who paid up, and there were a couple who fed the kitty more than once. The weather remained clear, bright, and beautiful for the entire period. We all felt rather sad and somehow cheated when our final hours ended because we would not be able to soar with abandon as the instructors could when they had no students in the back seats. Still, the end of our orientation flights in the Cubs meant readiness for the beginning of the next stage.

Early in June, two buses drove us the 13 miles for our very first look at the Tuskegee Army Airfield. We disembarked from the buses and "fell in" with our duffel gear into four columns. After the roll call, we moved to assigned rooms in the Lower Preflight barracks building that stood at one end of the headquarters quadrangle, the quad being shaped like a horseshoe. At some point we marched to a quartermaster's building where we were issued different shirts, dress coats, and hats. The caps, banded in blue, had wings and propeller on the crown. We received white name tags with our last names on them in plastic holders and at that point we really became aviation cadets and our first station, Preflight.

What we did not know was that we had suddenly become less than dirt and not fit to let our shadows fall on another human. Our names were "Mister" but that is not how the upper classmen treated us, upperclassmen now in their Basic and Advance phases of training. They also called us "Dummies," especially when an upper classman was all primed and ready to give you a good dose of hazing. Cadets in Basic wore light blue-colored name tags while the Advance ogres wore pink.

All of the classes were divided into upper and lower units and the movement upward from one unit to another required actual physical moving, a change of quarters from one barracks to another. Lower Preflight where the most hell was dished out or caught, depended on your class ranking, that being were you doing the dishing or the catching. The intense hazing served at least two purposes. One, it allowed the upper classmen to vent some of the pressures they were subjected to during the day, and, two, it accustomed the rank, slimy Dummies to the pressures that lay ahead when it became their turn to run the gauntlet. That is not to say there were not two or three masochists among those doing the dishing out of either physical or mental hazing, or both. Physical hazing taxed you in the most stressful manner because you actually reached the limits of your physical endurance and beyond. Sitting on the little Red Stool, for instance, required squatting in the position as if you were actually sitting on a stool. When your legs began to tremble with fatigue the upper classman might sneer and say, "Dummy, you don't look comfortable, so why don't you just rest yourself and relax on the little Purple Chair!" That meant staying in the same position you had assumed except now the legs had to be crossed and the arms held out as if on the arm rests of a big easy chair. For the simultaneous execution of both forms of torment the upper classmen might then ask you the time while you comfortably lounged in the Purple Chair. Your reply would be, "Sir, I am deeply embarrassed and greatly humiliated but due to unforeseen circumstances over which I have no control the inner workings and hidden mechanisms of my poor chronometer are in such a state of discord with the Great Sidereal Movement, by which all time is commonly reckoned, that I cannot with any degree of accuracy state the correct time. However, Sir, without fear of being too far wrong, I will state that it is approximately five minutes, eight seconds, twenty ticks and four deviatory vibrations past the hour of nine, Sir!" This recitation takes place while you look at your watch with the hour stated being the time actually indicated.

There were eight so-called "DoDo Verses" that had to be memorized and regurgitated when ordered by an upper classman regardless of your position or what you were doing. In explanation: a DoDo is an amoebae of an army flyer to be properly chastened and subdued by an intricate course of a predetermined and idealistically integrated formula for the purpose of impressing upon the unused convolutions of the cerebrum the correct and proper duties and functions and instantaneous assimilation of the compound in aggregate wisdom by the previous initiated intelligence in direct control of movement. And double woe to the miserable Dummy who missed a line or word from any verse called for by his masters.

Lots of "Re-Dee-Deating" up and down the halls of Preflight barracks further heavily taxed our physical limits. To perform the aforementioned required donning your dress uniform, your heavy wool overcoat, your gas mask, and your hat. Thus attired you then, on command, duck walked up and down the halls yelling "Re-Dee-Deat" over and over in that gas mask until you were ready to fall over. If that became too boring for the upper classman you might hear the words, "Pop to, Dummy or Mister!" which meant stop whatever you were doing and stand at immediate attention. And there were various degrees of attention, the actuating word was "Brace to" or "Brace up" which meant to get into a position of rigid attention, or more so, with chin tucked tightly inward, chest thrust outward and the arms in an exaggerated position at your sides.

In the mess hall at least one upper classman sat at each table. There would always be one in ready position to command and harass the Dummies. Dummies must sit in rigid position on the front halves of their chairs, they could eat only when given permission and meals had to be eaten with square motions. The fork came vertically straight up from the plate and then made a right angle to the mouth, it returned to the plate in the same manner.

Beds had to be made with forty-five degree tucks at the foot and be so tight that a quarter, held a foot above and dropped, bounced back up to a specific height. Should the quarter not reach that height the bed would have to be torn up and remade which meant almost certain failure on the second attempt. Your roommate often would be ordered to show you how it should be done, and of course his making of your bed would usually pass the quarter test. The bed would again be torn down and it would have to be as neatly remade as your roommate had successfully demonstrated. The next time it might well be the roommate's turn to be the goat or if it was some upper classman's bad hair day it could very well be yours again.

Another matter of degrading took the form of shining the upper classmen's shoes, their belt buckles, fetching them cold drinks, ice cream, or cigarettes. And just so they could have more free time their rooms had to be cleaned, cleaned well enough to pass the white glove test. Periodically, the cadet officer of the day, with two adjutants, would scrupulously go over each room searching for dust with white gloves. The finding of any dust could lead to demerits and five demerits could earn you a walking tour of duty around the headquarters quadrangle shouldering a heavy rifle wearing your own white gloves. We meticulously scrubbed floors with brushes and GI soap on hands and knees and as a Dummy it meant that not only your own room had to be spic and span but also the upper classmen's.

Lower Preflight for our class began with a total of 80 men and right away, with the drilling, stiffer physical examinations, the cross country running, and class work, cadets began to be eliminated. Upper Preflight was more of the same and included a trip to the pressure chamber at Maxwell Air Base near Montgomery, Alabama. We dramatically saw what happens when oxygen deprivation occurs, even for a few seconds; a cadet easily unties one shoelace but is unable to retie it. His hands go through the motions, aimless motions that never get completed. The demonstrations proved that being deprived of oxygen could kill you but not because of not breathing, the cause would come from unconsciousness and crashing.

A serious incident occurred in Lower Preflight that could have been made messy had headquarters wished to mete out punishment. After 9 o'clock at night almost everyone had gone to bed from a full day. Suddenly all the lights in the barracks flashed on followed by shouts of, "Hit the deck, Dummies, hit the deck!" That got everyone out of bed. The entire barracks was ordered to assemble outside in five minutes. Anyone late would receive five demerits. Only the subdued brightness coming from the outside barrack's porch lights provided illumination in the darkness. The cadet captain always came from the Advance class. This time it was John Whitehead, nicknamed "Mr. Death" because of his severe gaunt facial features. Whitehead's class had just come in from night flying exercises and they were ready to have some fun. Fun they had at our expense by keeping us up most of the night in continuous hazing, the Purple Chairs, bed making, duck walking, pushups, and reciting verses. Later that morning, about half of the class flunked the medical exams that had been scheduled. This unusual circumstance prompted questions and the answers pointed directly to Whitehead's class. There was a verbal reprimand. But that reprimand rolled right back to Lower Preflight with more shoes to shine, more errands to run, more rooms to clean, and more beds to be remade. But all of that hazing stopped once we advanced to Upper Preflight, a physical movement to the adjacent barracks. Gratefully there now appeared a brand new batch of "cruits" to take our places, the "re" being shaved off because a "cruit" was so low and disgusting that he would have to climb upward to get to the bottom level of a snake's track in the dirt.

Wakeup came at 5:30 am, which allowed 15 minutes for showering, shaving, and brushing teeth, the last 15 minutes was for making beds, getting dressed, and falling out for reveille at 6 am sharp! As we became more acquainted with military life we began to find loopholes and subterfuges to make life seem a little easier. Many times roommates would rotate in falling out for reveille in the early grey darkness of the new dawn while the others slept in. It required shouting "Here!" using a different tone of voice, to answer at roll call for yourself and the missing roommate. There was always roll call at reveille but not for retreat, the time of assembly for the lowering of the flag for the day. It was a dangerous game to miss either call but more so for retreat because the cadet officer of the day and his aide would check all barracks thoroughly, and they checked everywhere except in the upstairs ceiling crawl space. After they departed you could safely come out and flop down on your bunk, but being caught would bring enough demerits to keep you walking tours each and every weekend.

Once a month all barracks, the upper classmen first, would have to fall out for payday which meant lining up outside of the mess hall wearing nothing except your shoes and your overcoat. There were civilian women working in the kitchen of the mess hall and they would crowd their windows because some of the cadets would flash, or pretend they were flashing, to the delight and squealing laughter of the female spectators. Inside, you would receive your pay in bills only after you had performed a satisfactory "Short Arm" inspection, which was a visual inspection by an officer of your private parts to insure that you were free of any social disorders. The inspection was all very embarrassing but your pay could be seen neatly stacked on a table only a step away and besides everyone did the same thing.

There was no flying during Preflight but we nonflying cadets were kept mentally juiced up by the sights and sounds of those in Basic and Advance piloting those shiny silver planes overhead. Ground school proved far from boring because all the subjects related directly to airplanes or flying and that alone kept interests soaring. While the entire class trotted out on a cross-country run an incident occurred while we stopped for a five minute breather at mid-point of the run. From where we had stopped you could look down on a major runway of the base. As we stood there looking down at the scene, a shiny AT-6 trainer ran up its engine prior to taking off. It moved to line up with the runway, ready to open throttle. Just then another AT-6 entered the traffic pattern and came in on its landing approach as the one below slowly began to move forward. The cadet pilot of the incoming plane failed to see the one below him because of carelessness and because of the wing blocking his view. The cadet in the plane on the ground failed to see the landing craft in the traffic pattern, and then could not as it approached from behind him, as he prepared for takeoff. The incoming plane slammed across the top of the other craft stopping it dead in its tracks then proceeded to smack into the ground farther down the runway. Both pilots appeared uninjured as they climbed from their respective planes but the two AT-6s were heavily damaged. We never learned what happened to those two cadets although it seems more than probable that one or both were deemed at fault regardless of what the tower's instructions may have been. The tower may not have even given any instructions to either plane. During those days any mistake at all could send you packing. Each day, it seemed, someone in the class lost a roommate and the loss came for nothing quite as drastic as a crash.

In Upper Preflight we no longer had to cater to the upper classmen who were now able to feast on a fresh bunch of dummies. There was still much learning to absorb such as keeping belt buckles shiny, having your shoes so shiny the toes were like mirrors, and having your shirts either tailored or, as was the usual case, tucked in at the sides so they fitted your shape. Your trousers were supposed to be sharply creased so that you literally cut the air as you walked. The shirt buttons had to line up with the middle of the belt buckle and the tie had to be tucked into the shirt at the third button. We did have some thin men in the group but no fat ones. Fat was not allowed to stay around with all the calisthenics and cross-country running we endured. The instructor gave the rear man in the group a whistle to blow if anyone dropped out as he trotted along leading us. No matter how tired or winded you were it was best not to drop out because there would be more so-called conditioning exercises waiting for the dropouts while the rest of us were free to hit the showers at the end of the run. Of course, the one giving these exercises was none other than the instructor who had run back in leading the group. It was a sort of rub-it-in–your-face punishment lesson showing just how in condition the instructor was. In running the cross country, we all ran or jogged in step, not fast, but onward at a steady constant pace.

With the basics more or less behind us we were now learning the spit and polish phase of military life. We were moving farther and farther away from the ordinary and the casual, nonchalant aspect of civilian life. We were all doing the same things at the same time and in the same manner or in a single accurate expression, in unison. The intensity of our purpose each day began to swell and grow with increased fervor. Each day became a problem to solve and another step upward to accomplish. We were being challenged mentally and physically and some began to fall by the wayside unable or unwilling to successfully meet the challenges.

Preflight was like the infancy of first learning to walk. There were many more difficult challenges ahead to negotiate individually and as a class. Those who failed did so as an individual, the class, like the "moving finger" of Omar Khayyam moved on not looking back and unable to change what had been written. Except for lunch time we moved from place to place as a group but rather than having some sergeant giving the orders of movement one of our class was appointed by headquarters for that purpose. We could see the airplanes as they flew overhead and we could hear their engines roaring but we could not get close enough to touch one. That mental state was far more enticing than the carrot dangling in front of the donkey because each day, each week brought us that much physically closer to that desired goal of flight.

We were a class and individuals made up that class, so there was competition among and between each of us, but there was also a certain cohesion that bonded us together. When we marched from one location to another it was as a group that looked good marching with crisp precision while we sang or recited one of the numerous ditties reserved for marching. In running cross country the same sort of cadence was used; uphill and downhill we were all in step with one another just at a faster pace. Even in running we always sang or called out one of our ditties. By the end of Preflight we were probably in the best physical shape possible, what with the drill instructors demanding exercises. We did not have just plain old pushups. It was necessary to spring up off of the ground and to clap your hands and feet together before completing the next pushup. The "Biloxi Booster" was sort of a reverse pushup with the arms and hands behind you. If a particular exercise by itself was not really physically demanding the instructors kept the drilling going long enough to make sure that it you were pushed to a limit. They led from a raised platform so that the entire group could be surveyed and those in the back rows could not fudge by not being fully observed.

Each phase of training beginning with Preflight lasted from nine to ten weeks and each stage was further subdivided into Upper and Lower units. We were literally being honed as one would sharpen a good knife. Sharpening a knife is only a physical act, we, in fact, were being honed both mentally and physically. Eighty young men, none over the age of 25 and none under 18, were focused on meeting the challenges and successfully finishing the course, the course that would put us into the cockpit of a warplane.

Since we could see airplanes but not yet be allowed to touch any, the total occupation was divided between the books and physical training. The pressures that would later appear were at this point still standing to one side, waiting for the arrival of the cockpit, the aerial classroom. At this stage in our training, there was no thought of considering the loss of classmates through elimination. I believe the general train of thought was that we were absorbing all that was being thrust at us and asking for more. Yet, insidiously, classmates were silently disappearing. They were not hanging around after elimination so they could be seen as reminders. They vanished quietly without fanfare, drum roll, or the sound of trumpets. Still, collectively, one-third of our class was silently removed before we had advanced on to the next step. This was determined by knowing the number beginning Preflight then counting noses early in the Primary stage.

Losing classmates obviously had the greatest impact on roommates who had developed close buddy relationships because then the associated idea develops thinking of whether that particular room is marked for washout, or who is next from that room. It can almost be likened to a game of bingo where no one knows which numbers are going to tumble out next. Usually there seems no order, rhyme, or reason that can be counted on to prognosticate what is to follow. And the washout factor, once started does not stop until the very end. Even then the possibility exists, albeit, not strongly, but it does exist. There was a very long road ahead in Preflight; we still had three more phases to cover and each one increasingly more difficult and demanding.

As disturbing as it was to lose roommates or classmates it can only be imagined how those who fell by the wayside felt in having to write home to inform that they had failed to succeed, that they had stumbled in trying to reach their goal of flying.

The weekends did belong to the cadet so there was enough leisure time to unwind and move aside from the pressure. The origin is not known but at about this time a practice grew that was called the "Dozens" or more correctly, the "Dirty Dozens." It was primarily played among and between friends because otherwise some serious physical eruptions could have taken place. The object, usually, was to mouth off, if you had lost a bet or some game, about some trait of your friend's mother. It could get started by telling your buddy that his mother wore two left shoes or she brushes her teeth with a scrub brush. If it were known that the buddy had a sister it was not uncommon for her to be brought into jousting of words along with the mother. Perhaps because of the tender thoughts of mother and sister the accusatory battles would often come close to having books thrown at the one who could low grade the other's the best. Of course, there were some who absolutely refused to play this insulting words game and those who did not or would not let it be known early on. His positional words would simply be, "I don't play that!" Then there was the position of the "Signifying Monkey" ditty. If one or the other would make some challenging statement, a retort might be issued to remember the Signifying Monkey. This related to the story of a monkey high up in the trees yelling down at a lion what he would do to him if he were to come down to the ground. The monkey taunted the lion and called him a number of bad names. All of a sudden the monkey's foot slipped and he fell to the ground in front of the lion he had been bad mouthing. In the lion's mouth the monkey began to cry and plead and apologize for ever saying anything bad about his friend, his old buddy. Many of the words used in this ditty would not be appropriate in mixed company but its total primary effect was to cause laughter and that would relieve pressure and tensions.

# CHAPTER 5

# Learning to Fly

By the time our Preflight training had advanced to the Primary phase, in clear numbers, 27 men out of the original 80 eager cadets had fallen by the wayside. The major move to Primary represented the first stage of actually learning to fly a large plane, compared to the orientation flights in the little Piper Cubs. The advancement also meant a move from the Base back into a Tuskegee Institute dormitory. Phelps Hall had been set aside for cadet quarters during Primary training. The 66th Army Air Forces Flying Training Detachment was then commanded by Major H.C. Magoon. The Primary training unit, technically called the 2164th Army Air Force Base Unit, under Major Magoon, was commanded by First Lieutenant Daniel J. Sorrells, who despite having a distinct southern drawl, was well liked by all the cadets because of his fairness and impartiality. Within one week, for some unexplained reason, I was appointed as Color Sergeant which meant that after the cadet captain and his adjutant, I was next in command. This positional move came totally unexpected and really unwanted because it put the skids to my missing retreat, a practice at which I had become very skilled. Now I had the responsibility of hoisting the flag in the mornings and hauling it down in the evenings. Each morning, after reveille, Lieutenant Sorrells would give us a short pep talk and then tell us what the uniform of the day would be, including whether we were to wear "high top shoes" or "low quarters" before dismissing the group for breakfast. The way Lieutenant Sorrells pronounced "hah top shews" had that distinct southern lilt which I still remember. And because the air seemed fully infested with tiny gnats outside of the dormitory, he constantly swatted at them with both hands as he gave us our orders for the day. Breakfast, in fact all meals, took place across the street on the ground floor of a building, Tompkins Hall, which also served as our ground school with classes on the second floor. Ground school now became more intense with the study of such things as how carburetors functioned when an airplane flew upside down, how the magnetic compass lagged in one direction and ran ahead in another as well as how cross winds could affect an aircraft while it attempted to land.

The really big item now though was flying. We flew every day except on the weekends. All of the Primary instructors were black and all of them exhibited a very strong interest in squeezing every ounce of flying ability from each one of us. This group of truly dedicated men had eventually swelled to 40 in the number of months before we arrived. These were men who could not only fly they had become masters of their profession. Many of these instructors had tried earlier to enlist in the Army's flying program and had been turned down despite all their qualifications. So, for some instructors, this unwarranted slap in the face drove them to train just as many cadets as possible to advance on to the next flying phase. That facial slap was one of the elements that added fuel to their determination. One of those determined instructors was Wendell Lipscomb, now a noted psychiatrist, who had gravitated close to retirement at the time of the interview. He had earned his instructor and commercial pilot's ratings in San Diego, California, in 1940 from a private flying school. Lipscomb had become hooked on aviation when, as a newspaper boy in Oakland, California—he had won an airplane ride in an old Ford Tri-motor airplane. He spent six months at the Coffey Flying School in Chicago as an instructor until he heard rumblings and rumors that Tuskegee was getting ready to train black military pilots. He, like many others, had tried unsuccessfully to enlist in the Army Air Corps. The turn down was blatantly ignominious. "The recruiting sergeant told me there was no place in the Air Corps for me because they weren't taking 'night fighters' yet," Lipscomb recalled with a grimace. You could almost hear his teeth grinding in disgust. At Tuskegee the Primary instructors were tigers without their stripes. Lipscomb said, "It was awful, they (the Primary instructors) had no rank, and no title, they were really nothing except they could fly. We were all determined to turn out as many students as we possibly could. The 'Experiment' was designed to fail, and we were determined that if it failed it would not be because of us." Coming from the West Coast, Lipscomb had more than a little bitterness to swallow. For example, a simple thing like going to the bank or a clothing store was humiliating. "You thought you were waiting your turn but a bank manager's assistant's assistant would come up and say, 'boy, you have to wait.' In the store you were not allowed to try anything on so you had to eyeball the fit and make certain that you didn't hold the shirt or jacket too close to your body."

The world's mightiest conflict raged on but gradually, at some point, the allies began turning the tables on the Axis powers and Lipscomb saw tiny changes creep forward. With the war winding down, the military was finally going to accept the civilian instructors as warrant officers, some of them with thousands of flying hours. But he said, "Some went for that but I stuck my finger in the air and said to hell with you...it would have been more tempting had they offered to give us commissions as Majors or even Captains. I was mad as hell about being turned down from joining the Air Corps in the first place. I had knocked on doors, written letters to congressmen and I wound up in the newspapers." Lipscomb said the instructors fought the existing system of segregation, racism, prejudice, and all the cankerous manifestations of white-superior, black-inferior attitudes by teaching as many to fly as they could. "We were trying to train young men from all over the country, many of them with no mechanical experience other than a shovel or 40 acres and a mule. Surprisingly, enough of them came out to do exceedingly well...but I did not envy the guillotine guys like Charlie Fox who had to chop off the hopeless ones, those who just didn't have it at all." He pondered thoughtfully for a brief moment, "I hope that as history books are updated, the history that was actually generated down there at Tuskegee will appear as it was, as it actually happened."

Lipscomb shook his head slowly as he remembered back through the mists of years. "I must admit that there were a number of students that I set up to go through with their final check rides with my fingers tightly crossed. Then there were some, not very many, who were in a category that should never have been introduced to aircraft. There were some guys who had two left feet who could barely walk let alone fly. All of us instructors had to face the tough decisions of whether to put some borderline cadets in the wringer for washout or let them go through hoping something would happen to allow them a chance to survive and graduate."[1]

The very sturdy biplane that we flew in Primary, the Stearman PT-17, a tough, take-a-lot-of-abuse airplane, had supplanted another Primary trainer, the Fairchild PT-19, even though the latter looked more like the Basic trainer that followed. They finally determined that the PT-19 was too underpowered to consistently reach a safe altitude above the tall pine trees around Moton Field. Moton Field was named in honor of the second president of Tuskegee Institute, Robert R. Moton. The PT-17, a real workhorse, was fabric-covered like the Piper Cubs but it could absorb the constant and intense punishment meted out by some slightly inept students who had difficulty learning to round out in landings reasonably close to the ground. Later classes would fly the Stearman PT-13, a plane exactly like the 17 but having a more powerful engine.

With the little yellow Piper Cub, someone, like a cadet awaiting his turn to fly, had to turn the propeller by hand while the pilot sat inside. The person spinning the propeller would yell, "contact," and the pilot would call back loudly, "switch on," at that point the propeller person would crank down on the prop hoping the engine would start, but if it did not, the pilot would yell, "switch off." Failure to turn off the switch could have the engine start as the propeller person adjusted the prop for the next start attempt. On the other hand, the PT-17 was not only bigger and more powerful, the starting procedure proved much safer, if not easier. Instead of the prop being spun by hand, the starter person had a big hand crank that he inserted into the inertia starter on the left side near the nose, but safely behind the propeller. It usually took almost a half minute to get the stiff-turning inertia wheel rotating fast enough to turn the engine over. The yelling of "contact" and "switch on" remained the same. Keeping your eyes open and being alert around a spinning propeller or one ready to turn was standard policy.

The more Lipscomb talked, the more he began to remember. "That whole aura of black-white, Dixie oppression, suppression and just downright meanness was terrible to contend with, that business of black-white water fountains and separate waiting rooms at the train stations was more than just deplorable." In their spare time, he said the instructors would visit the "block," a slice of the Tuskegee campus that had a grocery store, a barbershop, and a soda fountain. "The block was where you could find out where things were happening like the house where you could buy a setup to go with the illegal booze you had acquired elsewhere ... the county was dry." As in Mississippi, a setup was usually a big bowl of ice, lemons, and, more often, bottles of Coca Cola.

Lipscomb edged the coaster around on the table with the bottom of the bottle of Heineken I had brought as a bribe for his story. "I remember when Wendell Pruitt came back from combat with the 99th as a Captain. He was a real 'hot rock.' And the guys were horsing him into flying the AT-6 with a victory roll over the runway. He pulled the AT-6 up like he would have done with the P-51 with all of its horsepower and into the ground he went. I remember that very, very well."[2] The coaster stopped moving and a hardened look set into his eyes. He had knocked on all the tightly-closed doors of the country's airlines, he had flown charter flights down to Mexico and he had flown the sister ship to Lindbergh's "Spirit of St. Louis." The country, America, the land of the free, still was not ready for a black professional pilot to join the mainstream of commercial aviation.

Another dark, terrible image about one of his students still stuck disturbingly in Lipscomb's mind. The student, he said, came from one of the leading black families of Tuskegee and he was learning to fly on heart alone. He said, "The student was never really comfortable flying but he had to live up to the family name." One day during transition training in the P-40 fighter he made a big gaping hole in the ground. Lipscomb said, "I remember riding out to the crash site and seeing some of the crash crew picking up the pieces while others were salvaging the plane's Allison engine. Later I talked to some of his classmates and they told me that he never really wanted to fly." He admitted that even his own brother, an artillery officer who had transferred to the Air Corps, became an unwilling victim. A fellow instructor had pulled him aside one day and told him that his brother did fine except when it came to crosswind landings. He proceeded to give up several of his lunch periods to help his brother learn to land in a crosswind but he never quite got the hang of it. "After he almost ground looped me, I threw up my hands and said, that's it, no more." His brother, Ira, did, in fact, make it through Primary but was quickly eliminated in the next phase, which was Basic.

More than half a century later, Lipscomb still retained some very poignant memories of his instructor years at Tuskegee. "I remember many Sunday evenings just as the sun was setting and our mingling with the students around the statue of Booker T. Washington, there would be fire flies flitting here and there. There was a kind of haze the color of which can't be really described. The students would begin singing a cappella and the songs would be so moving that it would make you cry."

The muscles in his jaw suddenly tightened. "You know we instructors stayed and we operated under the white stress burden of 'niggahs' can't fly and got no business being around airplanes anyway'; that had a tremendous influence on the instructors." His jaw relaxed into a smile in remembrance. "Of course some instructors were tougher than others, you could hear them screaming at some student while the plane was 15-hundred feet in the air and some of the language was as foul as you would hear anywhere." His smile became a low chuckle.

Lipscomb eventually returned to California and finished medical school at the University of California at Berkeley. But racism still would not leave him alone, it snarled at him again after two weeks into internship at Kaiser-Permanente's Oakland hospital with a firing by none other than Mr. Kaiser himself. Seems that he had failed to include a picture of himself with his application and Mr. Kaiser said, "Your loyalty to this country has not been proven to the satisfaction of . . . ." However, pressure from the International Longshoremen Workers Union (ILWU) labor union which then had a huge health plan with Kaiser caused a reversal of those words and Lipscomb went on to become a highly successful psychiatrist.

Although I had not fed the buzzards during our CTD orientation flights, I made up for that, one fateful morning when, after eating two bars of peanut brittle instead of regular breakfast, my instructor began to teach me the elements of aerobatics for the first time. When he tried to turn the controls over to me, my head was already hanging over the side of the cockpit cowling, my eyes rolled back in my head. I was spastically out of it. My instructor headed back for the field, landed, taxied to the wash rack between the hangars, climbed out of the front cockpit, pointed to a long-handled brush and said, "Clean up your mess, we'll do it again tomorrow." To this day, I have never eaten a peanut brittle bar before going up on any flight whether or not there were aerobatics.

In Primary, the instructor always sat in the front seat and at times he would attempt to communicate by voice through a funnel-like device that connected two rubber tubes that ran to both sides of your helmet. But that was like using two cans connected by a string. Even with the engine not running it was virtually impossible to hear much of anything through those tubes, so to be absolutely certain, when the instructor wanted to take control of the plane, he would pat the top of his head. That meant let go of the stick and get your damn feet off of the rudder pedals!

The most soul shaking day of my life came after eight hours of flight instruction. After taxiing out to prepare for the usual takeoff and checking the magnetos, my instructor suddenly unbuckled his safety belt, climbed out of the front cockpit, and said, "It's yours. I want you to take it around once and land here." I was extremely anxious. The anxiety to show what I could do had surfaced after the first three hours but with the instructor in the cockpit you always knew that even with his hands and feet not on the controls, he could take over in a split second to correct a mistake. That is when the mind began to swell and explode with exhilaration. The rush and pump of adrenaline forced the taking of slow deep breaths as you poised ready to spread your wings and soar with the eagles. You had control of this big airplane! You would take it off the ground! And you would land it safely just like your instructor! The first solo touch down bounced a little bit, not a perfect three pointer but each succeeding one became better and better. After that the gravy began to pour in, the instructor would show you one or two maneuvers, you would land and immediately go back up alone to practice what had been shown. The next day the instructor would see just how well the previous lesson had gone. If you had absorbed the teaching he would go on to the next more difficult tactic. If you failed, he would repeat the series again and again for a total of three days teaching the same lessons. After that, depending on the instructor, you might be given a check ride by another civilian Primary instructor or the Air Corps check pilot who had the final say about who stayed and who was "washed out" (eliminated). Some instructors were more lenient than others, in other words, if they felt your difficulty only temporary, they would try harder and longer to keep you in the pack even though you were now behind the rest of the class.

Another of that venerated cadre of instructors was Adolph Moret, born in New Orleans, Louisiana and the oldest of five brothers. "Dolphy" as his friends called him, helped in his father's printing shop, worked for the Pinkerton Detective Agency, and finally became a U.S. postal service worker. All this was before he learned from his close friend Octave Joe Rainey that they had a good chance of getting into flying training at West Virginia State College under the CPT program. In 1940, Moret earned his private pilot's license and proceeded to get married in October 1941. The day of Pearl Harbor came while Moret was up flying with his new bride and another couple. He landed to take the two women up but the airport manager came running out and told him that all planes had been grounded. His first thoughts were that racism had raised its snake head again and hissed but he did not argue about the grounding. On their way home the car radio blared out what had happened at Pearl Harbor. Moret said, "I was newly married, 24 years old, hell, I didn't want to shoot at anybody or be shot at." He quickly applied for secondary training under CPT at Tuskegee but because of his height, G. L. Washington, Director of Aeronautics, did not want to admit him. Nevertheless, after a check ride with Chief Anderson and an Army physical four days later at Maxwell Field, he made it, but it was not all that easy. "I was tall and thin so I started loading up on as many bananas as I could eat and practicing how to scrunch up my height to get down to the maximum of five feet nine and a quarter inches."

"I never had any trouble with Mr. Washington. I never saw him. I stayed out of his way...so I did well in the program. I was also there when Mrs. Roosevelt came to the campus. To the consternation of the Secret Service agents, she wanted Chief Anderson to give her a ride in this plane...I helped her into the plane and I saw later that they had cut me out of the picture that was taken of them."

Moret became a flight instructor but with just his second group of students the first mishap occurred. "We were going to make a simulated forced landing with the student at the controls. We were coming in over some tall trees and I could tell that he was going to under shoot (land short). You're supposed to clear the engine every so often to keep the carburetor from loading up and I waited just a fraction too long, hoping he would see his mistake. When I hit the throttle the engine didn't even cough, we just mushed right down into the trees. We tumbled down about a hundred feet and were upside down. After we got out it was a long walk out of there, and when we reached the field I took the full blame for the accident. When we returned to the crash site you could see that the wings had been sheared off and just the fuselage (body) was stuck up there between the tree trunks. Oh, they reprimanded me, of course, but later, you know, that same student was credited with shooting down a German fighter."

Moret remembered another simulated forced landing, one that gave him a lot more pleasure and satisfaction. "We were letting down into this nice flat field when lo and behold there was some guy down there standing up in his wagon throwing rocks up at us. We pulled up and away from him but it teed me off for some clodhopper, some hayseed, trying to throw a rock into my propeller. I went around then came in again about a foot off of the ground and headed straight at him. All of a sudden he jumped off of the wagon to safety but I came so close that the mules hitched to the wagon took off too; they bolted off so fast that they broke the traces and left the wagon standing where it was. Nothing more came of that." Moret smiled broadly and looked as if he were watching the frightened mules bolting from the farmer's wagon again.

Moret, like his fellow instructor Lipscomb, had two dark water memories that still remain with him. "I had a student who was a nice kid, a real likeable boy who did everything right except he could not recover from a spin ... everything he did well but he just could not recover from spins. After carrying him along for a long time I sent him up for elimination, and Charlie Fox, the guillotine, wrote him off as well. But the Air Corps check pilot a Captain Ports, ordered more time for the kid. The youngster was still unable to recover from a spin when the Air Corps check pilot took him up and let him solo." He said, "Capt. Ports soloed the boy in the evening when the air was nice and calm and no other planes were nearby to cause any problems. Then he gave the student to another instructor because I refused to carry him anymore. The other instructor sent him up to practice solo spins, the boy spun in ... just eighteen years old. Capt. Ports never looked me in the eye after that. I never talked to him and he never said another word to me. I'll never forget that young man."

Yet another tragic incident occurred during Moret's career as an instructor. He did not really want to talk about it but his wife, Eline, prodded him, even telling part of the story herself to get him started. One afternoon, with Moret scheduled for instruction, he had left home feeling a little sick and it worsened to the point of being unable to fly. Another instructor took over his students and while the substitute and one of Moret's students were up practicing, another student, flying solo, collided with their plane in midair. There were no survivors. "My Guardian Angel was watching over me that day," he said slowly, his brow furrowed. Later, as the outcome of the war became more evident, Moret was sent to the Tuskegee Air Base and given a commission to be an instructor in, first the BT-13 and then the AT-6, the Basic and Advance trainers.

Moret continued his story. "As soon as the war was over I used to go to New Orleans every time I got a chance and I'd land at Keesler Field, Mississippi. My brother would come to pick me up. One day I took a Captain with me, a Captain Braden who was a doctor. Someone else heard that I was going to make this flight so I was handed four, one hundred dollar bills and told, 'Dolphy, one of these is yours, just bring back $300 worth of booze.' Well, Macon County, Alabama is dry and New Orleans is wet. This trip I flew past Biloxi and Keesler Field on to the New Orleans Naval Air Station where I had been on training flights. You could only land there on official business so I called their tower and they wanted to know the nature of my business. Before I could answer Capt. Braden picked up the mike and said he had business at the Goodrich Hospital, a colored hospital. The tower cleared us immediately. When we returned we had two flight bags loaded with 300 dollars worth of booze. I know the seaman who drove us out to the plane must have known what was in those B-4 bags. I took off, turned the plane around and dropped it right down over the middle of the main street of town at rooftop level and kept on going."[3] Moret's wife gave him the eye when he remarked that it was his first effort at being a flying bootlegger. His buddy, Rainey, later became one of the approximately 60 black Army Artillery Liaison pilots of WWII. Most of the others in the final liaison group sooner or later received their commissions and Rainey finally received his early in 1944. It is not known if Rainey"s buddy Elvatus Morris ever received his. Both Rainey and Morris had been eliminated from flight training at Tuskegee. Just past the mid-point of Primary training, the first serious incident took place to press home the understanding that we aviation cadets were black and in the Deep hostile South. In Primary, if you had no demerits or tours to walk, it was standard procedure to be issued a pass that was good for a radius of 50 miles from Friday afternoon until Sunday night. Your only duty, sign your name and the time of checkout to be issued that priceless piece of paper. Although the campus abounded with pretty girls, Tuskegee Institute officials discouraged fraternization, which, in turn, caused most cadets to head for Montgomery, the closest large city. My roommate and I had spent a wonderful weekend in Montgomery relaxing and having fun. Late that Sunday afternoon as we stood in line waiting for the bus that would carry us the 40 miles back to Tuskegee, two white MPs accosted us. We were in dress uniforms, the right sleeves of our coats held the distinctive round black patch with a gold propeller in the middle of the wings. Our hats had the typical dark blue band with large gold wings and propeller on the front. The two MPs, both wearing .45 caliber side arms, pulled us out of the middle of the line and forcefully escorted us to a detention cell in the basement of a building two or three blocks away. The ringleader of the two asked what we were doing in Montgomery to which we replied that we were returning to Tuskegee from a weekend of leave. He asked to see our passes. We handed them through the bars and he promptly tore them up and dropped the pieces on the floor outside the cell door. An hour later he opened the door and said something like, "get the hell out of here and you needn't bother to come back to Montgomery!"

Both, shaken and angry my roommate and I returned to the bus station thinking dangerous thoughts filled with bad intentions at having been subjected to such openly spiteful and unwarranted treatment. We returned to Tuskegee late but we marched directly to the commandant and explained the full story, including the missing passes. Lieutenant Sorrells nodded slowly in understanding and told us he would take care of the problem. As it turned out, for the rest of the months we were stationed on campus and at the base proper. No further incidents or encounters arose with white MPs.

At the time of our group photograph in Primary, there were 53 cadets remaining of the original 80-strong that had started out in Preflight. Our flight instructors would meet with small groups of us after classes on the campus in impromptu bull sessions. We knew from their encouraging words that they were doing all they could to train as many as possible. But the "washing machine" kept taking us, one or two at a time. Unless it happened to be your roommate the only notice was an empty bunk here and an empty bunk there as you passed a room. Then you had to think back as to who had last occupied that bed. It all happened very quietly, unobtrusively and the insidious result that grew began to spread and work on your mind—who would be the next to have to pack up and leave. To the day of graduation I never talked to any cadet, not even a former roommate, to find out explicitly what he had been told as to the reason for his elimination. They seemed to disappear, just fade away while the rest of us were in class, having lunch, or doing calisthenics. You could not pretend that they had never been there because just the day before you had been laughing and joking, having a soda together, maybe planning to do something on the coming weekend. With two weeks to go in Primary, my running buddy and I collaborated in concealing a sworn to silence secret. Following a very hearty weekend of frolicking in Montgomery, we went to one of those military prophylactic stations for preventative treatment. My buddy fainted and when he came to, he confided to me that he had a heart murmur. Even if he had not extracted a promise from me, I would not have said anything because an infraction of any kind could be grounds for elimination. At the back of my mind, how-ever, a nagging thought grew, coupled with the hope that he would never lose consciousness while at the controls of a plane. Knowledge of his physi-cal condition could have put him at serious risk of elimination.

An unfortunate incident occurred near the end of flying training in Primary. One sunny afternoon as I taxied out and waited for a clear break to take off, another classmate sailed in for a landing. Prior to take off it was standard procedure to park just off the runway at such an angle that the magnetos in the plane could be checked without interruption and that position also allowed you to check the traffic pattern. If a plane entered the pattern to land, you had to hold your position until it was down. My classmate landed, then to my horror, when well down the runway, he started to ground loop; not only did he ground loop first to the left, but he overcontrolled and proceeded to ground loop to the right, damaging both wing tips in the process. I could not see who had committed that unforgi-vable error but it probably meant that cadet would pack his bags very soon after being given the feared check ride. Usual practice was if the plane were to be seriously damaged you were gone, washed out.

Standard practice also dictated that if you failed to learn a maneuver or made a serious mistake, such as a ground loop, you would be given at least one check ride, sometimes three, but typically, any check ride at best was not good. In Primary, the final check ride was given by an Air Corps officer and the only Air Corps officers assigned at the time were white. In another instance my instructor noticed another cadet flying under us as we climbed to reach altitude to do some loops. This fellow was completely out of the area to which he had been assigned and seemed to be nonchalantly skimming merrily along just above the treetops. That cadet never finished Primary because of a very serious infraction, one which could have led to a collision with another craft that readied to practice aerobatics in the same area with the errant plane. Even though you were taught to clear the area before beginning any aerobatic maneuver, which meant circling and looking all around, above and below for the presence of other planes, it did not prevent another aircraft from zooming in from a distance to make instant hamburger of both planes.

Several women interns worked in the Moton Field hangars learning to be mechanics. One of them was the chief instructor of parachute rigging as well. But these ladies were far out of reach of mere cadets, so any thoughts in their regard would be pretty much wasted. From the numerous excursions to the city of Montgomery a much-used expression made by eligible young ladies for dating, not only in the USO Club but outside as well, still sticks in my mind. As a rule most dates seemed to begin with at least two ladies hanging together, which meant, for best advantage the same number of cadets would have to approach this clique. Once conversation began one of them would invariably ask the others, "are you fer it" and usually there would be giggles and a nodding of heads. The next step would find us pairing up and determining what to do and/or where to go. Most often the same group would stay together as dates for at least the day or the weekend depending on when you had met. I do not recall any group of women with which we were trying to date in which any of them had said that they were "not fer it." With the war in full swing there was a critical shortage of men and for those of us privileged to spend recreation time in a city where there was a super-abundance of ladies, seldom did we see "Jodie." This was a fictitious name given to those males who, for one reason or another, were not in one of the armed services. "Jodie," that mythological enemy that each of us had to worry about if there was a girlfriend back home, caused fiction to seem real because he was that conceptual smooth talking critter who would steal your girl while you were absent. In the mind's eye you could see or create a "Jodie" because every town or city had at least one such character or at least so you imagined. We even had a marching expression sung to the cadence of the step telling how there was no use in going home because "Jodie" had your girl and she was gone. Although it was only an expression created by someone, it strangely did have an effect during mail call and other times, as will be elaborated on later, especially if your girlfriend had not written when you thought there should have been a letter. It seemed that we constantly marched or drilled wherever we went. We marched to classes, we marched from class back to the barracks, we marched to the mess hall and back, and wherever else there was room, we marched. There were a number of little ditties that we sang in cadence as we marched along, such as, "My gal's a corker, she's a New Yorker, I buy her everything to keep her in style; she's got a pair of legs just like two whiskey kegs; Oh boy, that's where my money goes"; or, another tune sung to the same cadence, "I've got six pence, jolly, jolly six pence, I've got six pence to last me all my life; I've got two pence to lend and two pence to spend and two pence to send home to my wife, poor wife." When you have 80 to 100 men marching and singing these little ditties in unison, it had the effect of causing you to march with a crisper brisk step.

Primary training was a very special time indeed because we had no hazing, no purple or red chairs to sit on, and no square meals to eat at the table. However, inspections were still carried out periodically with the dreaded white-gloved affair thrown in once in a while. At white-glove time, Lieutenant Sorrells would accompany the cadet officer of the day, the one actually wearing the white gloves. The neatness of your bed would be checked but there were no more quarter bouncing tests; your footlocker would be inspected from top to bottom to see that everything was neatly stored in proper place. Your hanging clothing would be checked for proper order of hanging and the white gloves would be swiped here and there but nothing like in Preflight, so "gigging" (demerits) was rare. I do not believe any of our class received enough demerits to do tours or be restricted to campus for the weekends. A tour required you to be in full dress uniform with white gloves and shoulder a rifle to march the quadrangle or another open prescribed path. On the base that path had the shape of a horseshoe; to march from one leg of the shoe around to the other end and back totaled one tour. When flying began our pay scale increased by a whopping 50 percent. It jumped from 50 dollars a month to the grand sum of 75 dollars a month. They based flying pay on a minimum of four hours of flying during any given month. Four hours of flying each month satisfied the flying scale requirements for all pilots, graduated or not.

All too soon Primary ended and those of us who remained, gathered up our meager belongings, which had now swollen to the complement of a footlocker, for the trip back to the base to begin phase three, Basic Training. Basic was an entirely new ball game. My best guess is that when we entered Basic, 45 cadets remained in the class to continue the fight, the grueling challenge. Ground school now included the link trainer, aircraft identification, mastering the Morse code, navigation, and for the first time instrument flying under a black hood in the rear seat. The black hood unfolded to completely cover the rear seat shutting off all outside light. Only the lighted instrument panel and the controls were visible. The conditions were such that the cadet had to fly the airplane by instruments alone. Unlike Primary, all of the flight instructors in Basic were Air Force pilots, all were officers and all, until some time later, were white. The instructors now sat in the back seat, except when you, the student, went under the instrument hood. The BT-13, or "Vultee Vibrator" as it was dubbed, was much bigger, heavier, faster, and more complicated. An all-aluminum, low-wing monoplane, the "Vibrator," had a radio, a canopy over your head, more instruments to read and decipher, a variable pitch propeller, and for the first time, flaps. In the old PT-17 you became used to a certain angle of glide as you settled downward in the approach to landing. The BT-13 changed all that, especially with the flaps set at full, the nose of the plane slanted sharply down instead of up. The airspeed would have been slow enough to stall but the flaps provided extra lift. In addition, the nose angle would have increased the airspeed far above normal landing speed. The BT-13s nickname "Vibrator" came from the fact that in the air, at cruising speed, the aluminum covering of the wings waffled and wrinkled as you flew along. The instructors quickly pointed out that the wing's skin waving back at you was strictly normal. And the instructors also firmly warned you never to attempt to make a power off dead stick landing by turning back to the field you had just taken off from, in the event of engine failure. In case the engine quit, the standard procedure was putting the nose down and landing straight ahead no matter what lay in the way. We were told we would have far better luck turning a rock around to land back on the runway than trying to force the BT-13 to do the same. The landing gear on the BT-13 was so wide apart that I do not believe you could ground loop that craft even if you wanted to and tried very hard to do so.

There was another major difference in regard to the new instructors. Although not spoken, there came a feeling that these instructors were not going to get behind and boost you like the Primary instructors or go out of their way to help you over a rough spot in the flying training. That feeling later proved to be false in more than a few instances because some instructors did go out of their way to help. Another new thrill greeted us, the introduction to night flying. With night flight came another one of those stern do-not-do-that dictums. In this case, you were never to stare down at the lights on the ground because eventually you would lose orientation with straight and level flight and head for the ground.

Now, as a part of navigation, came the introduction to the link trainer. The link was a simulated little stub of an airplane that sat on the ground on a swivel-type pedestal and had all of the controls of a regular airplane with the cockpit covered by a hood. In other words, in the link all you could see were the instrument panel and the instrument chart with its symbols on a clipboard which rested on your leg. The link could probably be called an earlier version of the simulator. Because the link's controls operated much like a regular craft you could also, if careless, get into a spin although spin recovery at night or by instruments would definitely not hit the list of recommended things to try. You really had only one choice, either fly well by the instruments alone or fail. Outside of the hooded link sat the link instructor at a large table where he controlled the direction and velocity of the wind as he watched you attempt to establish a desired course and stay on it. What he actually monitored was a slow moving crab like device that rolled around on a chart identical to the one you were using, making a trail of ink of the course you flew. The instructor, in reality, could make or break you. If you made mistakes he could coax you into the correct move by radio or stop and take you through the same maneuver again with helpful suggestions. He could keep the wind blowing from one direction at one speed or he could change its direction and hurricane you off the chart. His skillful instructions, with the aid of that little mockup airplane, made the art of learning to fly by instruments much easier. In that little ground-bound stub of a plane you learned how to bracket a beam and fly from point A to point B without ever seeing the ground and hopefully, passing over from point to point, what were called cones of silence. Hitting a cone of silence indicated that you had passed directly over the beacon transmitting station. Those stations would be marked on your chart and silently told you where you were or at least where you were supposed to be.

Aircraft identification was a system of flashing, for just a split second, the side view or head-on view silhouettes of planes, both enemy and friendly. The objective pressured you for instantaneous recognition. You had to know quickly if you should or should not arm your guns in readiness to fire. Learning to instantly identify those little black shadows on the screen was critical, because should you mistake an aircraft approaching you as friendly when in fact it was the enemy, it could be your last mistake. So they drummed into us the danger and the urgency of getting the identification correct with the first blink of your eyelids.

Learning the Morse code proved different, if not a bit harder, since most of us were not used to translating the sounds of dots and dashes into letters and numbers. The minimum speed of translation was 25 words a minute but the ear quickly learned to accommodate that and even faster speeds. We were not required to send at any given rate, only to be able to receive at a minimum. The code also helped us in the hours of link training. In flying from beam to beam and from one cone of silence to another, you were guided by identifying the Morse code, the signal "A" (dit-dah) on one side of the beam and the signal "N" (dah-dit) on the other side. That stubby little link trainer helped us in learning to trust our instruments, regardless of what it looked like outside. We were taught that if the ground could not be seen, trust your instruments, not your senses; the senses could be easily fooled, rattled, and disoriented, none of those states being good.

All of our ground school instructors were black and all of them highly skilled in what they taught. I remember one in particular because of his prominent gold front tooth. Whenever you were required to make a verbal answer he would always flash that tooth and ask, "You say that to say what?" Another instructor was extremely skilled at chewing out dullards and sluggards. Chewing out meant having your behind chewed out for some infraction or mistake. This teacher's chewing techniques were so polished and surgically precise that he could deftly chew around your behind and then let it fall out on its own.

Several important incidents occurred while we fought our way through Basic. The first came when I stayed too long in Montgomery on a weekend and missed the bus returning to the base on a Sunday night. A feeling of near panic rose up to torture me with images of being drummed out of flying. There were no more buses that evening for the 40 plus miles back to the base. I spotted a white cab driver parked near the front of the bus station and cautiously approached him. I explained what had happened and asked if he would drive me to Tuskegee. I also told him that all the cash I had was the two dollars that would have been the bus fare, but I tried to assure him that I would get whatever it cost from my roommate. He looked me up and down than asked if I was certain I could get the money from my roommate because the charge would be seventeen dollars. I nearly wilted with relief because my roommate tended to hoard his resources while I splurged everything. I said yes. But even if he did not have it, I intended to wake up the whole barracks to scrape up the deficit fifteen dollars. The driver had me give him the two dollars and sit on the front seat next to him. His next move was to open the glove compartment and he took out a shiny pistol which he opened, I think for my benefit, showing that it was loaded. After the pistol demonstration we took off on our way and I began mentally kicking myself for ever allowing this to happen in the first place. When we arrived at the main gate the cab driver seemed very surprised because the MPs were armed and black. It never occurred to me when I ran up the stairs of the barracks to just stay inside and not bring the cabby his money. Ole' honest Sam woke up his roommate and paid the driver his honestly earned money knowing that he would have to go very slowly through the main gate again passing out by that armed sentry. I ended up being doubly penalized the next weekend by having no spending money besides owing my roommate fifteen dollars from my next month's pay.

The next incident came when the base commander, Colonel Noel Parrish, ordered the Basic and Advance barracks to assemble in the mess hall. After we were all seated, Colonel Parrish briefly talked about the struggle and the quality of the struggle in being a cadet at Tuskegee Air Base. Then he told us to take a good look at the cadet to our left and then at the cadet to the right. He said take a good look now because tomorrow neither of them may be there. Then he said, "I want you men to know that we will wash out better cadets from among you than will graduate from Randolph or Kelly Fields." His words were important, vitally important, but with my immaturity and dampness behind the ears the real importance, the significance of what he said did not really strike home until much later. What he could have said directly was that a quota number of cadets would be washed out no matter how good they were. That Colonel Parrish's statements would be true, I witnessed over the next several months.

About midway through Basic we faced the challenge of another two-part examination or evaluation test. The first part consisted of the standard Rorschach Ink Blot Test. You looked at a series of cards that had various shapes and forms printed on them, shapes that looked like scraggly drawings by a two-year-old. You had to state what you saw in each drawing and/or what, if any, meaning lay in whatever you saw. The second part was much more demanding. It consisted of a bucket airplane seat rigged to a cluster of arms mounted on a table-like device. The way it was mounted reminded me of a miniature octopus ride at the carnival, except there was only one seat. After being strapped into the seat you were given a clipboard that had questions and an answer sheet. The first question might ask if the tenth word in the fourth sentence had three n's, put a three in the ninth box on the answer sheet. Or it could have been, if there are seven letters in the next to last word in the second paragraph, place a "c" in the twelfth box of the answer sheet. That was all good and fine, except the operator, while you were figuring out what to put where, was jerking the bucket seat forward and backward, sideways, bouncing you every way except out of the seat, only because you were buckled in. This last test measuring concentration under extremely distracting conditions may have aided the so-called experts in deciding how to separate those better suited for single or twin engine training.

Each day that we flew I became better and better and more proficient as a budding pilot. I was not the first to solo in Primary but that honor became mine in both Basic and Advance. To be the first to solo brought small bragging rights but they were not heralded with bravado, only realized and mentally noted within the group. And in all fairness all the instructors differed, some held onto you like a mother hen while others readily kicked you out of the nest as soon as your tail feathers dried. As for proficiency, the entire class was like a chain. There were no weak links, each segment being much like those connected to each of its ends. Near the end of Basic something happened that could have ended my hopes very abruptly. In moving from the simplified instrument panel of the PT-17 with its magnetic compass we encountered the gyrocompass in the BT-13. While the magnetic compass moves around and runs ahead or lags behind, depending on the direction you are turning toward or from, the solid gyro keep a steady pace no matter what the direction or how steep the turn. But the gyro has faults of its own. Before beginning aerobatics, to prevent damage to some of the instruments including the gyro compass, standard procedure required caging (locking) them. When you finished doing snap rolls and Cuban eights the caged instruments were then unlocked and you were obliged to reset the gyrocompass to match the heading of the magnetic one.

The class, near the end of Basic, was to fly a three-legged cross country course from Tuskegee to Birmingham on the long first leg, then fly to Anniston for the short leg, and then return to Tuskegee. At both checkpoints you were required to call in to the check plane and he would acknowledge seeing you by giving you an okay "some number" on the radio. On the Anniston back to Tuskegee leg my troubles began. I had hit my checkpoints and had turned on the final leg heading home to Tuskegee in beautiful late afternoon weather. There were very few ground checkpoints (water towers, railroad tracks, or some other easily identifiable permanent object) so I relied on my gyrocompass and ignored periodically checking the gyro against the magnetic compass. The gyro began to precess. That means it began to turn on its own ever so slightly that in its faulty turning I failed to notice the movement. Two hours later, when Tuskegee should have been right in front of me, it was no where in sight. I had no idea if I had flown to the right or to the left of the field. In plain words, I was completely lost, and near panic, rose again. Up to this time the class had not received radio instrument instructions. We had flown by instruments in the link and under the hood in the back seat but to put the whole package together and operate the radio to establish a course still lay ahead of us in instruction. I knew I had flown far enough that I should be directly over Tuskegee. I had drifted to one side or the other, but to which side? I decided as my first choice to turn left and fly for 20 minutes and if that produced nothing I would turn right and fly for 40 minutes.

At the 20 minute mark I spotted a single grass runway and a building with the word "Macon" painted in large black letters on the dull corrugated roof. I also saw a single man on the ground; he waved to me as I flew over the field. Temptation strongly urged me to land and ask where I was, but a little voice whispered, "If you land you'll be washed out." Later, I learned that little grass field was Macon, Georgia, the first small town, east of the Alabama state line. My second move was to make a 180-degree turn and gain altitude; the third was to pray, which I had never done before even though my father was a minister. I had heard many prayers, though with head bowed, I had never uttered a single word in prayer. Then as though being guided through the correct procedure, I reached down and pulled the radio book from the chart case and looked up the frequency of Tuskegee's tower. I turned on the radio and rotated the coffee grinder, as it was called, to the frequency given for Tuskegee and instantly heard that frequency in my headset. What I heard told me that I was right in the middle of the radio beam heading for the field. By the time I arrived darkness had fallen and after receiving permission to enter the traffic pattern I landed and taxied to the ramp parking space. Just as I reached to turn off the ignition, the engine coughed and died. I realized that had I landed in Macon on that little grass strip and gotten instructions on which way to turn I would have run out of fuel before reaching Tuskegee. At night that would have meant bailing out, with the plane crashing somewhere and I would have surely been washed out.

My instructor and most of the class were waiting in the ready room to hear some word of my whereabouts. As it turned out I was congratulated by the instructor and patted on the back by my classmates. I have never mentioned those prayers before putting that plea in writing. Realizing now the complicated combination of things I had done without training along with the engine dying when I had parked the plane forever made me a believer. A popular aviation magazine used to carry a column entitled

"I Learned About Flying, From That." Stories from private pilots who learned valuable lessons the hard way, from their mistakes. Mine would have been to frequently check the gyro compass against the old reliable magnetic one to make certain the gyro was staying on course and not subtly creeping off leading me to parts unknown and not planned.

As had been happening from the very first a few more of our class were eliminated but the rate of washout in the last two weeks of Basic dropped to zero. Those who remained were being promoted to Advance, sent to the next barracks and given the desirable pink nametags instead of the blue. For me it was both a happy and a sad time again, happy because I was going to the super AT-6 and sad because I was losing my roommate who had decided to choose the AT-10, the twin engine phase of Advance. Saying that I was anxious to get my hands on the AT-6 would be a gross understatement. That plane stood just one step away from the real fighters. The T-6 was sleeker, faster, had retractable landing gear, and it just looked like it separated the men from the boys. As before, the move forward also meant a physical change of barracks, a huffing and puffing of moving clothing and footlockers to the new building.

Eugene Jacques Bullard, the first African-American combat pilot, was one of 200 Americans who flew for France in World War I.
*Source*: Wikipedia's Web Encyclopedia

Bessie Coleman with her Curtis Jenny-4 in the mid-1920s.
*Courtesy*: Ellis County Museum, Waxahachi, TX

Author's multi-engine segment of Class 45-A at Tuskegee.
*Courtesy*: Author's Collection

Grover Nash, first black pilot to fly the U.S. Mail.
*Courtesy*: National Air and Space Museum, Smithsonian Institute (S199-15414)

Aviation cadets on parade at Tuskegee Institute, May 1944.
*Courtesy*: Tuskegee Airmen Photographic Collection, Air Force Historical Research Agency, Maxwell AFB, AL

Author's class of fighter pilots graduating from Tuskegee in March 1945.
*Courtesy*: Author's Collection

Reviewing student checkpoints prior to a cross-country flight at Tuskegee.
*Courtesy*: Tuskegee Airmen Photographic Collection, Air Force Historical Research Agency, Maxwell AFB, AL

First class of black bomber pilots to graduate from Tuskegee in November 1943.
*Courtesy*: Leslie Alan Williams

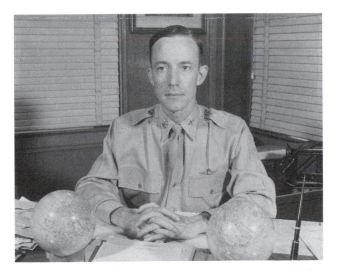

Colonel Noel F. Parish, final commanding officer of Tuskegee's Army Air Base.
*Courtesy*: Tuskegee Airmen Photo Collection, Maxwell AFB, AL

Wendell Lipscomb, Tuskegee primary flight instructor, eyeing one of his students.
*Courtesy*: Ellen Gunther

Photo # USN 1146845   Ens. Jesse L. Brown in cockpit of an F4U-4

Jesse L. Brown, the U.S. Navy's first black pilot, in his F4U-4 Corsair.
*Courtesy*: U.S. Naval Historical Center

Neal Loving with one of his self-designed and constructed planes.
*Courtesy*: Special Collections and Archives, Wright State University

Guion F. Bluford, first black astronaut in NASA's space program.
*Courtesy*: NASA photo division

Mae Jemison, first black female astronaut to join the NASA program.
*Courtesy*: NASA photo division

Ronald E. McNair, physicist, perished in the 1986 Challenger shuttle explosion.
*Courtesy*: NASA photo division

Charles F. Bolden, piloted the shuttle that launched the Hubble space telescope.
*Courtesy*: NASA photo division

# CHAPTER 6

# Making Changes

At Tuskegee, from the very first class, 42-C, through the class of 43-I, if you washed out you went back to your point of origin, that is, if you had come from the infantry, that is where you returned. When white pilot cadets washed out they had the option of going to navigation or bombardier schools for training. Before class 43-J no programmed training of black bomber pilots took place, so there was obviously no need for black navigators or bombardiers because they would not have been permitted to fly with white crews.

LeRoy Gillead was in the first class of 30 black navigator cadets to ever train at Hondo Field, Texas, or any other site in the United States. He had washed out of pilot training in class 43-G after that class had been advanced in an upward consolidation move from the class 43-H designation. A New Yorker, Gillead had grown up primarily with a grandmother, an older sister, a younger brother, and seven cousins. In January 1941, when the Air Corps announced that blacks were being accepted, Gillead enlisted three months later and was sent to Mitchell Field, New York. He and a number of other black enlistees took the written and physical examinations. About 40 of them passed and were sent to Chanute Field, Illinois for technical training. Gillead recalled that when they first arrived at Chanute they were given coffee and sandwiches and then trucked to the far side of the base to be quartered in old WWI tar paper barracks. The next day they found that their white counterparts were housed in nice, fairly new brick buildings.

Each morning they marched about a mile to their classes in the newer brick buildings and the white trainees would line their route to shout slurs and jeer at them. A couple of days of those taunts proved more than enough. Their flight leader, Big Jim Reed, one day gave the order for "right flank, March!" that turned the whole unit in the direction of the jeering spectators who quickly dispersed. There would be no further taunts after that. After some six of months training, Gillead—who had trained as a mechanic—and the whole group, were scheduled for shipment to Tuskegee with high expectant hopes. But Tuskegee was not nearly ready so, as mentioned earlier, they ended up at Maxwell Air Base. At Maxwell they were assigned every possible menial chore except house cleaning. Gillead remembered those loathsome chores with a degree of bitterness. "They had us sweeping the streets, we cleaned rifle ranges, we, in fact, had to clean everything except the barracks that the white cadets were staying in." And even though they had a pressing need for mechanics at Maxwell, these newly trained mechanics were not allowed to service any of the planes based at Maxwell.

There were a few tradeoffs that Gillead remembered, such as at night, the men would put on civilian clothes, sneak under the fencing and head for a good bar in Montgomery. While the men languished at Maxwell, Pearl Harbor erupted. This prompted the immediate transfer of the group to Tuskegee even though they were to live in tents until the first barracks were finished. Thinking back, Gillead remembered, with a smile, playing in the fresh snow that fell on Tuskegee. He recalled it as a pleasant, unforgettable memory because he had one of the best ever frolics in the snow. He said, "That snow lay untainted by man or beast unlike it was up in the crowded North, the blighted sooty snow in the big cities." The group stayed in a tent city for almost three months before the barracks were ready for occupancy and since there was still no flying training on the new base this group of trained technicians faced more menial type duties.

Eventually flying training began at Tuskegee and Gillead's first technical duty was to begin "turning wrenches" on the AT-6 as a mechanic. Soon after the first class of graduated cadets had advanced to the transition plane, the P-40 fighter, he recalled, "I became an electrical propeller specialist. Months later I entered the pilot training program but I failed to advance beyond the Primary phase." Of the nine cadets who advanced to class 43-G, including Daniel "Chappie" James who had been in class 43-I, only Gillead would be washed out. James would go on to become the country's first black four-star general after combat missions in Korea and Vietnam. With his fourth star, came command of the North American Air Defense Command.

It was standard practice to move a very small class of cadets up to fill out and complement a small class ahead of it. Lee Archer could also be counted among those in 43-G. Archer later became the only Ace among all of the 450 black fighter pilots who would see combat. Archer's fifth credit was only grudgingly recognized many years after WWII had become history. An Ace is one who has officially been credited with the destruction of at least five enemy aircraft or, as was commonly stated, had five confirmed "enemy kills."

Gillead retained a very strong feeling that he had been caught in the washing machine of quotas imposed on black cadets, quotas based strictly on race. He remembered an incident that happened in Montgomery, Alabama, where being unused to traffic lights, he had jaywalked and had been caught by a burly, red-faced policeman. The policeman had called him "Boy" and had asked him where he was from. Gillead pretended to have a southern accent and replied that he came from Champaign-Urbana, Illinois. The officer then asked him, "Don't they have any lights there?" Gillead told him yes but he very seldom ever got to that part of town. The officer then growled, "Well, down here you better pay attention, you hear me, Boy?" He responded. "Yassuh!"

Being in the very first class of black navigators to be trained gave Gillead some sense of accomplishment and satisfaction but that was not his first love, he felt cheated in not receiving the wings of a pilot. Gillead easily remembered that although all of their training was equal at Hondo Field, Texas, at the close of training the black cadets received a different version of flight scheme than their white counterparts. The graduating black cadets charted the courses of their planes eventually to La Guardia Field in New York. Gillead remembered the event. "We were greeted by then Mayor Fiarello La Guardia and they even gave us a ticker tape parade to city hall." They were escorted to the Savoy Ballroom where Gillead, now itchy and in home territory again, decided it was time to test fate by sneaking away to see his girlfriend. He managed to slip back just in time for the reception with only his roommate being aware that he had taken off on the sly. After the class had been given a short leave, the next stop was to attend bombardier school at Roswell, New Mexico. The three months at Roswell were segregated but the black cadets had tables in the same mess hall as the white trainees. Gillead recalled, "The food was good and there were no particular racial problems for our entire training period there."

A smile came to his face as he reflected back. "There happened to be some Chinese cadets in pilot training at Roswell at the same time and our two groups would associate with each other. The Americans taught the Chinese cadets how to gamble and lose their money while the Chinese taught the Americans a lot of Chinese sex words."

After bombardier school there was gunnery training at Yuma, Arizona where the group received air-to-air, air-to-ground, and skeet shooting to sharpen their eye skills. Of the original 30 cadets that began training at Hondo, 24 graduated to earn their officer's bars. Immediately after graduation, Gillead and his buddy Arnold Galimore, also a New Yorker, decided to integrate the base theater. Two burly MPs in the company of the base commander soon called them out of the theater. The commander sternly told them to make sure they got their "black asses" off his base before another night fall. Both Gillead and Galimore already had their travel orders in hand so they bid goodbye to Hondo for good the next day. He continued,

"We all had almost a full month's leave before having to report to Godman Field, Kentucky for assignment to the 477th Bombardment Group, the all-black bomber unit." The very first officer that Gillead would see when he reported to Godman for duty was his old former classmate Chappie James. James looked at him and said he did not think Gillead looked as enthusiastic as he did when they had last seen each other months earlier. Gillead, in explanation, said, "I told him that all the racism and discrimination that I had been forced to swallow had sorely angered me and caused me to become bile bitter."

Another memory fiber vibrated and Gillead recounted a less pleasant event. He remembered being involved in a running battle with the operations officer of the 616th Bombardment Squadron because the operations officer was forcing the crews to do things that Gillead thought were unnecessarily dangerous. Finally, after four months of battling, he transferred to another squadron. The 477th then moved to Freeman Field, Indiana in March 1945, where the black officers refused to submit to discriminatory treatment and 101 of them were put under house arrest. Gillead stated that a majority of the group later shipped to Walterboro Air Base in South Carolina to temporarily become part of the 126th after they had been kept under house arrest at Godman Field, Kentucky for more than two weeks. Gillead remained thoroughly convinced that the Freeman Field incident, sometimes referred to as a mutiny, was a successful assault on what he called the white power structure. Without being asked, Gillead rated the attributes of the final TAAF base commander, Colonel Noel Parrish, as having all super "A" pluses without question or flaws.[1]

In Primary and Basic training we were taught a few simple maneuvers that could be called aerobatics. In Advance everything was about to hang out, everything in the book and some things not in the book. Again, there was a change in instructors but now there were fewer of them because the class had been divided into single engine and twin engine, which for my class put 24 in single engine and 16 in the twin side. My instructor came from Brooklyn but he did nt seem to have that readily identifiable Brooklyn accent. He was very dedicated and sincere in his efforts to make certain you learned what he was trying to teach. We had been in Advance only one week when one of my classmates asked the Director of Advance for a transfer to twin engine class. His request was most unfortunate because two or three check rides later he was gone. Just before he made his request a few of us asked him why he wanted out and he merely replied something to the effect that the AT-6 was a little too fast and the landing gear too narrow. I have no doubt that had he stayed with the group he would have graduated with the rest of us. There would be one more casualty at the end of Advance after all instruction was over and we were allowed to fly pretty much as we wished. It is a very disturbing remembrance that will be related later in its proper place.

There was plenty of flying in Advance including more precision maneuvers and the demanding and exacting skill of formation flying. Then there was instrument flying, no more of the partially flying by the seat of your pants. It so happened that my instrument instructor was Director of Instrument Training and this part is important because of an incident that occurred during my final instrument check. When I reported for the instrument flight check the check pilot appeared surly and disagreeable to the point that he made it quite plain he did not like me even a little bit at first sight. In the air near the end of the check ride, without warning, the control stick was suddenly yanked out of my hand and banged hard repeatedly across my knees, hard enough to be painful. The check pilot immediately ordered me to open the instrument hood and raise my seat. For instrument training the student sat in the back seat under a black hood so that only the lighted instrument panel could be seen. In order to close the hood the seat had to be lowered. When I opened the hood and raised my seat I could see him carefully watching for my reaction in the mirror. I could sense he was waiting for me to swear at him or show some anger for his having battered my knees with the steel stick. I mentally gritted my teeth and refused to give him the satisfaction of showing any facial anger or uttering a word that could in any way be interpreted as insubordination. Either of those responses could have meant instant washout. When we landed and climbed out of the plane the check pilot, with a spiteful sneer, told me that I had flunked the test. My instructor looked at the report and told me to climb back into the cockpit and get under the hood. Up we went again in the same plane for the same test. As I went through the required maneuvers I suddenly heard in my earphones, "There's nothing wrong with your instrument work. Let's go home." If my instructor had not been the head of instrument training the treatment by the check pilot would probably have washed me out. But I had this strange feeling that my instructor already knew of the check pilot's biased attitude and the tactics that he was capable of.

There was a more humorous occasion when the class had a night solo flight. Night solo, in this instance, was nothing more than going up to a certain area and holding in that area at a designated altitude. Since we would be up for quite a while we all had been given one sandwich and an apple to eat. At mid-point I decided to chomp on the sandwich and so as not to be accused of cluttering the cockpit with garbage, I cracked the canopy open. I intended to start unwrapping the wax paper with my teeth then stick the sandwich through the canopy opening and let the wind blow the paper away. That plan did not work; just as soon as I stuck the sandwich through the opening the wind whipped both sandwich and wrapper from my hand leaving me with an apple for lunch. Another one of those, "I Learned About Flying, From That," experiences.

In Advance and in Basic we wore only our underwear and flight suits; to have worn more would have been too hot and bulky along with the traditional parachute. As a rule you removed everything of value from your pockets and transferred all to the zippered pouch pockets of the flight suits just below the knee. On this particular day, as I started to practice aerobatics, I had forgotten to zip up the pouch that contained all of my pocket change. I began a slow roll and immediately all the change flew out of the pouch and landed on the canopy just above my head with me upside down. If I continued to complete the roll all the change would end up in the bottom of the plane to be scooped up later by the crew chief. My only solution was to remain upside down until I had plucked all the quarters, nickels, and dimes one by one from the canopy and held them in one hand before I completed the roll. I managed to carefully retrieve all of my treasure of coins, leaving none for the crew chief.

A condition was drummed into us beginning with Preflight—you were never to "quibble." As a cadet, "quibbling" was an attempt to offer an explanation, excuse, or a reason, valid or not, for something you did, said, or failed to do or say. In order not to quibble to an upper classman or to an officer your only utterance could be "Yes, sir, No, sir or No excuse, sir!" To attempt to explain any situation, regardless of the nature, opened the door for more hazing from the upper classman or contempt from an officer.

As we progressed in the Advance phase, instructions became more exacting and precise. You had to show your instructor or check pilot just how much you had polished and perfected the things you had been taught. On one occasion my instructor took over the controls and flew over a tiny auxiliary landing strip called "Shorter Field." That is all it was—a single landing strip in the middle of some farmer's crops. An old barn stood at one end of the strip and to land on that strip you had to clear the peaked roof of the barn with very little wiggle room. Too low, you would hit the barn, too high and you would not be able to stop before hitting the trees at the far end of the strip. All at once my instructor ordered me to land on that little strip of ground. He gave me no advance warning or chance to drag the area. Dragging is a method of first flying very close to the ground to check for tree stumps or ruts should you have to make a forced landing. And of course, that barn's roof stuck up high enough to make it interesting as a test of judgment and precision. Following my instructor's order I set up an approach and came in to land. As we cleared the barn roof I could readily see that someone, on some prior landing, had ploughed two nice healthy wheel troughs through the pitched roof of the barn. We landed so softly that it could not be felt we were on the ground. My instructor suddenly yelled at me over the radio, "What the hell was that?" I was startled. I had no idea what I had done wrong. In a split second I had checked my cockpit landing procedures and found nothing wrong. Then my instructor growled again into my headset, "Do it again!" Immediately it hit me that the landing had been perfect and he wanted me to show him that it was no fluke. I took off, went around and landed again. This time it was very, very soft, almost as good as the first time but not quite. Those two landings told my instructor that I had mastered the T-6.

Just past the mid-point of our training in Advance we learned the technique of precision formation flying. That required, among other things, crossing under the lead plane to change from a Vee formation to a stepped down configuration called an echelon, to the left or to the right and pushing the planes in extremely tight. In following the lead plane the following planes always followed slightly lower and behind the ones they were keyed on. Knowing that the propeller of your craft whirred very close to the wing of the plane to your left or right meant that you did not dare blink. Out of the corner of your eye you could peripherally see on the side away from the plane you were glued to, but your eyes never wavered for even a split second. After this training phase when your instructor had given you all he had to teach you were left to your own to practice over and over what had been imparted. In single engine you were encouraged to develop what was called the "Messerschmitt Twitch." Advance training included having roving instructors in other AT-6s flitting around the skies looking for a chance to sneak up on you and theoretically shoot you down. Your only defense was to constantly keep your eyes moving all over the sky, no matter what you were doing, checking to see that another AT-6 did not get close enough to shoot you out of the sky. If you spotted such an imagined enemy you waggled your wings indicating that you had spotted the sneaky enemy. If you happened to be caught unawares you were destined to wear an orange armband with the word casualty printed on it, and, of course, be in line for some ego deflating ribbing from your classmates. I had my chance one sunny afternoon when I spotted an AT-6 to the right and below me. It headed my way so I immediately began to waggle the wings signaling that I had spotted it. But it kept coming so I waggled again and then again. The other plane finally passed under and to the left of me. In the front cockpit I could see Captain Bruce Walker, the Director of Advance and my own instructor, Lieutenant Perry Dillman, in the rear seat. When I finished my air work I returned to the field and entered the ready room. Captain Walker stormed out of his office and braced me up in front of some of my classmates. He yelled that if I were not such a good pilot he would first wash me out and then court martial me. Captain Walker was simply livid with anger because he thought I had attempted to engage him in a dogfight, an act totally forbidden in training. As it turned out another of my classmates had been slammed with the same accusation, but all we could say without "quibbling" was, "Yes, sir and No, sir"! I could not tell him that I thought he had not seen me which was why I had continued to waggle my wings and that I was definitely not trying to get into a dogfight. I had to write an essay on the dangers of attempting combat actions in Advance while my classmate had to verbally describe a radial engine in front of the rest of the class.

The rest of Advance went smoothly and uneventfully until the very final week. Instruction had ended and those left in the class knew we were going to graduate and earn those treasured silver wings. We had already received our officer's uniform allowances and a tailor was customizing the purchased uniforms. Pink shirt and pants, green shirt and pants along with a green coat and a stiff hat that would only be worn for graduation and returned to the box. That final week we flew at our leisure to practice whatever we wished or just to go up and "lollygag" in other words to do nothing with any real meaning in the air. That last week became a disaster for another of my classmates. He made just one mistake, one that could have been fatal for him but actually ended with his elimination. My classmate, now poised and ready for graduation with the rest of us, attempted to take off perhaps a half minute too soon following the takeoff of a twin-engine AT-10. The turbulence created by the larger craft proved so severe that when the trailing AT-6 rose some 10 to 15 feet above the runway its slow vulnerable takeoff speed caused it to stall and crash nose first. I watched helplessly and in horror as it happened not knowing who the pilot was but sensing that what he had done surely created another washout. I had been waiting next in line with clearance for takeoff after my classmate. The tower ordered me to use a different runway.

When I returned to the field I learned who had been involved in the crash. The wreck had been removed and the pilot had a knot the size of a golf ball on his forehead but was otherwise all right. Two check rides later the cadet disappeared. His elimination had come so late that the graduation list had simply a blue line drawn through his name. But for that one single unforgivable blunder my classmate would have graduated with the rest of us.

Instruction was over and all that we were required to do was a little air work until the end of the week and then the wings, those elusive hard-won silver wings would be pinned on the left chest. In the case of my eliminated classmate, the tower could just as easily been at fault for not reminding or telling him to hold until the AT-10 had fully cleared. How much time should have been allowed before his takeoff would have been safe? The same question could have been asked of the previous crash. The tower could have told the AT-6 on the ground to hold until the craft entering the traffic pattern was down which would ordinarily be the normal course of events. The plane preparing to land would have the right of way over one preparing to takeoff. The tower knew there was a plane in the landing pattern because you had to receive permission to enter the pattern. The plane readying to take off could have or should have been warned to hold for the landing craft. But it was apparently standing policy that if you were involved in any accident you were kicked out with no analysis or fact-finding as to who or what should be actually blamed. There was no real traffic control other than receiving permission to enter the traffic pattern at which time you would be told the direction of the pattern, left or right, and the runway to land on.

I also had a minor mishap during the final week, in fact it happened on my next to last flight. On a clear calm afternoon the moment I touched down on a routine landing I felt the tail section drop and the plane began to swerve left in an honest to goodness genuine ground loop. I had full flaps down and I knew that if I allowed the ground loop to continue the flap under the right wing would be wiped out. Only sheer muscle power on the control stick enabled me to end up completely off the runway, pointed directly in the direction I was originally headed without any parts of the wings or flaps touching the ground. My instructor had been watching me from the porch of the ready room. He hurried out there to examine the wings and the flaps by the time I had shut off the engine and climbed out of the cockpit with the logbook. I made a notation in the logbook that the tail wheel had malfunctioned. My instructor looked at me, smiled and said simply, "Lots of strength." The crew chief came out to look the plane over and when he saw what I had entered in the logbook he said, "No way," not his plane. He wanted to badger me into changing the entry until he looked at the tail wheel. He was muttering as I walked away heading for the ready room holding my parachute up behind me.

In about the second week of Advance a coined expression began circulating in the class. It was called having your "head up and locked." Basically, it referred to the plane we were now flying which had retractable landing gear. When the gear was retracted or up and locked it was, of course, nonfunctional. That expression carried over to any cadet who committed a senseless or stupid mistake. That cadet was said to have his head up and locked, meaning his head must have been up his rear end and his rear end locked around it to have committed something so dumb!

When we had been given the hours of orientation in the Piper Cubs no one wore a parachute. Beginning in Primary you had to learn to walk with the front edge of your parachute unsnapped and tucked up behind you against your buns until you reached the airplane. Without doing that simple act you would have had this 10 or 15-pound seat cushion slapping each leg as you took a step. The front two straps were snapped just before climbing into the cockpit and easing down into the bucket seat because the parachute was, in fact, the only cushion available until graduation into combat aircraft. For the fighter pilot that combination of seating became even more uncomfortable because there was now an additional very hard life raft that had to be fastened to the parachute. Bomber pilots had the same life rafts but the exception was that multi-engine pilots could get out of their seats and walk around or stretch. In addition they did not have to wear their parachutes while at the controls. Fighter pilots were given recommended bun exercises because there was no standing, walking around, and stretching. The equivalence would be likened to sitting on a very, very hard cushion then inserting a board between your buns and the hard cushion.

On the leisure side, at Tuskegee, every Friday evening the sandwich man would come to the upper Advance class' barracks with a huge cardboard box of ready-made sandwiches. The sandwiches were edible but that was not the main reason for the sandwich man's appearance. Beneath the piles of sandwiches were bottles of booze that looked like whiskey and tasted like whiskey but what was really in those bottles only the sandwich man knew for sure. Each bottle had its cap secured with scotch tape, so whether the sandwich man brewed it in drums, bought it in drums, or diluted each bottle will forever remain a mystery. I am sure the MPs at the main gate were aware that the sandwich man had more than sandwiches in that big box in the trunk of his car. He probably rewarded them with a jug of taped Scotch delight as his entry fee. I also recall that he never went to any other barracks, only the upper Advance unit located next to the street. With that particular portion of Alabama being dry I am sure he had more stay-in-business payoffs to take care of before he even reached the base.

Heading into our final week, someone who should have provided the single engine group with better scheduling failed and failed miserably. It turned out that we should have had three weeks of skeet shooting in the previous month but now, because of timing, those three weeks had to be completed in one day. Some of the class had never even seen a shotgun before let alone fired one and that spelled painful disaster for some. In skeet shooting there were three stations from which you were required to shoot, one in the center and one on each side. At each post there was a low bird (clay pigeon) and a high bird. The operative words were "Pull" and "Mark." When you yelled out one of those words, operators in one of the two little huts would release a clay pigeon that rapidly flew up and away from you. The so-called clay pigeon resembled a thick salad plate turned upside down. The shooter had to be quick enough to draw a bead, give the correct lead, and fire to hopefully pulverize the bird with a direct hit. Twelve gauge shells, as we were using, obliterated the clay pigeons with ease, if the aim was correct. The idea, for us in shooting skeet, was to estimate the spot where the bird would be when the buckshot finally caught up with it. To fire directly at the bird would mean continually firing behind an object on the move. We fired all afternoon and after all of the shooting ended, several of my class-mates ended up in the hospital with severe contusions in the shoulder area. Everyone had been instructed to keep the butt of the gun pressed firmly against the shoulder in order to lessen the slamming effect from the recoil. However, after hours of firing round after round, fatigue and carelessness seeped in. Near the end of the firing a careless mistake occurred that could have taken a life. The same classmate who had brilliantly described the radial engine vocally, stood at the center position ready to fire when the operator in the "mark" house told him to wait a moment. I watched the classmate lower the gun, still cocked and ready to fire, as he grabbed it by the barrel to lean it against the center post while he waited. Instead of putting it down gently, he dropped it and the gun discharged into the air less than a foot from his head. I saw it happen because I was waiting to fire the next set from the same station. He appeared outwardly nonplused and unruffled by that very near miss but even today I remember just how close he came to blowing away his head.

On March 11, 1945, we had our graduation day and for one more time the entire class, in spanking new officer's uniforms, but no wings, marched as a unit behind the post marching band to the chapel for the graduation ceremony. The splendid, crisp sounds of the band and the realization that finally graduation time had arrived made it seem that we were actually briskly marching on clouds. There were 38 very proud young men who marched together from headquarters to the chapel, 22 in single engine and 16 in twin engine. We would become the largest class to ever graduate from Tuskegee although we did not know that at the time, and except for the two crucial mistakes there would have been 40 strong.

In the chapel the base commander, Colonel Noel Parrish, praised those who were ready to receive their shiny silver wings and be called pilots. He said we were the cream of the crop and our accomplishments would be admired and cheered by others who could only faintly imagine the adversities we had overcome. With those wings came the bars of an officer and that combination caused our steps to remain several inches off the ground. In addition, the left breast, where those glorious wings proudly sat, automatically moved upward and forward. But the next step, after all the jubilation and cheering, slightly deflated our balloons. We were not to go on leave home to family and friends as we had thought. We had been scheduled for our first real taste of aerial gunnery practice. There was some disappointment in not being able to rush home and show off our newly won silver wings, but a huge helping of anticipation at the prospect of pulling the trigger of a machinegun while controlling the airplane beckoned.

There is another phase or aspect in the training of black military pilots that took place before President Harry Truman ever signed the executive order ending segregation in the armed services. That order was issued in July 1948, and although the services generally delayed and stalled coming to grips with integration in terms of years, the Air Force, previously one of the staunchest services against integration, began another experiment. It may have been noted by some ranking Air Force officials that an excellent team work had developed between pilots of the 99th Fighter Squadron and the 79th Fighter Group when they were placed together under near integrated conditions. It could have been some far-sighted Air Force visionary who could clearly see the writing on the wall and who acted with open intelligence. Down through the years it had been irrationally assumed that black and white soldiers could not fight shoulder to shoulder against some common enemy. This meant there had to be trial research to determine whether the two racially different Americans could be trained together.

That would have to be the first step in overturning years of ingrained racial attitudes. We can only speculatively raise the question at this point—was the real attitude one of wait and see or was it another one of expected failure.

Though Texas born, Big Sandy, to be specific, Harold Hoskins, did most of his growing up in the fairly liberal Northwestern state of Oregon. An aunt in Los Angeles began to raise him following the death of his parents. This thoughtful aunt shipped him up to another aunt in Portland when he appeared headed for trouble by running with a small gang in the Watts area of Los Angeles. Hoskins volunteered for the Air Corps just before graduation from high school because he had developed an early attraction to airplanes and disdained the thought of slogging around in the infantry. The Air Corps called him in February 1945, the month after he received his high school diploma and sent him to Ft. Lewis, Washington, for induction. During his five days of processing Hoskins remembered the German and Italian prisoners of war being able to enter and shop at the main PX on the post but the black personnel were restricted to a little one-room separate building that stocked just a few items. On his train ride to Tuskegee the train pulled into Athens, Georgia and Hoskins hopped off the train to get a drink of water. He had not noticed the "White Only" sign over the fountain. He said, "A white female employee at the train station saw me and went positively ballistic, screaming and pointing her finger at me. Oh, she was ready to have a stroke." He beat a very hasty retreat back to the train and out of harm's way. He recalled the earlier part of his trip on leaving Washington. "Every thing was fine then. There were even a couple white pilots who had just graduated and they were telling me what to expect when my training began. But as soon as we hit the Mason-Dixon Line they put all the black soldiers in a separate car, the closest one to the engine's coal car. In the dining car they had put up a curtain around the first two tables separating us from the rest of the car."

Hoskins spent several weeks in Preflight training living in Sage Hall on the Tuskegee Institute's campus. After Preflight his class designated as 46-A began actual flight training at Moton Field in the sturdy PT-13, a plane duplicating the PT-17 but sporting more horsepower. Soon the class transferred to the Tuskegee Air Base to begin their Basic phase of training. In a drastic change from earlier stages, Basic training began in the AT-6 rather than the old BT-13 and by this time all the instructors were black former combat pilots who had completed their tours of action. While all of the instructors were now black, Hoskins recalled, "All of the check pilots were white and those guys didn't have any combat experience." Hoskin's class had just begun instrument training when the war ended. They were all afforded the choice of staying in and finishing the training or going home. He remarked, "I didn't like the South. I sure didn't like Alabama so I decided to get out and go home." He waved goodbye to Tuskegee and flying training in November 1945, and headed back to Portland.

In Portland, Hoskins and a newly found buddy, Lawrence Campbell, were attending the University of Portland when their GI benefits well ran dry forcing them to drop out of school. At just that time they happened to learn that the Navy had openings in its pilot training program. After taking and passing the required examinations, Hoskins and Campbell received letters directing them to report to the recruiting office where the exams had been administered for assignment. All seemed normal except that on their arrival the recruiting officer told them that the Navy had no place to train them. The date was September 1947, and the two men found out the blunt way, that the Navy, at that time, still had its doors closed to black candidates. Both men were more than a little puzzled by this development of taking the examinations in the same office that was now saying "thanks for your time but no, thanks."

The historic executive order desegregating the armed services would not come for another nine months and even then the actuality of desegregation dragged along for more than two years after the signing. This unexpected snub caused the two men to take the Air Force exams again at McCord Air Force Base in Washington. There the two were given kinder treatment and allowed to enter a trial program that took them to Randolph Air Force Base in Texas. Joining them at Randolph were two other cadet candidates, Vernon Burke and Milford Craig and two Second Lieutenants, Paul Lehman and George H.O. Martin. These six men would be the second batch of black pilot trainees to be placed in an experimental program to see if blacks and whites could be trained together. The first group had nine black cadets and only one would survive to graduate. Claude Platt who had been an instructor at Tuskegee and had accumulated some four thousands hours in the PT-13, not only survived but showed some of his instructors a thing or two about the PT-13.

As soon as Hoskins and the others arrived on base they were called to the commander's office for a briefing. He remembered the Colonel's words. "He told us that we could go anywhere on the base and do anything we wanted just like everyone else. But he also said that because the training would be so tough we might want to room with each other rather than with a white cadet, in case we needed support." A humorous tone inflected his voice. "Then he said on the weekends he would prefer that we not use the swimming pool because the girl friends of the other cadets came to the base then and it might cause some problems if we were at the pool." Hoskins suddenly laughed outright. "The Colonel said he couldn't order us not to use the pool but he hoped, so as not to cause any trouble, we would refrain from doing that."

Hoskins became a cadet officer in his group and did not readily recall any unpleasant racial incidents at Randolph with one minor exception. It came during a touch football game and Milford Craig had the ball running for a touchdown. He said, "As Craig broke for the goal one of the white cadets yelled out, 'stop that niggah'! But just as soon as it came out he immediately showed his embarrassment and he apologized." The only other problem Hoskins recalled arose on their first trips to the post barber shop. "The barbers on the post had not been used to cutting black folks hair so they really butchered us the first couple of times we went in there. But they soon learned the knack and everything after that was fine. And because Craig came from Utah the barbers used to call him the 'Black Mormon.'"

There was the customary hazing by upper classmen but according to Hoskins, hazing by these upper classmen was a walk in the park compared to what he had endured at the hands of the upper class monsters at Tuskegee. When graduation time came there was still no place for black pilots other than at Lockbourne Air Base, which by then had been winnowed down to the P-47 fighter. This meant that the five graduating black pilots would be sent to Williams Air Force Base for fighter training while about half of the white graduates ended up in bomber training, a fact that made a number of them very unhappy because it would be a rare bird indeed who did not yearn for the exciting thrill of becoming a fighter jock.

At Williams, the men received a couple of hours in a piggyback (two-seater) P-51 and then more hours in a "captive air" P-51, a full-sized plane set in concrete that the trainees could fly without leaving the ground. In addition to finally getting training in the real thing, P-51s not anchored in concrete or having two cockpits, the cadets were treated to some other training, how to handle a pick and shovel. Their ground skills were used to help dig the huge hole that would later become the officer's swimming pool. Final graduation came October 8, 1948, and the class held their party in the Westward Ho Hotel in Phoenix, Arizona. The hotel also established a first in its history by allowing the black graduates to enter the establishment with their white classmates. Hoskins remembered getting just one dance with his date, a gorgeous young lady, who was rushed by all of his classmates. Following a short leave, the first assignment as an officer took him to Lockbourne Air Base in Ohio and to a new plane, the hulking P-47. Combat veteran Colonel Bill Campbell was in charge of base operations and the flying transition training in the P47s. With the desegregation order now in full effect Lockbourne could no longer stand as the nation's only segregated air base but before it closed, Hoskins recalled another galling incident. A number of white officers were routinely enrolled at Ohio State University taking advanced courses. While they were there, in order to maintain flight pay status, they would come to Lockbourne and fly C-47 transports to various other bases around the country. He remembered, "It happened on a flight to Jacksonville, Florida. We were transporting a plane load of enlisted men. I was flying as the junior officer to log some hours and we ran into some terrible weather and had to land at the civilian municipal airport. Those enlisted men had no money and in the hours waiting for the weather to clear those men had to be fed. The white officer came up with seventy-five dollars and I produced fifty dollars to pay for their meals in the terminal restaurant. That's when a major hitch developed. The enlisted men were served but they refused to allow me to enter the front door and eat with the other military men. Even though my money had helped provide almost half of the food for the hungry white enlisted men I had to go to the back door to get my portion." On the return flight from Jacksonville, they landed at Maxwell Air Force Base in Alabama. Hoskins then found out that in 1948, being a black officer had rather limited privileges despite a fresh presidential desegregation order. "I found that they wouldn't allow me to eat in the officer's club. They sent me down to Squadron 'F' the black enlisted men's club. And there they really treated me royally."

Just before the closure of Lockbourne, Hoskins was reassigned to Bergstrom Air Force Base in Texas. He arrived in a cab at the base main gate and the sentry refused to salute him saying that he did not salute colored officers. This disrespect took Hoskins immediately to the commanding officer. Although the offense would have been subject to court martial the CO decided to give the offending airman an opportunity to apologize or face the court martial. The airman made the wise choice and apologized for his offense of disrespect.

Hoskins left the service in January 1950, but was recalled three years later and assigned to Lackland Air Base in San Antonio, Texas. On a night cross-country refresher training course to Malden, Missouri, he landed at the Little Rock, Arkansas municipal airport. Tired and famished, he once more had to go around to the back door for his food, the restaurant operators refused to serve him after he had seated himself at the counter.[2]

There were many others just like Hoskins who had to suffer the indignities and humiliation in serving their country while much of its white majority desperately tried to cling to the old, deeply entrenched inferior-superior racial attitudes. The change would not come and pass easily or cleanly without pain, anguish, and bitterness. There would be no soft, gentle transition replacing the past openly raw contempt with the new tempered understanding of humanity as a collection of individuals who were created equal. Naomi Greene had happened and passed during war time, the confrontation of Rosa Parks still lay ahead in the future. Plans for the "March to Selma" ordeal barely glimmered in the back minds of the downtrodden. Racism would just not collapse and readily capitulate without demanding and exacting a scarring toll on its enemies. The bold American concept of freedom and justice for all would be extremely difficult to apply evenly and far more strenuous to actually share than the founding fathers ever dreamed of in formulating the two basic documents that severed all ties to England. The documents were designed to give freedom and independence to all the people of a new nation. The statement that all men are created equal remained fully blurred during slavery. Bringing into proper focus the intent of the Declaration of Independence and the Constitution would require many decades of mental readjustments. For some that re-focusing continues to shuffle along too slowly and for others it briskly hurries past at much too fast a pace. One thing is certain, regardless of some preferred rate of re-focus change that change does move on and it moves on in a constant state of flux.

Although Harold Hoskins and Lawrence Campbell were rebuffed by the Navy in 1947, it finally did open its doors to black pilot candidates a year later. Jesse L. Brown became the first black Navy pilot in 1948. As an ensign, Brown was shot down and killed while flying on a close air support mission in the Korean War becoming the first black Naval Officer to lose his life in a war. Fellow pilot Lieutenant Thomas Hudner performed a very dangerous landing under hazardous conditions and unsuccessfully attempted to free Brown from his wrecked plane. Twenty-three years later, the Navy, after posthumously awarding the Distinguished Flying Cross, Air Medal, and Purple Heart to Brown, commissioned the USS Jesse L. Brown, an escort ship, in his honor. Lieutenant Hudner was awarded the Medal of Honor for his attempt to save Brown.[3]

While Brown's flying and fighting had been in the propeller-driven Vought F4U-4 Corsair, another black pilot, Ensign Earl Carter, had the distinction of becoming the Navy's first black jet pilot. A New Yorker, Carter had completed his advanced carrier training less than three months before the untimely combat death of Brown.[4]

Inspired by Ensign Brown's career in the Navy, Frank E. Petersen, Jr., carved his own niche in U.S. military history by becoming the first black pilot and later the first general in the U.S. Marine Corps. After high school Petersen enlisted in the Navy as a seaman apprentice then got a chance to enter the Naval Aviation Cadet program. He received his wings in October 1952, and accepted his commission in the Marine Corps. His first tactical assignment came with a Marine Fighter Squadron in the Korean conflict. Petersen earned a Distinguished Flying Cross and six Air Medals for his 64 combat missions. On returning home, following a number of assignments, Petersen would become the first black officer to command a tactical squadron in either the Navy or the Marines. He later commanded a fighter attack squadron in Vietnam and was shot down on his seventy-fifth mission but his rescue came quickly. That timely rescue allowed him to complete 205 more combat missions before the ceasefire came in Vietnam. Petersen was promoted to flag rank in 1979, to major general in 1983, and finally to lieutenant general in 1986. He became Commanding General Marine Corps Combat Development Command, Quantico, Virginia and then as Special Assistant to the Chief of Staff until his retirement in 1988.[5]

Slightly more than two decades later black women would pass through the rigid portals of military aviation. For the Navy first came Jill E. Brown, a former home economics teacher in Maryland. Brown began her training near the end of 1974 and continued on to later become the first black female to be hired by a major U.S. airline, Texas International Airlines.

Brenda E. Robinson became Ensign Robinson in June 1980, making her one of less than fifty women earning Navy wings. Robinson had already acquired her private civilian license prior to enlisting in the Navy. Macella A. Hayes became the Army's first black female pilot in November 1979 by earning her wings as a helicopter pilot and finishing the rigorous training of a paratrooper to pin that vaunted badge on as well.[6]

The U.S. Air Force has unquestionably produced the lion's share of black pilots including women. This is not surprising since the Air Force is the only U.S. military service whose greatest thrust is doing things in the air. Of course, there were many other black men and women who successfully entered the very broad field of aviation and were not pilots. The essential professions of flight attendants, mechanics, FAA controllers, airport security, baggage handlers, ticket clerks, and so on, all share in vital roles in the world's safest and quickest mode of transportation. While air tragedies, when they do occur, seem disturbingly spectacular, federal statistics show that for numbers of persons per thousands of miles, air travel is still the safest way to proceed from one point to another.

# CHAPTER 7

# Fighter Training

For two weeks our single engine group was restricted to base at Eglin Field, Florida. We found some immediate new pluses in being officers. For example, at breakfast we had choices, such as, how would you like the eggs, would you like bacon or sausage, one or two slices of toast. These little differences began to multiply as we learned to adjust to a new status, the status of rank.

The planes we were to fly for practice gunnery at Eglin would be the reliable and versatile AT-6s with a single 30-caliber machinegun firing through the propeller. And, yes, there was one plane that had a bullet hole in one blade of the propeller, the result of synchronization failure. When not flying, we had freedom to do anything we wanted except leave the base. They never bothered to explain why we were so restricted during training, but for all of us except one man, there were enough things to do such as playing cards, shooting pool, playing ping pong, or just reading. Dissatisfied, one classmate decided he would really like some female companionship, but in order to get off the base he first had to remove his officer's insignia and pretend to be an enlisted man. It worked for a couple of hours; he did manage to get off the base and go downtown to mingle but it ended when the only identification he could produce was an officer's which meant being out of uniform. What we soon learned and understood from this unwritten and unspoken order of conduct was that they wanted no Tuskegee graduates meandering around in that southern town.

Our gunnery training consisted of two phases, air to air and air to ground shooting. In the first phase, a cargo plane such as the C-47 towed a banner-like target on a long cable and each of us, in flights of five, would make side approaches and fire at the towed target. Accuracy was determined by inspecting the target after the tow plane dropped it back on the ground. Each pilot's bullets were painted a particular color so that if you hit the mark, your color left its imprint as it passed through the white banner target. The ground targets were big square objects tilted backward so as to be nearly perpendicular to your line of flight as you approached down from a slanted firing position. Again, each pilot's bullets were color-coded, that is painted some solid color. The exercise began by dropping out of a flight of five that circled at 3000 feet above the target area. At an altitude of 500 feet you would approach the target dropping lower as you came closer. At a distance of about 400 yards there was a marked firing line on the ground which indicated that you could begin firing as soon as you crossed that marker. By the time you reached the marker your plane would be less than 100 feet above the ground. I recall being told that some previous eager beavers had been so intent on hitting the target that their tailwheels had actually smacked the top of the target as they pulled up at the end of the firing run. None of our group could be charged with that kind of recklessness. As a matter of fact, the same classmate who tried his surreptitious foray into town did so well in target practice that he was sent to Texas to compete against others from all over the country. We later learned that while he did not win first prize he came in either third or fifth which was darn good in open competition of any kind, especially when he was not supposed to even be able to fly in the first place.

Change for us did not come gradually; it came quickly, like flipping a pancake. Training now went from intense noncombative action to pulling the trigger in the cockpit of a plane that now spewed out bullets that could kill. I think the first time any of us fired and heard that special clatter of the machinegun was the first time that it clicked! This is now for real, no more playing and posing, you are getting ready to take someone out! Those two weeks went by in a flash and before we realized it was time to go home on leave for two weeks. I received two weeks because of the travel time back to the West Coast; the others received varying amounts of time depending on how close or far away their homes were from the next assignment, Walter-boro, South Carolina. At home, I stayed forever on the move proudly showing off my new uniform adorned by those precious silver wings. On my last night before heading back to duty I got a promise of commitment from my girlfriend that she would not let "Jodie" take over while I was away. At the last minute, parting became a monumental effort when it seemed as though I had just arrived moments before. After all it had been almost a year since we had last seen each other, but with promises to write often and send pictures we grudgingly made the break, our outstretched fingers reaching and reluctantly pulling apart.

Although departing from home again after a seemingly very short leave created some lip pouting and disappointment, anxious anticipation nudged us along toward the next step, the transition into the actual fighter plane, the move to the aircraft for which all previous training had been preparing us. Transition would take place at Walterboro Air Base at Walterboro, South Carolina. The unit was classified as the 332$^{nd}$ Replacement Training Unit (332$^{nd}$ RTU) of the 126$^{th}$ Army Air Force Base Unit (126$^{th}$ AABU) and our Military Occupational Specialty (MOS) number was further reclassified as 1054, fighter pilot. Arrival at Walterboro began a brand new ball game; no more aircraft with training wheels, we now headed into the serious stuff. It would be our first encounter with a real fighter aircraft, no instructor in the back seat or the front seat, just one plane and one pilot. There would be many other firsts demanding complete absorption and assimilation. We lived in low-lying, single-story, camouflage-painted buildings called revetments that were irregularly staggered in placement and at odd angles to each other. On our arrival, the entire class of 22 was quartered in the largest of the buildings that had entrances on each end and center, with interconnecting doors between each living space of six beds. A month later, we would be broken up and housed in smaller revetments of four two-man rooms with a windowed front hall that ran full-length across the curtained entrance of each room.

We spent the first week in ground school classes learning all about the P-40 fighter aircraft, its specifications, and operating limits. Its real in-the-seat characteristics would be learned only by actual flying, the hands on revelations that would be shown by sitting in the cockpit. Perhaps because of earlier mishaps or complications, we received our first two hours of flight in P-40s that had been modified to hold two men, so-called piggybacks. Since we were now full-fledged pilots, those imparting information to us no longer were called instructors but supervisors. The supervisors were combat veterans who had completed their missions and duty tours and had been rotated back to such stateside duties as teaching neophytes like us the ins and outs of fighter pilot tactics. The next big thrill following the first solo flight in primary had to be climbing into the cockpit of that two-seater P-40. Olive-drab painted, its liquid-cooled engine sported about twice the power as the radial-engine training planes we had last flown. Even though the P-40, by now old, outmoded, and unable to equally compete with such enemy planes as the German ME-109 and FW-190 or the Japanese Zero, nevertheless was still a full-fledged fighter craft that could do plenty of damage. Those first two "get acquainted" hours went by "Whish" and then time came for one pilot in one plane. All of the planes at Walterboro had a big white-colored letter "E," followed by a number painted on both sides of the nose. That made for easy identification from almost all angles, from the ground or from the air.

One of the first things we learned about the new plane fitted a descriptive word. Squirrelly, or more accurately, very squirrelly on the ground, meaning that, with its narrow landing gear you had to be constantly watchful for as long as the wheels were in contact mother earth. The P-40 also did not like to stay on the ground idling for very long, even with the oil cooler wide open. To not pay attention to idling on the ground could easily push the engine temperature needle into the red that at best was less than good. Another item not in the text books was the fact that we would be spending a lot of time flying over water wearing a Mae West life jacket and sitting on an almost rock-hard life raft. The raft sat on top of the already hard parachute. For unknown reasons these life rafts had been known, on occasions, to suddenly inflate and if one should inflate while you sat in the cockpit your head would suddenly be smashed up against the canopy, if it were closed. That condition would emphasize the physical fact that two solids cannot occupy the same space at the same time. This is not to imply that one of those objects is completely solid. At any rate such an unenviable position would make it difficult, if not impossible, to control the airplane and thus lead to all kinds of problems trying to maneuver back onto the ground in one piece. To solve this potentially dangerous dilemma, some enterprising mechanic had come up with the idea of hanging a homemade stabber made of a short pointed-blade of sheet metal with a wooden handle in each cockpit. If the raft started to inflate, hopefully, you would have time to quickly grab the stabber dangling from a frame member to your right and poke a hole into the rapidly inflating thing that was now much more than a hard seat. After seeing that setup I began to wonder how many pilots had previously been done in because of having their heads squashed against the canopy by a malfunctioning life raft. On the other side, part of our standard issue was a pair of extremely soft kid gloves that looked and felt like something from the ladies' wear section. Not only were they soft, they flared well up over the wrists, a thoughtful protection in case of a cockpit fire.

While in ground school, besides learning some of the unique characteristics of the P-40, we also had to learn such things as not flying below 1,000 feet, except on training missions, not doing snap rolls or outside loops, and not making simulated attacks on any friendly military or commercial aircraft. All of these "No-Nos" had to be signed items and then became a part of your file with the threat of being punished under the 64$^{th}$ Article of War or in other words court-martialed if violated. I specifically mention this in leading to an incident that occurred after logging the big total of about six hours in the P-40. On a beautiful, bright, sunny day, feeling good and flying alone off the coast of South Carolina, still getting to know this airplane, I was jumped by four Marine Bearcats or Hellcats from the Cherry Point Marine Base. These guys apparently knew when each new bunch of neophytes had arrived at Walterboro and they could not wait to pounce on and embarrass the hell out of the untrained newcomers. But even with training and full familiarization of the P-40, there would have been no match against either the Hellcat or the Bearcat. These four guys, one on each wing, one behind and one above me, rode me all over the sky taking me where they wanted to go, when they wanted. After about five minutes of this, the ringleader on my right gave me a "thumbs up" signal and took off with his buddies. Obviously, each one of them must have signed similar orders as we had, forbidding simulated attacks or not approaching closer than 300 feet unless on a training flight. They might have just considered that hazing incident as a special training flight for me, but it was not one anticipated or appreciated at the time. Even so it was all in good harmless fun, with me being the butt, like positioning a bucket of water over the doorway for an unsuspecting roommate.

The days and hours began to build up in the P-40 and with the increase of hours so did the confidence in handling and learning by feel and trial and error, just what that aircraft could do and should not do. Again, on a lovely cloudless day I managed to get into an unexpected and unwanted position. Somewhere at around 12,000 feet over land I suddenly found myself in an inverted flat spin. Try as I could, nothing I had been taught about spin recovery worked. I tried some things not taught then tried mixing them together, and still nothing worked. I remained still spinning upside down and getting closer and closer to the ground in what I thought was going to be a death ride or an inverted bailout. Then just as quickly as it had begun, the spinning mysteriously stopped, allowing me to get upright again. More puzzled than frightened, I gave myself an extra cushion of 3,000 feet and went back up to over 15,000 feet. I deliberately tried to see what maneuver, and what degree of cross controls would put me back into an inverted flat spin. But trying everything did not work, nothing produced another inverted flat spin. To this day I do not know what caused the recovery or even what had thrown me into that uncontrollable position. Years later, I learned from an experienced Air Force pilot flying F-16s that a flat inverted spin with one side flame out meant eject time because there was no chance of recovery. In fact one of the specific forbidden maneuvers in the P-40, along with outside loops and snap rolls was inverted flight, so, apparently, that made being inverted and in a spin at the same time a double "No-No."

One of the most pleasant changes of our transition was the presence of the officer's club in which, except for weekends, we generally spent most of our free time. The club, located about a block away from the revetments, contained dance hall, game room, ample card tables, and a bar. You could buy all the whiskey or scotch you wanted as long as you purchased a bottle of rum with each bottle of whiskey. No one particularly liked the rum so the floor space at the bottom of some wall lockers was half-filled with unopened rum bottles. Beer was also available but it tasted so green and bitter that after one sip even the rum tasted better than good. The food was excellent and we found that officers were afforded choices in the selection of more than one fare, and we did not have to stand in line moving a metal tray along to have the server glop whatever into one of the spaces of the tray. We actually had real plates and silverware that we then placed on our trays and carried to four-person tables.

There were two pool tables, a ping pong table, easy chairs and sofas along with the card tables. While the club was less than a block away, there were no sidewalks, gravel, or even asphalt around the revetments or on the main dirt paths leading to the club. The casualness of dress made transition training even more attractive. No necktie, just open shirt collar or t-shirts was standard attire during off-duty time, our flight suits remained in the flight line lockers when not flying and on the base. Typically, buses would transport us to the flight line and if a supervisor had some particular training maneuver that he wanted to show us, we would take off in groups of five, including the supervisor. These sessions generally lasted a couple of hours but if you took off on your own, the flight could be longer or shorter, at your decision.

Walterboro housed four transition classes at a time, two classes ahead of mine and one behind us. Each leading class had accumulated more flying hours than the one behind since each leading class had graduated a month earlier and had arrived at Walterboro in the same order. One day, after training had gone on for about two months, I was pleasantly surprised by the appearance of a classmate from the twin-engine group. The twin-engine boys were taking their transition in the B-25 and a training flight had brought them to Walterboro for several days. My classmate really itched to see what it would be like to be at the controls of a P-40, a fighter plane. It so happened that the two-seater 40s were still around so I readily agreed to take him up for a ride, a rip-roaring ride that came so very close to being a major mistake.

My classmate's nickname was "Apple" because he had started to become prematurely bald at the front of his head. I put Apple in the back seat and we took off. Out over the ocean, off the resort area of Myrtle Beach, I gave Apple the controls and told him to get his "kicks" in and enjoy the ride. Apple took the controls and instead of attempting loops or rolls or some other maneuver that he could not do in the B-25, he immediately swooped down to just above the surface of the water. That got my immediate attention, no loops or rolls at that level! We were about as low as you could get without hitting the water. But that went from bad to worse; Apple headed straight for the resort beach at wave-top level. I remember seeing these two little boys who looked up and saw this huge whirling propeller headed directly for them at their height and after starting to run left then right, they ran straight backward to safety. I grabbed the controls. We were at ground level fast approaching two towering hotels and not clearing them would never be an option. We cleared the top of the building immediately in front of us but not with a lot of room to spare. As we pulled Gs (i.e., the extra tremendous pull of gravity on all parts of the body in making a high speed change of direction, and the tendency is to pull all the blood from the head to the feet. The first stage could cause blacking out and the second stage would be the loss of consciousness) going up over the building, Apple yelled in delirious delight, "Cream time, buddy, cream time!" I never found out if Apple had deliberately tried to scare those kids or not. The first thought that flashed in my mind when the hotels fell below and behind us was who would phone in a report of the buzzing of a resort beach and hotel. That big E12 on the nose of our plane was a lot more prominent than Rudolph's red nose. Being the pilot in charge, I had visions of being cussed out, losing my flight pay, being grounded, or all three of the above. I let Apple know I was more than a little unhappy with what he had done although I did not ask why he had done it. Fortunately no one called the base to complain about chasing children from the beach or skimming over the tops of their buildings. Perhaps they had already been indoctrinated by the marine fliers who jumped me. Needless to say, Apple did not get to hitch any more fighter plane rides for the rest of his stay at Walterboro.

In our training before graduation, we had spent many hours flying in formation, starting out with the traditional and beautiful Vee formations of five planes then changing the formations with echelons to the left and echelons to the right. All this required very strict, precise movements, staying close with your wing tucked into the plane on your right or left. Changing from one formation to another meant crossing under another plane without losing your place or chopping off its tail as you stuck your wingtip in as close as possible. All our precision formation training sort of went out of the window in transition. From now on we would be taught the rudiments and reasons for flying a scattered formation called line abreast. In line abreast, the flight leader would remain ahead with the other members of the flight about 30 feet or more apart and at slightly lower or higher altitudes with no one plane in a neat fixed formation position. The combat vets told us that the German 88 antiaircraft gunners were so good that to remain in a nice, precise formation would allow the gunners to go from one plane right down the line shooting gallery style.

One supervisor knew exactly where he lived off base, and one day, as part of the training, he led all five of us down to roar at rooftop level over the backyard of his house while his wife hung up clothes to dry in the air. The wife obviously knew because she waved energetically as we zoomed one after the other over her clothes line. We soon found out that flying line abreast also had other advantages. The same supervisor led us down to very low level, far below the tree tops, skimming just above the ground, and cutting grass, as we gleefully called it. Hugging the ground would put you below any snoopy enemy radar beams and that would, of course, keep the element of surprise in your favor in approaching a target without detection. On a subsequent ground level training mission I got my first real shakeup. Flying line abreast and hugging the ground, I approached a tall windbreak of trees with the object of staying as close to the ground as possible. I cleared the tree tops and very quickly dropped back to ground level on the other side. As I came down I noticed a man and a woman hoeing their crops right underneath me. I could not have cleared the couple by very much. It had happened so quickly and I could not see behind me but I do not believe they waved as the supervisor's wife had done. I honestly thought and had the very uneasy feeling that I had hit them.

As in our previous gunnery training we started out with more air to air shooting except this time our weapon was a genuine former frontline fighter. The tow plane trailed the target and we would peel off and attempt to make cheese cloth of the simulated enemy. On this particular day, my wingman and I had wrapped up the shooting but we still had quite a few rounds remaining in our magazines. South Carolina has numerous canals or waterways leading inland from the ocean. On one of them a tugboat had four barges under tow and that sight sorely tempted my wingman beyond redemption. He radioed me that he was going down and try to sink one of the barges. Down he went, while I purposely turned tail so I could not see what he was doing. I could hear but not see. I could truthfully swear that I had not seen him fire on the last of the barges being towed up the channel if a court martial developed later. I think if he had actually sunk one of those barges there would have been later repercussions but nothing ever came of the incident.

Other training for us included dog fighting with the supervisors and with each other. Of course, flying the same type of plane would give neither opponent in these practices an advantage of turning inside the other, so I quickly figured out how to grab the initial edge. As a result I was able to shoot down two of the combat veteran supervisors. As a rule the plane with the greatest maneuverability, the greatest altitude, or the fastest speed would have the advantage. Since our planes were identical, only one element of the three could possibly be used and I used it to quickly gain one-up-man-ship.

My class had moved from the larger revetment building to make room for another incoming class which had not yet made its initial acquaintance with the P-40. On a daily basis, members of my class would be assigned to man the portable control tower near the end of the landing runway. Our job was to control the landing attempts of the new men. I recall that on my own very first landing attempt in the P-40, and this just after the two-seater orientation flights, I quickly realized that I was too high and coming in too fast. That set of conditions meant pulling up gear and flaps and going around so as to settle down in a good and acceptable approach. In the portable tower there was no radio contact with the landing planes. Our only contact was two very pistols with red flares. If a red flare burst across your path it meant you were wrong, you must pull up and make the attempt again, with corrections. On my second day in the tower, the very first candidate to come in for a landing try was far too high and too fast, the only landing he could make would be in the middle of the trees at the other end of the runway. I fired a bright red starburst flare right in the middle of his glide path just as he began to round out about 30 feet too high. He either ignored the flare or had his eyes glued to the instrument panel and continued his approach. I did the next best thing to make him aware of his horrible predicament. I fired the next shot directly at his open cockpit and it came close enough to grab his complete and unswerving attention. He poured the coal to the engine and pulled up in a hurry to go around for a second attempt. As it had been for me, it was just an acknowledged misjudgment; these planes were much faster and more demanding than the trainers we had been used to flying. I reloaded both pistols to be ready just in case my man decided to make the same mistake on his second try. On the neophyte's next attempt he came in at the right height and speed to keep me from shooting flares at him again but it also meant that he would not end up in the trees at the end of the runway.

A very welcome bonus became evident early in our transition training. All during our cadet days we had to be alert as to the direction we had taken when leaving the base or we had to be observant of the landmarks so as to know in which direction to head after the aerial practice was over. In transition that was no longer necessary. We could fly with full abandon and confidence in any direction without being concerned where we were with regard to the base. Walterboro's Base call name was "Aztec." Flying out over the ocean with no idea of where you were and not minding if land lay behind, ahead, or to the side of you, made it as easy as it gets. To return in a beeline to the base only required calling "Aztec" and giving a long count of ten followed by a short count of five. A heading, navigationally splitting the middle of the base, would be given in less than one minute.

We were all having fun doing what we loved best—flying as well as carousing with buddies in our free time on the ground. That soon changed to a sad note. One of the men who had befriended me as an upper classman while I had struggled along as a Preflight dummy lost his life. I learned that the traditional five-plane flight had flown into a heavy cloud formation under rainy low ceiling conditions and he had not come out to join up with the other four planes. A phone call to the base informed that a crash had occurred and a later check confirmed that my friend had not survived. In a mentally sad frame of mind I mused that he must have suffered vertigo, a deadly condition coming out of a low ceiling of clouds. There would be no time for recovery. What made the tragic news even more depressing and hard to accept was the fact that we were all instrument rated pilots and vertigo should not have been a factor.

The low grey clouds and rain stayed with us for a couple more weeks. A few days after the accident the ceiling lifted enough for us to fly and on this day it was flying on an individual basis, no supervisors or scheduled group training. I took off in the rain and in less than a minute an enveloping grey thickness wrapped around me like a soggy, close-fitting blanket. As I climbed, the thought of what had happened to my friend kept me focused on what the instruments were showing. In another minute I broke through the top of the thick cloud layer to be filled with sudden and unexpected awe. All around me the purest, untainted pristine color of blue that I had ever seen and below me as far as the eye could see the whitest and purest of whites. I thought this must be an example of heaven. Close to shocking, this sudden climb from the grey and rainy foreboding space down below, up into the heavenly, inviting spotless world above.

The next day we were told that there would be no flying, the ceiling had dropped too low again. That day, being confined to the ground brought another eye opener. The rain continued and it meant either staying in your revetment or going to the club to play cards or a game of pool. The rain pelted down hard enough to make wearing a raincoat necessary As I looked out of the window there popped a sudden bright flash and a bolt of lightning streaked between the revetments followed by the heavy roll of thunder that shook the building. My eyes opened wider when another seemingly smaller bolt, several feet above the ground, but as horizontal as the first zapped through again. In the foothills of Northern California I had seen numerous lightning strikes during the winter months but never had I seen a bolt travel horizontally across the ground. Dumbfounded and downright too scared I made no attempt to reach the club. After what I had just seen, any thought of going outside to be speared by a horizontal bolt of lightning would have been, to my way of thinking, suicidal. Off came the raincoat and I for one did not dare venture out until dinnertime when the jarring peals of thunder and the flashes of light had long since moved away to some other area. I have seen plenty of heavy lightning strikes since that time but I have yet to see any more horizontal streaks.

As our training continued, so did the urge to get off the base and raise hell as we had during out cadet days. The nearest large cities were Charleston, South Carolina, and Columbus, Georgia. My buddy and I, on weekend leave, were treated to some despicable historical information in the city of Charleston. While walking with our two dates in a Negro residential area, the two girls pointed out the "Hanging Tree." It was an old scraggly-limbed oak tree in the middle of the street that had its trunk painted with white-wash and surrounded by a low picket fence also painted white. The girls said that in past days of slavery, six black men had been hung in that tree. It had been kept and preserved as a grim reminder even though it stood in the middle of the street and forced traffic to go around it. In our continual search for dates we later learned that even closer at hand was Orangeburg State Teacher's College in Orangeburg, South Carolina. Word of mouth, we learned that a plethora of female students attended that institution with a notable lack of males. These words floated symphonic music to the mental ears, lilting stanzas that beckoned with strains so fetching and alluring that to attempt to describe the pulling, enchanting appeal would fall painfully short in understatement.

That music flooded my mental state of mind as I stepped out of the bus door into the college town of Orangeburg for the first time. It was already getting dark and I knew nothing about the layout of the town although I now knew there had to be a Negro section and a white section. Not having met any friends by the time of full darkness meant it was time to find quarters for the evening and begin my search anew the following day. I spotted a sign that said "Rooms for Rent." I knocked on the screened door of the front porch. A woman's voice came from a front window asking me what I wanted. I replied that I was looking for a room for the night. The voice asked me if I was alone, I said yes. The voice said the room would be two dollars and to leave that amount in the bowl on the hall table. Inside the room, with the light turned on, I noted there was a closet, a bureau, a bed, and a chair. A door opened to a bathroom. As I was hanging up my jacket I noticed movement out of the corner of my eye that came from the darkened bathroom. There was another door leading into it. Immediately the woman's voice told me I would have to leave because the room had already been rented. I protested reminding her that she had just now rented me the room. But the voice, strident and insistent, repeated that she had made a mistake; the room was rented and would I please pick up my money from the bowl. It suddenly hit me that the voice was white! I was in the wrong house for my color even though the money was green. I hurriedly left the premises and headed back to the Negro section which could be seen across the vacant lot a half block away.

The dull yellowish illumination coming from the street lights faded sharply toward the darkness in the middle of the block as I walked quickly toward a dimly lighted storefront window. I was definitely certain that this was the Negro section. Past one edge of an ill-fitting green shade covering the big window I could clearly see the barber cutting a customer's hair. Needing information I rapped repeatedly on the plate glass window. The barber and his customer ignored the rapping apparently because the shop was closed and this was a Friday night. I looked toward the darkest part of the block and back to the brightest area at the corner. Not a soul in sight, in either direction. But that condition changed in a hurry. From a little green hut that I had failed to notice before, as if by magic, a police officer appeared and approached me. "What are you doing out here this time of night?" he asked. I told him that I was trying to get the attention of the barber to ask him something. He grabbed me by the arm and said, "You got no business being out here after dark. You're coming with me!" With that he started walking down the street holding me tightly by the arm. I had no idea where he was taking me or why he acted as if he had a robber or shoplifter in tow. Two or three blocks later we climbed the stairs of the Orangeburg police station where he turned me over to the desk sergeant and left to return to his now vacant station in the little green hut.

I repeated my story to the sergeant expressing my unhappiness of being brought to the police station for trying to find out where I could get lodging for the night. The bespectacled sergeant leaned back in his chair and asked for my identification which I produced and handed to him. He studied the photo and the information typed on the folded brown ID pass and then asked me where I was stationed. After I said Walterboro he casually informed me that Negroes were not allowed to be out on certain streets after dark, curfew, and that there was a rooming house for "Coloreds" around the corner from where the officer had detained me. He handed the pass back to me. I left the building and began to retrace my steps on a path toward the rooming house. Less than a block away from my destination, a black patrol car passed me on the opposite side of the street then made a sudden U-turn and parked at the curb near me. From the darkness of the opened window on my side I heard, "What you doin' out here this time of night, boy?" The doors on both sides of the cruiser opened and quickly two blue-uniformed officers appeared, the gun belts around their waists studded with visible silver bullets in the fashion of western gunfighters. I wore my dress pink topcoat, hands dug deeply in my pockets. The one doing all the talking spoke again. "I asked you what you're doin' out here this time of night." I explained that I had just left the police station and that the sergeant had sent me to a rooming house. The spokesman said gruffly, "Boy, don't you know how to say, sir?" By now my anger had steadily climbed to a point of recklessness. I stated very slowly and clearly that I only said "sir" to my superior officers. The two looked at each other then the leader said, "Well, you better git on down the road and git fast!" I squeezed the fingernail clip in my right pocket as I turned and began to walk toward the rooming house. The voice behind me barked, "That all the faster you can go, boy?" I continued at the same pace but now I half expected to hear a gunshot; none came.

Over the entrance to the rooming house hung a medium-sized faded wooden white sign with one word printed in black letters, "Rooms." An elderly black lady opened the door, gave me the room number and collected one dollar in advance for the night. In the room, an old, scarred, and well-worn bureau stood against the wall at the foot of the bed but there was no chair. A single light dangled from the ceiling over the bed with a string tied to the end of the bronze chain to turn it off and on. As I stood there I seethed with anger, the same kind of bad-intentioned anger I had felt in the Montgomery incident. I had been humiliated not once but twice for no other reason than being black. After I had undressed and climbed into bed my mind raced from one illogical scenario to another on ways to get even, to recapture my elevated status of being an officer in the U.S. Army Air Force. Suddenly revenge went quickly flying out of the mind's shifting window as a new threat captured my attention. Something had sharply stuck or bitten me. I reached for the string that turned on the light. I looked carefully but there was nothing. Yet as soon as the light went out the vicious attack began again. This would be my first and last encounter with Cimex Lectularius, commonly called bed bugs. They have been known to survive for up to a year without eating, which means some very serious attacking would take place should a warm blooded creature be within striking distance just before the end of a year's famine. The sneaky little critters only came out when the light went out. I knew the area under attack so I kept the light string in hand for quicker reaction. When I first spotted them scurrying back into hiding, I did not know what they were except they were taking turns biting me. It took three efforts before I could yank on the light cord fast enough to catch and eradicate the little vicious critters one by one and finally get a good night's sleep. All thoughts of revenge had been momentarily sidetracked. The next morning I realized that despite their insidious torment the now departed bed bugs had so completely occupied my thoughts and activities that the rapidly forming ideas of revenge had been abandoned at a good moment.

By the time I returned to the base Sunday evening, the anger had begun to simmer again and rise to the point of my resolving to purchase a gun; my roommate had a revolver. I told him what had happened and what I intended to do. Advised by his wise counsel that I must just simper and bear it otherwise the strongest possibility pointed toward my own demise. At first I angrily balked saying I would take one or two with me. In the end he convinced me to bitterly swallow my sense of pride and absorb the humiliation. And this was the same buddy who wanted to sink some tug boat operator's barge after gunnery practice. I had brought what was called a Chinese dirk from home, a huge heavy knife in a wooden scabbard that I intended to wear when we went into combat. Smaller than a machete, the scabbard had a leather strap that allowed me to wear it slung down on the flat of my back. I had already tried it out on a couple of flights but found that after an hour or so it became uncomfortable. I kept it safely hidden in the bottom of my footlocker.

Having met one of the abundance of female students in Orangeburg, I subsequently made numerous trips there for weekend dating but never again had trouble with the police. This may have been, in part, because I now knew not to be out on certain streets after dark and also the fact that I now had a native resident to advise me away from any potential conflict or source of police danger.

Back on the base, trouble erupted on both sides of my class. One pilot in the lead class of transition trainees deliberately, for reasons we speculated on later, made not one but two low level high speed passes over the middle of the base with the big E 39 on the nose of his craft clearly visible. A couple of us happened to be outside at the time heading for the club and a rubber or two of bridge, when all of a sudden Lieutenant "Buzz Boy" made the first low pass right over our heads and the roof tops. He then flipped around and roared over again from the opposite direction. His second pass had many pairs of eyes turned skyward wondering who that crazy fool could be. It was as if he were saying, "if you didn't see me the first time, here I go again!" As is usual with liquid-cooled engines the whine and roar of the inline engine is only loudly heard after the exhaust ports have passed you. He could probably have gotten away with it had he kept going with 15 or 20 other planes in the air and it could have been any one of them. But that was not his intent. We found out later the name of the "Buzz Boy" upstart because he was restricted to base and had a nice deduction taken from his monthly pay. Because his forbidden actions had been so blatant and then repeated, we reasoned that he really just wanted to be taken off flying duty and he got his wish.

Although we no longer had to get up at 5:30 in the morning to stand reveille, there were occasions when we were ordered out for roll call, a counting of noses so to speak. On this one afternoon two names failed to answer. The commandant of training sent a classmate to the large revetment to look for the missing officers. The classmate returned with the two absent officers who sashayed toward the gathering area loosely and casually attired in shorts and unlaced boots. They had apparently been logging some off-duty sack time. The errant men stood at attention before the commandant. After a mild upbraiding for not falling out to be counted, their classmate was then told to drill the two offenders in front of us. Both men stood still refusing to obey any drill instructions. The shorter of the two muttered something about a regulation against drilling an officer for punishment. The commandant turned toward headquarters and ordered the two to follow him. Although the rest of the group had been dismissed we stood around to find out what was to happen. In a short time the two emerged from the commandant's office and were heard saying that if they did not follow his orders they would be facing a court martial. I do not remember seeing them do any close order drilling and I do not believe that the threat of court martial was actually carried out. But I have often wondered if one of those two had been at the controls of the plane I had shot with the flare pistol. After all, there is quite a difference between being a raunchy, cocksure fighter pilot and being just plain stupid. Who, after all we had gone through to finish our cadet training, would want to deliberately encourage any kind of court martial after becoming an officer for only a meager two months.

There was no question that the move up to a combat-type aircraft from one used strictly for training was a very major move, a high step in accomplishment. It amounted to moving from the benign to the ruthless, the unforgiving. You now had bombs and bullets at your fingertips and they were all designed for destruction without regard or selectivity on their own.

The P-40 had started becoming old hat to us when a rumor began to circulate that the sleek new P-51, that darling, outstanding descendant of the long obsolete "40" was coming in. What had begun only as a mild rumor quickly swelled into a higher wave of probability. Not too many days passed before the only planes left on the flight line were the four two-seater P-40s and several AT-6s. A clamor arose for those few cockpits and a waiting list grew before the new planes arrived. To our complete surprise, what did come were not the anticipated shiny new P-51s but old razorback P-47s, still adorned with their olive-drab colors after seeing many earlier hours in combat. By comparison to the P-40, or any other single engine fighter at the time, the P-47 was a huge monster of a plane and, of course, we now had more hours of ground school to learn the operating characteristics of this new blockbuster weapon.

The "47" was much faster, heavier, had more firepower, and instead of having an inline engine, it boasted two back-to-back Pratt and Whitney radial engines with almost twice the horsepower of the P-40. In both planes we had to do the blindfold test. That meant being so familiar with the interior of the cockpit that you could put your hand on any asked for instrument or lever while blindfolded. The P-47 had more of every thing, not squirrelly on the ground, it did not tend to overheat during extended taxi time and it had landing gear so wide it would take an act of congress to ground loop.

My first few flights in those well-worn, very tired old D models were not all that encouraging. For one thing, the canopy operated manually, so did the P-40's, but the P-47 used a hefty cast iron counterweight on a lever that had to be pulled down to both open and close the canopy. With the canopy in the closed position, the counterweight was in front of your head and when open, it normally locked behind the head. Standard operating procedure in landings required having the canopy open and the seat in the raised position. In attempting to land in one of those tired old gals, the canopy refused to lock in the open position and with the seat raised on final approach the counterweight kept grazing the top of my helmet as the canopy slammed shut. Another half inch raise and I would have had a nice throbbing lump on the back of my head just for trying to land by the book! Much later we learned that some of the later D models did have the bubble canopy but all of the other refinements still waited for the final N models. Another old lady— we never knew which planes would be ours for the day—had another flaw more annoying than serious. On takeoffs and landings the tailwheel remained locked until the landing had been completed and the time arrived to taxi off the runway. With the tailwheel locked, it was virtually impossible to turn from a straight line no matter how hard you held on one brake and revved up the engine. The last razorback that I flew absolutely refused to unlock her tailwheel. The only way to turn was to manually unlock it, fumble around down on the floor to the left, find and then pull up on a trip wire. Of course, that fault would not be revealed until the landing had been completed and the plane was at the very end of the runway. There would be no more runway left and no easy way to turn left or right. That was always embarrassing—to have landed, be at the end of the runway ready to taxi off, and have the plane behave like a stubborn donkey and refuse to budge until the trip wire could be found. Nevertheless these big ladies did not sail or float on landing. When you lowered the landing gear and dropped the flaps they knew you intended to land without equivocation or misunderstanding. Down they came just as you had intended.

All of our fussing and fuming at, and over, those well-used flying tanks soon changed. Before long, it seemed almost overnight, the old razorbacks were replaced by brand spanking new N models. The P-47 Ns sparkled as they had come fresh from the factory assembly line, silver, turbo-charged and with push-button canopy control. Thus began my serious love affair with the Republic Thunderbolt or "Jugs" as we called them. The Jug label came from the outline of the "47," if you stood it on its nose, the only thing missing would be the handle from a gallon glass jug. That statement actually belies the truth because the Jug was infinitely more beautiful than the shape of a glass bottle. Besides the superheavy firepower of the P-47, eight 50 caliber machineguns, the most of any fighter craft at the time, there was another feature that had been missing in the old P-40s. In the Tomahawk and in the Kittyhawk, two of the later models of the Curtis P-40, in the event of being shot down, you had to push two separate buttons simultaneously to destroy your radio equipment. In reality, often a plane would go down without the pilot being able to press these two buttons. What replaced that tenuous manual operation to keep valuable radio elements out of enemy hands, was a plastic-type ball that rested on a pedestal. The ball would remain on its pedestal until the plane had a very hard jolt, such as would occur in a crash. If the ball were knocked off its resting place the radio equipment would, in a word, self-destruct.

Now the Jug, as I mentioned earlier, came as close to being a tank with wings as you can get; it was heavy, the old razorbacks being listed at about seven tons of big mean machine. The newer "N" models were even heavier, for in addition to being turbo charged they also had water injection designed to give you an instant 50 mile-an-hour boost. The flip of a little toggle switch nestled on top of the throttle accomplished this.

A humorous incident occurred in our second week of delightful flying in the new mint condition "47s." A classmate and running buddy of mine and I had taken off to individually do more air work and to continue learning to master this wonderful fighting machine. An hour or so later, by chance, I spotted down in some farmer's field, the shiny form of a new airplane, one of our Jugs. My first thought was that someone had made an emergency landing so I went down to take a closer look. I dropped down to tree top level and began to circle the downed craft. On the left wing I recognized my running buddy calmly sitting there smoking a cigarette. He looked up and waved as I circled around him. I was still not certain whether he had been forced to make an emergency landing. After all, these were brand new birds and there could have been a glitch. It did not initially occur to me that he had taken the chance to land in a strange, untested bean patch just because he hungered for a smoke. He could have hit a soft spot, a deep rut, a hidden wire, or any of a dozen other dangers that could have prevented him from taking off again. But there he sat very calm and cool getting his needed nicotine fix on the wing of his brand new Jug. Perhaps, this only serves to point out the brazenness, the brashness, the egotistical elitism, or the downright unflappable flying skills embedded in each of us. The new Jugs were said to cost about five hundred thousand, an immense figure at that time but not even small peanuts compared to today's fighter craft that run into the millions.

While we were not aware of the so-called Freeman Field Mutiny in Indiana, the effects of that monumental disturbance carried all the way down to Walterboro. A number of the men in all four squadrons had guns, personal weapons that they intended carrying into combat along with the general issue 45 caliber automatic handgun. On any given day you could ordinarily see one or the other of them having target practice between the revetments, taking potshots at cans, handmade paper targets, or whatever else could serve as a target except bottles. They did not shoot at signs, posters, or other such items.

One of my classmates habitually spent much of his free time listening to classical music and drinking bourbon in his room. He played his 78 rpm classical records on a portable record player and he listened undisturbed in solitary peace and quiet as he sipped his favorite beverage. This same classmate had been the one who came dangerously close to blowing off his head during the skeet shooting finale. Dissatisfied with his own record player he elected to go to the white officer's club a few blocks away because that club had a big standard style record player. We had not attempted to integrate the white officer's club since our own seemed more than adequate, with the exception of a big standard style record player. My classmate insisted that the record player in the other club made his music sound so much better than his little suitcase box. As mentioned earlier, we, at the time, were not aware of the explosive situation at Freeman Field. That serious chain of events had caused the house arrest of 101 officers who had refused to sign an illegal statement as issued by the commanding officer. Colonel Robert Selway, the commanding officer, had drawn up a brand new regulation, Base Regulation 85-2, which essentially forbade "trainees" from attending the club reserved for so-called base personnel and supervisors. All the 'trainee' men were black and almost all the base personnel and supervisors were white so CO Selway had, by subterfuge, attempted to keep Freeman segregated by his new order.[1] Colonel Selway deliberately tried to subvert and skirt Army Regulation 210-10, which gave base club membership to all officers, meaning that an officer was an officer and color did not define one.

# CHAPTER 8

# Changing Cockpits

The troubles at Freeman obviously had been telegraphed or phoned to Walterboro because the very next day after my classmate had invaded the white officer's club the Provost Marshall, with truckloads of appointed officers and MPs, suddenly swooped down on each revetment. Each entrance was guarded by an armed MP while an officer went through each room and searched for weapons. When the searching officer found a weapon, he recorded it and gave its owner a receipt. He informed the owner that it would be returned to him when he left the base. The search officer promised good care would be taken of each weapon confiscated. My roommate had hidden his pistol in one of the two front hall corridor pot-bellied stoves. This being in late April or early May, there would be no fires in the stoves. My own weapon, the dirk, already lay at the bottom of my footlocker but I had thought to scoot it in a tiny bit from the very back.

The officer who searched our room looked through everything. He noted that the top tray of my footlocker held nothing and had me remove it while he checked the bottom. I held my breath, still holding the tray, when he began to probe, fearing he would discover my trusty blade. Although he searched, he failed to do more than slide his hand straight down to the bottom around the edges of my clothing and did not reach in and under. He came up empty in our room, no gun and no dirk. We were all inward smiles when the guards at each door left and neither of us had been handed a receipt. I can say that the Provost Marshall's confiscation swoop ended all the target practice for the rest of my stay at Walterboro.

The situation for the members of the 477th Bombardment Group at Freeman Field who had stood up for their rights ran similar to our incident at Walterboro but there was a major difference. The 477th was deliberately being kept from combat, despite continually logging thousands of flight training hours and being on the verge of combat ready. The fighter pilots had an outlet—they were being sent into action. So the bitter frustration of the pilots and crews of the 477th festered like a huge boil, bulging, tight, and more than ready to burst. And break open it did, causing an ugly blight that took many years for the Air Force to erase and even with the erasure the forever tender scars could still be felt and remembered by those who were there. Much bitterness still remains because of the way they were mistreated and humiliated. Expunging records and printing apologies many years after the terrible wrong, did little to remove the indelible permanence of such a terrible stain. Fortunately or unfortunately, the actions of Freeman Field did not happen at Walterboro's base. The base commander of Walterboro, having had numerous racial problems before these last four classes had arrived, must have felt that he was pulling any dangerous teeth before there could be an armed confrontation at his supervisor officer's club. Although up to that time, and during my entire tour at Walterboro, there had never been any talk of plans to repatriate the white officer's club. My classmate's entry apparently had stirred up enough concern to cause worry that such a move might be in the offing since it had already occurred at Freeman Field. Even though the classmate's action and only intent was simply to get the best sound from his records on a machine only available in that club, it must have been felt that this could be just a precursor of more undesirable things to come. Again, perhaps it was thought easier and safer to confiscate weapons rather than provide a similar big record player in the black officer's club.

Months before we had arrived at Walterboro, racially instigated troubles had exploded at Selfridge Field, Michigan, where the 477th had been previously based. In fact, the 477th had been shuffled and shifted around to numerous fields including Godman Field, Kentucky, and Walterboro besides stays at Selfridge and Freeman. All this shifting and moving around to keep the pot from boiling over produced just the opposite effect, the pressure shot up into the dangerous red zone. Earlier at Walterboro, several black officers came close to causing a riot by their protest against not being served in a white restaurant in Fairfax, the largest town near the base.[1] This incident may have conditioned some of the thinking after the Freeman blowout. Probably the most damaging effect of this cat and mouse game, this moving the group from base to base after base, eroded the morale of the men who soon became aware that they were pawns being shuffled about. There were also thoughts that the constant moving was a deliberate attempt to disrupt the morale so as to make sure the 477th became a failure. As a matter of record, during its first year of operation, the men of the 477th built up more than 17,800 hours of flying time in their B-25Js and had only two minor accidents. That number of hours is equivalent to flying a plane 24 hours a day for two years—a remarkable achievement!

When VE (Victory in Europe) Day came in Europe, rumors soon gathered that the 477th, with its four squadrons, could be sent to the Pacific. Those rumors failed to materialize because although General George Marshall and General Douglas MacArthur were ready to accept these black birdmen, the commander of the Pacific Air Forces, Lieutennant General George C. Kinney turned them down with the backing of Air Force Chief, General Arnold. Although Kinney already had medium bomber units in the Pacific, he felt it would complicate his war efforts by having to segregate any of his bases.[2] One can only imagine the tremendous cost that was expended to train all of these men in the special jobs that they had more than mastered. To view this expense and all of the training as being wasted and totally squandered because of racism during a war far exceeds reasonable and fair belief. If the pressing military need was not for the use of the medium bomber why then was this talented group of airmen not shifted over into the heavy stuff, the four-engine B-24s or the B-17s. It seems almost criminal to think that a four squadron bomber group is formed, trained, and then jockeyed about for the sole purpose of taking the heat and pressure off the White House, the War Department,and ultimately the Air Force.

For the men of the 477th, a cunning conniving enemy fought them through concealed venues of hatred, much like the Trojan horse drawn up to and then into the gates of Troy. How difficult it had to be in training for war, in girding for battle, and to have their leaders stealthily and covertly plotting their defeat from within their own camp. But unlike Troy's defeat, and sacking the determined endurance and intelligent persistence by the men of the 477th served to bring the enemy down despite the treachery.

Our training continued in the new Jugs and I reveled in every airborne minute much as the owner of a new car might be enthralled by that distinctive new car smell and feel. Just sitting in a new car without touching the key or moving it, feels good. By now the allies had pounded the vaunted German war machine into full submission and VE Day arrived. Our flying did not miss a beat until August 6, 1945, when the Enola Gay, a B-29, dropped the world's first A-bomb on Hiroshima. It seemed something so unreal and devastating that we began to discuss all the uninformed possibilities this could have on our last remaining enemy, Japan. Then, just a few days later, Nagasaki received the same horrible treatment and within hours, while on the way to the flight line, the portable radios announced VJ (Victory over Japan) Day. Some whoops and hollering filled the air but in the bus there was also a suppressed air of disappointment. We had trained and trained and now we had no one to fight, no one was left for us to defeat, to show just how good we were. The bus deposited us at the flight line as usual but all the air had been let out of the tires, going up would not have the same meaning, that thrill of expectancy would be missing. Without war, military flying would be reduced to a form of pleasure flying; there would be no need of the quarter-inch armor plating of protection around the cockpit and no need of loaded 50 caliber machinegun canisters. We had been honed and whetted to a fine edge, like a good pocket knife ready for good use, but now this fine edged tool was useless surplus, an unnecessary excess.

When I had enlisted at the age of 17, I agreed to remain in the service for the duration of the war plus six months. Soon after the announcement of VJ Day, we were told that to remain in the service we would all be expected to perform some additional jobs behind a desk. Those were definitely not the kinds of words a fighter jock like me wanted to hear. I could not imagine sitting at some desk pushing a pencil, not after my training! The training commandant also informed us that under a special regulation for demobilization (RR1-5) those needed at home could sign a statement and be released within a week. For a couple of weeks after that announcement, a group of five of us, in collusion, would isolate certain of our classmates who had girlfriends back home and work on them. We would suggest in a very informal, offhand manner that the various girlfriends were starting to date "Jodie" or the guys who were getting out of the service before our victim. Since we did not seem to be conniving against anyone these disarming statements worked each and every time. As soon as we had finished our dirty work the unsuspecting victim rushed off to headquarters to sign that special regulation of release. However, what we had not counted on, was the fact that our concocted stories began to backfire and affect us, the story tellers, as well. Within the next week, I too had signed a release order to end my military flying career. Prior to our anticipated entry into combat, one of our classmates had printed our "Spookwaffe" cards. That concocted name had been genius'd up by taking the colloquial reference word "Spook" meaning a Negro and hooking it to the German Luftwaffe or German air force. The combination indicated, in the vernacular, black air force. The heading of the green card indicated that so-and-so (your name) had met the requirements for the "TS" Card (tough s____) with an expiration date to be filled in, on or before V-J Day by the puncher. Inside, were a series of numbers 1, 5, and 13 arranged so they could be punched out, conductor style with each mishap. In the center were the words "TUFF—Jack Pot" with a larger space for punching out. The understanding, to have the center punched out meant you would have been punched out, permanently! We never had thoughts of burning or exploding in mid-air; only of the possibility of crashing into the ground and for that we had coined the term "augur in" much in the same fashion that a carpenter's bit would cut into a piece of wood. Fortunately none would have their jackpot centers punched after my friend's untimely death months earlier.

Because of VE Day and the world's first atomic bombings, all of the members from Walterboro's last four classes missed the horrors of actual combat by two weeks. Most, I surmise, were bitterly disappointed after such intense training but we could take great pride in having passed all of the tests and standing poised at the ready. Contradictory to the AWC findings and conclusions mentioned earlier in regard to African-American men, we, as the original Army Air Corps song stated, were ready to live in fame or go down in flames. This concept, this rationale is apparently what glorifies and catches the eye, ear, and heart of the ground-bound enthusiasts and supporters of the fighter pilot. This daring do and caution to the winds has that certain charismatic attraction and appeal that sparks the imagination as controlled recklessness. Just the category of fighter pilot instantly makes that person a hero, a person to be lionized and wildly celebrated.

Many today now know some of the exploits of the famed Tuskegee Airmen, especially the fighter pilots since the release of a movie of that same name. Gradually, the fact that black bomber pilots, navigators, and bombardiers, who also trained under the same degrading circumstances is slowly being recognized. Still, as much as these other groups or classes of Tuskegee Airmen have been in such low profile for so long, there is yet another trained segment of men in the "Tuskegee Story" or "Experience" who are even less promoted. In fact, little has ever been mentioned of them and the role they were trained to perform. All but forgotten, are the black Liaison pilots, the putt-putt operators, the grasshopper drivers, the puddle jumpers, the skim the tree tops aviators assigned to artillery battalions. These hearty flyers piloted very slow moving, unarmed little planes, such as the Aeronca, the Piper Cub, or the Taylorcraft. They flew these planes with an observer in the back seat to spot the accuracy of an artillery battery's shells. Regardless of which plane was used they were all high-winged monoplanes, fabric covered, and had a maximum speed of less than 90 miles an hour. Because they operated at such low altitudes and such slow speeds they could easily become sitting ducks for small arms fire from the ground. Although the apparently preferred training plane was the L-4 Piper, used at Fort Sill and at Pittsburg, for some reason only the L-2 Taylorcraft was available for the training at Tuskegee.

The U.S. Army's Officer Candidate School (OCS), established in 1941, had commissioned a number of black artillery officers to keep pace with the formation of black artillery units. This had created a pool of black officers from which candidates for liaison pilots could be selected. Early on, the first black observation pilots trained in integrated units in both the primary and advanced phases. Charles Brown is listed as the first black field artillery officer to be trained as a liaison pilot at the Army Air Forces' flight school at Pittsburg, Kansas. Following his graduation from the OCS at Ft. Sill as a second lieutenant, Brown, the only black student in a class of 49, was sent back to Ft. Sill for advanced tactical training after earning his wings. He was assigned to the 350th Field Artillery Battalion, an all black unit, at Camp Livingston, Louisiana at the completion of his advanced training.

After August 1943, Brown was joined by two other black liaison officers at Camp Livingston, Lieutenants Ernest Davenport and Elvin Hayes. These two had received their primary training at Denton, Texas, an Army Air Force glider training site that had been converted into liaison training. Fort Sill also became their station for the advanced tactical training. Reportedly, Davenport and Hayes are the only two black liaison pilots to have been trained at Denton. Brown would later, in 1943, be transferred to the European Theater of Operations to serve with the 351st Field Artillery Group until 1945.[3]

Sherman Smith, born in San Antonio, Texas, the youngest of six siblings, was raised along with his younger sister by their mother. Smith, always an avid reader, after graduating from high school took the best job he could find, that of shining shoes in a white barber shop. Even after he had made a job change from shining shoes to doing janitorial work he knew that there just had to be something better than what he had found so far. That something better would be to enlist in the army but it came only after months of pestering his mother to sign the necessary papers. He was inducted into the army in August 1940, and sent to Ft. Sill, Oklahoma. There, after classification testing, he completed OCS, emerged a second lieutenant and was assigned to the 349th Field Artillery Regiment, an all-black unit.

The 349th did most of its training at Camp Gruber near Muskogee, Oklahoma but because there was no firing range at Gruber, the group did all of its practice firing at Ft. Sill. Smith recalled with amusement their first real firing training. "Our guns were located on one side of the base and the targets were on the other side. With a range of twenty-five miles we fired those guns right over Ft. Sill to the targets. Fortunately there were no short rounds or incidents from that, but can you imagine what it was like, here we were green artillery units firing live shells over a populated base." During one of those live fire training exercises he caught sight of some liaison planes flying overhead. Immediately the thought of becoming a pilot and operating one of those spotter planes away from the dust and deafening recoil explosions of the artillery pieces blossomed into an urgent desire. He applied and was accepted for pilot's training. Smith's class of 20 men began their training on October 4, 1943, at Tuskegee as the third and final class for primary liaison pilot training at that station. Of this third class of students, 18 would survive the approximately 60 days of rigorous training to graduate. The previous two groups to complete their primary training at Tuskegee, began with 21 students and graduated 15 and 18 men, respectively. All of these first three classes consisted of officers varying in grade from second lieutenant to captain. The first class began its training on August 2, 1943, and the second group began on August 23, 1943. While the third class was still undergoing training, on November 15, 1943, directive was sent to the Army Air Forces Training Command stating that no further black liaison pilots would be trained at Tuskegee. Thus the fourth and final group of students did not train at Tuskegee. Instead, about half of them received their primary instruction at Pittsburgh, Kansas but all finished with advanced training at Ft. Sill. Most of this final group of students consisted of enlisted men who were not sent to OCS and who would receive their commissions later.

Although three of these classes were stationed at the Tuskegee Army Air Base, their actual flight training took place at Griel Auxiliary Field about six miles away. To actually reach Griel by vehicle proved an ordeal arduously demanding for the truck drivers, students, and instructors because the road was unpaved and in many places almost impassable. Fuel, spare parts, and mechanics all had to be brought in by truck over that tortuous jolting route. Smith recalled that all of the instructors were white officers and each student received his training from the same instructor from start to end. Smith paused and rubbed a hand across his forehead as if trying to remember something then he exhaled sharply and said, "I'm six feet-four and my own instructor was about five feet-seven. During my training I guess I used to get some things wrong and my instructor, who sat in the back, had a habit of taking the controls, pushing the stick forward then quickly snapping it back. That, because of my height, would cause my forehead to hit the wing strut with a thump. It Hurt! Finally, one day he did it just once too often. When we landed and got out of the plane I grabbed him in his collar and told him that if he ever did that again I would knock the livin' stuffin' out of him." Smith laughed as the vision of what he had done came fully back. "He was a first lieutenant and I was only a 'shave tail' (second lieutenant) but after I released his collar he looked up at me and laughed and said, 'you know, I wondered when you were going to get tired of my doing that.'" He touched his forehead again as if recalling the thumping his head had taken until he had angrily decided he had had enough. "We became good friends after that. We corresponded with each other for years later."

Most of the graduates would eventually be assigned to black artillery units that were then stationed at Camp Gruber, two pilots to each battalion in either the 92$^{nd}$ or 93$^{rd}$ Infantry Divisions. The units practiced and trained going from Gruber to Ft. Sill and back and finally travel orders came assigning Smith's Division, the 93$^{rd}$, to the Pacific Theater. They disembarked on the enemy occupied island of Biak where an occasional shot could be heard but they had no real opposition to the landing. For the liaison pilots Smith said, "There were only two airplanes and the men struggled with each other to get in our minimum four hours of flight per month in order to collect our flight pay." More importantly, they had no combat duty, no one to fight. As Smith put it, they had essentially, months and months of island paradise duty but without any sign of a single hula girl. "All we did was lie around in the sand, go fishing and have fun," he said.[4]

The very first black artillery liaison pilot, Charles Brown, joined the Army Reserves after World War II and was recalled to active duty in 1948. He was assigned to the 74th Combat Engineer Battalion which ended up in Korea in 1950. Brown not only flew L-16s he also mastered the H-13 with the Engineer Battalion and was recommended for the Distinguished Flying Cross. He never got it. Reportedly, his commanding officer refused to sign the recommendation saying that he already had too many medals for a black man. Brown retired from the Army Reserves in 1965 and was later inducted into the Field Artillery Officer Candidate School's Hall of Fame at Fort Sill.[5]

Although the liaison pilots who were stationed at Tuskegee during their training could or could not be considered as Tuskegee Airmen, there are distinctions that should be noted. The two groups served in different branches of the Army. The Tuskegee Airmen were part of the Army Air Corps which later was designated the Army Air Forces (AAF) and then the U.S. Air Force, an independent service, in 1947. The liaison pilots although trained at Tuskegee were and remained a part of the Army Ground Forces (AGF) which included the Field Artillery Divisions.

For the liaison pilots, the Army provided primary training sites at Pittsburg, Kansas and Denton and Sheppard Fields in Texas as well as the Griel site at Tuskegee. Fort Sill, Oklahoma was the designated advanced training base for the final phase of these aerial observation pilots. The planes they were trained in were essentially the same ones the graduating liaison pilots would later use in combat.

The Tuskegee Airmen cadets were trained exclusively at the Tuskegee Air Base and Moton Field in planes entirely different than those used for the liaison training. The primary phase was conducted at Moton Field near Tuskegee Institute using first PT-19 Fairchild low-wing trainers and finally PT-17s and PT-13s, the trusted and durable biplanes. Those completing the primary training then returned to the Air Base for instruction in the BT-13 in Basic training and finally the more powerful AT-6 in the Advance phase.

Both groups of pilots earned wings upon graduation, the liaison pilots after completion of Stages A and B and the Tuskegee Airmen after 10-week sessions each in Preflight, Primary, Basic, and Advanced training. The flight instructors for both of these two groups of pilot trainees were also different, the liaison training included a number of civilians while with the Tuskegee Airmen, civilians were used only in the primary training phase and all of those instructors were black.

Prior to the introduction of liaison pilots, all spotting and observations for the artillery was done by balloon observers who did their surveillance from very dangerous vantage points that were fully open to enemy rifle fire as well as aircraft.

The 92nd Division would be eventually deployed in the Mediterranean area of Italy with its complement of liaison observer pilots. It is estimated that during WWII, a total of between 40 and 60 black liaison pilots were trained with approximately half of that total number being divided between the 92nd and the 93rd Divisions. There is still debate over whether the liaison pilots should be called Tuskegee Airmen because most of them had some training at Tuskegee, or whether they should not have that appellation because they were never a part of the Air Corps. The reader has the choice of making that ultimate decision or just saying the heck with it! Does it really matter at this point in time? It is, however, a matter of historical fact that some of the liaison pilots trained at or near Tuskegee, so, should we call only these gentlemen, Tuskegee Airmen and not those who trained elsewhere? I will take a sheltered step aside and let the discussions and argumentation begin.

Numerous other black men not destined to become pilots, navigators, or bombardiers found station at Tuskegee. A typical example of those accomplished and talented men and women was William Moulden. Born in Hanford, California, Moulden and his family moved to Palo Alto, California while he graduated from San Jose State College earning a degree in science and a two-year degree in radio engineering. When the war started he wanted to go to Tuskegee. "I already had earned a private pilot's license as a result of being a member of the '20 Flying Club' at San Jose State. I was the only black member in the flying club as well as the only black student in my graduating class." His problems began when he was turned down as a result of his medical examination. Moulden recalled that his friend Leslie Williams, who would go on to become a B-25 bomber pilot, had the same trouble until he, Williams, went to Chicago to take his medical exam.

Moulden eventually found out that his vision in one eye was 20/30 uncorrected, which, at the time, would certainly not have allowed him into the pilot ranks. So, based on his college degree, "I applied for a direct commission and was accepted for Officer Candidate School (OCS) at Fort Benning, Georgia. I enlisted as soon as Pearl Harbor erupted and was sent to Georgia for my basic training." During basic training he credits a white Major for advising him to enter and complete OCS rather than just accepting the direct commission. The same officer paved the way for him to get into OCS. For that reason he stayed in the infantry for four months after graduation and then transferred to the signal corps, the unit to which he had first applied for the direct commission. He was quickly assigned to the 717th Aircraft Signal Warning Company and became one of an abundance of signal officers. As soon as the signal company went on alert for the Pacific Moulden, along with one other black officer, was reassigned to the 332nd Fighter Group as communications officer.

Like so many others from the West and the North, Moulden remembered the shock of suddenly coming face to face with harsh discrimination and segregation on such a blatant and unyielding scale. He recalled going into the little town of Tuskegee, on one occasion, to the one movie theater where black patrons were forced to sit up in what was called the "Crow's Nest." One of his lasting impressions, with a degree of bitterness, of the South and its humiliating discrimination, remained vivid. "I felt that the college and university Blacks in the South were clannish and they made me feel all the more like an unwanted outsider." It certainly was not that he had not seen discrimination in California; he had, and then faced it head on with success. Moulden related that while in college, he and a friend, who was attending the University of California at Berkeley, were refused service in a San Jose restaurant. He said, "I sued the owner and won the civil case in my very first real eye to eye meeting with racism."[6]

Too often the thousands of military personnel, specifically the enlisted grades, without whose efforts and specialties the oft-mentioned pilots, both fighter and bomber, would have been perpetually grounded, are not mentioned or even given some of the credit they so richly deserve. It cannot be overemphasized just how critically important these men and women were in keeping this high flying branch of the service operating and functioning. While the pilots, by high profile, collected all the accolades, glory, and the headlines, the enlisted technicians were the ones who truly formed the real backbone of the Air Force. As a matter of fact, they still do. There are not enough words to fully praise the black mechanics, radiomen, and a long list of other technicians who under severe handicaps, the very same segregation, the very same racial hatred, mastered their specialties in much less time than even General Arnold had predicted it would take. What these men did has yet to receive the proper recognition for not only doing their jobs but doing them in such a superb manner in the full face of adversity. These were the men who did not actually fly either as pilots, navigators, bombardiers, or air crewmen. These were the expert technicians whose highly skilled abilities were critically essential, without which all planes would have become permanently grounded. Then, now, and as far as can be envisioned in the near future, fully maintaining and servicing airplanes could not be, cannot be, and will not be done in the air.

Oliver Lanaux became such a representative of this core of dedicated men, an aircraft mechanic at Tuskegee and very proud of it. Lanaux was born in Bay St. Louis, Mississippi, one of seven children.[7] He had graduated from high school and stood poised ready to enter Xavier University in 1941, but he had a feeling that war was coming. Lanaux recalled, "I did not want to be drafted so I enlisted and was inducted into the Army at Camp Shelby, Mississippi. At Ft. Bragg, North Carolina I received my Basic training and then I became a radio operator for gun positioning with the Artillery." Soon, because of his mechanical skills, they assigned him to the motorpool, servicing mostly trucks. He said, "My short stature prevented me from becoming a truck driver, but my good mechanical skills caused them to send me and my buddy David Glover to Flint, Michigan." There they became the only two blacks in a class of 40, to learn the Pratt and Whitney radial engine and they would become two of a very few to learn those skills under nonsegregated conditions. The two men graduated in April 1943, after six months of training and were sent directly to Tuskegee.

Lanaux stayed at Tuskegee working on the BT-13 and the AT-6 exclusively, and then when the love bug came on the scene, he married while on leave in October 1945. The couple managed to rent a room from a farmer whose property was near the black veteran's hospital. He proudly remembered that all of the crewmen were a rather close knit group and that they generally worked to help each other. Although he originally came from the South, dealing with segregation on a daily basis he and his wife remained completely uncomfortable. He bitterly recalled some of it. "My wife could only shop in Tuskegee on certain days. If she happened to forget some particular item then she would have to wait until the next week to go back on the 'Colored's shopping day' to pick up the forgotten item."

Numerous other instances helped to counterbalance some of those racial negatives for the young married couple. Lanaux had a twinkle in his eyes as he recalled the many Sunday afternoon sessions he had with the farmers. "The county was dry so many farmers made bootleg booze and on Sundays, after dropping my wife off to attend church services, we would all get a 'little pie-eyed' from sipping some excellent home-made spirits." Lanaux never had any real serious problems either on the base or off until he left the service in December 1945, following the end of the war. He eventually ended up in Oakland, California, finding work at the Alameda Naval Air Station. Lanaux said, "Despite the fact that here I was a skilled engine mechanic, I spent two years doing 'diddly work' before they allowed me to work as a journeyman mechanic." Once he had crossed that threshold he became an aircraft planner and estimator, and in 1977, he had put in 35 years with the government before he retired.

Ira O'Neal became the final Provost Marshall at Tuskegee's Air Base accepting that position in March 1945, under the request of Colonel Parrish. O'Neal related how terrible the relations were with the local sheriff's department. Although it was customarily expected that all military policemen would wear and carry weapons of some kind there was a bristling standoff with Pat Evans, the local sheriff. O'Neal said they had a leased building in town that they used to store surplus government materials. Sheriff Evans told O'Neal that it was okay for the black MPs to guard the building but they were not to have bullets in their guns. He further threatened that if any of the MPs were discovered to have bullets in their weapons he would arrest them. O'Neal quickly solved that nasty and potentially dangerous problem. "I told my immediate superior, Major Fleetwood McCoy of the impossibility of having my 52 men doing their duty with empty weapons." O'Neal remembered with a deep hearty laugh, an incident that happened not long after he had taken over the duties as Provost Marshal. In an aerial demonstration, the all-black paratroopers, the Triple Nickel group, were scheduled to make a daylight mass jump at the air base. O'Neal laughed aloud, "When those 600 black troopers began jumping out of those planes and coming down like locusts with weapons showing, the whole town of Tuskegee exploded with every sheriff's vehicle available sounding their sirens roaring up to the gates of the base. The sheriff's men were talking about the invasion that they saw." The sheriff and his men were refused entry and it took O'Neal's hurried arrival to explain that what they saw was not an invasion of black troopers but a paratrooper jump demonstration.[8]

Not all of the incidents involving Tuskegee Air Base personnel were as harmless or as humorous as those that occurred while O'Neal headed up the roster of MPs. In September 1942, a black army nurse stationed at the Air Base, Second Lieutenant Nora Green, received yet another infamous sample of the Southern treatment of blacks. On leave in Montgomery, Lieutenant Green committed an infraction that could have cost her life and/or started an armed riot. Just as Rosa Parks would do years later, Green paid her fare and had taken a seat on the city bus. The infraction committed was not waiting for all the white patrons to board the bus first. The bus driver ordered her off the bus to wait for the white patrons to occupy the seats first. She steadfastly refused and the angry bus driver left to call the police. Nurse Green was allegedly manhandled and beaten by the police as they dragged her from the bus. She had protested that she had to return to the Base at a certain time. Green was jailed overnight and also fined. The Justice Department investigated the incident and later reported that it found no grounds for a prosecution.[9] Had it not been for the polished brinkmanship of Colonel Parrish, an armed retaliation by angry black MPs could very easily have taken place after they had heard the story of what had happened to Nurse Green.

There are numerous other stories of violent and ugly treatment of blacks both in uniform in the service of their country and as civilians, and of course the preponderance of this maltreatment occurred in the Southern states, some more notorious than others. In 1943, the base commander of Selfridge Field, in a drunken fit, shot and wounded a black soldier. This was after he had allegedly stated a number of times earlier that he did not want a black driver.[10] The commanding officer later was given a court martial and forced to retire from the service but those measures did not erase his violent act of undisguised hatred. This still in the era of the "night riders" who could swoop down in the middle of the night to raid, ransack, burnout, and kill for some purported infraction against white rule. Blacks were not afforded the protection of the law as civilians and it was certainly almost as tenuous even if you were wearing a uniform.

Hannibal Cox's class that had graduated on April 15, 1944, completed their required transition training at Walterboro's Air Base and had received their overseas equipment. That equipment included the standard issue 45 caliber sidearm. Cox and his 15 classmates were taken by bus to Fairfax, South Carolina, where they were to board a train that would carry them to the port of embarkation in Virginia. In Fairfax, because they entered a white restaurant to buy food, some white patrons in the restaurant immediately became violently upset. Shouting racial epithets and curses, they drove Cox and the group back to the still dark and deserted train station. Being armed only further inflamed the white antagonists to the point of having some of them calling for a lynching. Only the chance intervention of a white officer home on leave and the arrival of the train quite probably prevented bloodshed and murder. Each of Cox's group was an officer but total disrespect for the uniform in the form of raw hatred was shown for these men who were readying to ship out and present their lives in the fight for the freedom of others.

A bewildering set of circumstances is presented to even the casual observer, and these elements are most certainly why German interrogators asked downed and captured black pilots why they fought for a country that hated them. It was almost as if the reality of full and complete freedom in America was based on skin color, religion, and just as often, on gender. This combination of facts raises another troubling question—how many other people would voluntarily fight for a country, a homeland, which in return for their patriotic spirit, showed them only abject contempt at best?

America, the world's idealistic melting cauldron of freedom, surprisingly retained some unyielding forces that coldly refused to willingly adhere to the wording of the Declaration of Independence which states that all men are created equal. All of the rules and guidelines were in place and carefully considered, yet exceptions were made and inhumanely kept in place. Dr. Myrdal searched for and found the real reasons for these illogical exceptions, exceptions that are still very much in evidence. It was through his acclaimed research that the unadulterated facts of racism were presented as he exposed and brought them to light.

# CHAPTER 9

# Combat

Altogether, it is estimated that approximately 933 to 960 combat pilots trained and graduated from Tuskegee. Included in this group of graduates were five Haitians who, although having French as their first language, had to be trained under segregated conditions because of their color. About one-third of the total number of men who received pilot's wings had the classification of multi-engine rated or bomber pilots. Four hundred fifty fighter pilots would see combat in the Mediterranean Theater of Operations (MTO) and sixty-six would lose their lives. The combat achievements and skills of the "Schwartze Vogelmenschen" (black birdmen), as their Nazi counterparts learned to call them, became all too well known and respected.

Although the 99th Pursuit Squadron had been authorized in January 1941, because of the Air Corps' stonewalling and foot-dragging it literally took many months before a full-fledged operational group would be formed. By then, the designation pursuit squadron had been changed to fighter squadron with all the other important elements, such as numbers of men and planes, remaining the same. As the nucleus of the 99th began to fill out and grow to its full complement of pilots and support crew, a monster question blossomed to nag and make life miserable for the Air Corps chiefs. Where were they going to put them, this all-black 99th? Could they be shipped to some island and kept out of the war or should they be thrust into combat, this first-ever group with no combat experience. The war raged on and so did the debate about what to do with this historic unit. One of the second plausible choices would be to send them to Liberia but that idea stalled, because Liberia, a black nation, refused to have them there as part of the Liberian Task Force to finish pushing the Germans out of North Africa. The first thought of sending the 99th to the Pacific to fly under General Claire Chennault's "Flying Tiger" experience quickly fell by the wayside when someone pointed out that to send a green squadron in already obsolete airplanes up against the Japanese and the highly maneuverable Zero fighter would not be very good thinking at best.

This "on again off again" where-do-we-send-them fiasco played havoc with the morale of the 99th. Their training continued and so did the number of alerts. Total flying hours steadily mounted with Lieutenant Bill Campbell leading the whole unit in P-40 hours. Campbell had graduated from Tuskegee Institute with a degree in business administration. His father was the chief field agent for the U.S. Department of Agriculture assisting black farmers of the lower 15 Southern states to improve their crops. After finishing his secondary training with the CPTP, Campbell was accepted for cadet training and earned his wings along with 14 of his classmates in class 42-F, the fourth class to complete pilot training at Tuskegee. 42-F went directly from CPTP into the Basic phase of training. Because Campbell, born in Tuskegee, knew all the ins and outs of the community and really had a gung-ho attitude about flying, he eagerly flew when any of the other pilots became ill or for any reason failed to fly on any given day. As a result he gradually amassed more flying time than any of the other men of the original 99th group. Campbell recalled, "I had a car, there were lots of girls, I was at home, I was flying so I had a real good time!" But the numerous alerts that had the men repeatedly poised to make ready to ship out, began to wear on their nerves and patience. When the real day finally did come, most of the men pretty much disregarded the alert and then had to turn on the steam in getting their gear ready to board the train. In New York, they boarded the USS Mariposa, a converted luxury liner, but no one knew where they were headed, some said the Pacific and others were betting on the long haul to Europe. As senior officer, Lieutenant Colonel Benjamin Davis, Jr. became the executive officer of the entire ship. There were also white officers and white enlisted personnel on board, but Campbell said there were no serious incidents with Davis in command. Officers were assigned the upper decks and the enlisted men to the lower. On board, was the entire complement of the 99th Fighter Squadron.

The ocean voyage took them across the Atlantic and after eight days with the men speculating about being hunted down by German submarine wolf packs, there was complete surprise and relief when the ship docked at Casablanca, Morocco. Campbell remembered the disembarkment well. "It was hot as hell and Col. Davis had us in full dress uniform to march down the street toward the area where we were to be bivouacked. Where we were to stay there were only wooden platforms to sleep on for the next two days." Fighting the heat and the pesky flies, the 99th then prepared to head north by rail. Campbell recalled that the passenger cars of the train, unlike the American style, had compartment doors that opened to the outside. The whole contingent boarded and spent the next full day slowly chugging toward where, the men still did not know although Campbell suggested that, "Col. Davis probably knew where we were headed but the rest of us had absolutely no idea of our destination." Their terminus turned out to be a little town called OuedN'ja situated between Casablanca and Tangier and almost adjoining the city of Fez.[1] Near the field used by the 99th was a white fighter-bomber group flying the A-36. The relationship between the two groups remained cordial and when the 99th received its P-40s they began to stage impromptu friendly dogfights.

Two weeks after arrival the men began returning in twos and threes back to Casablanca to ferry in the brand new P-40L models that they would use in combat. Lieutenant General Carl Spaatz, commander of the North African Air Force brought in seasoned combat veterans to help transition the new kids on the block, the 99th, into what would be in store for them. One of those seasoned American vets was none other than Lieutenant Colonel Phillip Corcoran, the depicted star of the comic strip "Terry and the Pirates." Corcoran was a noted expert on dive bombing and it was his duty to show the men just how it was done.[2] For a whole month the 99th participated in intense exercises designed to prepare them for the final jump into actual battle. Each day the men felt sharper and more confident in their abilities even though they knew the P-40, even this new model, would be no match for the FW-190 or the ME-109 they expected to soon be facing.

The intense training soon ended and the group moved to Fardjouna on the Tunisian coast of North Africa, its last near-the-front training camp, attached to, but not a part of, the 33rd Fighter Group under the command of Colonel William Momeyer. The 33rd was one of the fighter groups operating under the XII Air Support of the Northwest African Tactical Air Force. The 99th next moved to El Haouria on the Cape Bon Peninsula. From this site they began escorting medium bombers to the western portions of Sicily, the doorway to Italy, in the softening up process. Its first real assignment was to operate as wingmen to the veteran pilots of the 33rd and their first mission, dive bombing and ground strafing attacks against the heavily fortified Italian island of Pantelleria. This began the allied assault on Sicily. These strafing and dive bombing missions continued for a full week without a single enemy plane being sighted. During their first dive bombing attack, Bill Campbell, now a first lieutenant, flew as wingman to the leader of the four-plane flight. The white leader had earlier cautioned him not to lag behind and to stay in close. Campbell said he mentally had no intention of lagging, he intended to stay in the hip pocket of the leader. Over the target the leader peeled off and went down to drop his 500-pound bomb. Campbell stayed right behind him and dropped his own load, he did not see it explode or what it hit. When they pulled up he said, "The leader looked back to his right to see where I was. I was right there nudging his right wing. The leader then snapped a quick swivel look again as if he were startled and surprised to see me. I said to myself, damn it, you're not going to lose me!" Those seconds of flying by Campbell gave him the distinction of being the first African-American military pilot to drop a bomb on an enemy of America.[3]

When the flight landed at the base of the flight leader, Campbell had the misfortune to taxi into a shell hole with one wheel of his brand new P-40. That generated a tiny spike of embarrassment for him at the end of an otherwise successful first combat flight. Since his own plane was now damaged and required repair he had to borrow one of the 33rd's planes for their next mission. When they returned, Campbell studiously avoided the shell hole but then had to return to the 99th base in a jeep. Mechanics from the 99th base came to repair Campbell's ailing plane so it could be flown back to its point of origin. Obviously, no thought or consideration had been given or ventured to having the white mechanics already there to do the needed repairs. This was, after all, Colonel Momeyer's command and Momeyer became the first to criticize the performance of the 99th after it had later moved to El Haouria and had begun operating with the 324th Fighter Group. In his evaluation report to Major General Edwin House, Commanding Officer of the XII Air Support Command, Momeyer stated that the 99th "seemed to disintegrate" when enemy planes jumped them and he accused the 99th of a "lack of aggressive spirit." He further charged the 99th pilots of avoiding some heavily defended targets when they were dive bombing.[4] Momeyer summed up his criticism by saying, "...it is my opinion that they are not of the fighting caliber of any squadron in this group...It may be expected that we will get less work and less operational time out of the 99th Fighter Squadron than any squadron in this Group."[5] General House concurred with Momeyer's negative evaluation and recommended that the 99th be sent back to Africa to do patrol and convoy duties out of the combat zone. Their new P-40s would be taken from them and replaced by Bell P-39s, a fighter craft that performed even worse than the outdated P-40s. General House had the idea that, "[T]he Negro type has not the proper reflexes to make a first class fighter pilot."[6] So the distorted negative evaluation of the 99th grew larger as it reached farther up the chain of command. However, General Spaatz tended to temper his own observations slightly as he forwarded the damaging critique to Washington and to General Hap Arnold, commanding officer of the Air Force. The condemning negative report contained just the kind of ammunition needed to yank the 99th out of the air and to reemphasize the original "I told you so!" concept that General Arnold had maintained all along. All of the command fingers pointed in that condemning direction, except now there appeared a buffer, an Advisory Committee on Negro Troop Policies, would intercede. Colonel Benjamin Davis, Jr., now back in the States to take command of an all-black Fighter Group, the 332nd, was called to testify before that committee. Davis admitted that there had been some mistakes at first—after all the 99th had no combat experience and had entered the fight more or less in a partial vacuum.

General Arnold continued to press the attack to rid the Air Force of its unwanted black pilots. He ordered a draft memorandum to President Roosevelt saying that Negro pilots were no good in an active combat area and recommended that they be pulled back and reassigned to some rear defense area. Unfortunately, for General Arnold, a member of the Air Staff not only ambushed his negative memo, but revised it as well and then covered it with another memo. The cover memo urged serious reconsideration because of the consequences and strong negative publicity that such a drastic proposal would generate.[7] As a result of Davis' testimony, the Special Committee's findings and other questionable conclusions by the War Department, General Staff Operations recommended that the 332nd be formed and sent into action as a final just and reasonable test under the command of Colonel Davis. The big question that still remained unanswered on the table was, could black pilots fly and fight on a par with their white counterparts or were they, as suggested by the Air Force's top brass, useless inferiors, ill-suited for the rigors and exhaustive demands of combat flying.

While the formation of the 332nd was underway, the 99th would make yet another move, perhaps the most significant and fortunate in its short combat existence. The 99th was assigned to the 79th Fighter Group under the command of Colonel Earl Bates. Operating from a section of the Foggia Air Base as the fourth squadron of the 79th, the men of the 99th began to realize what had been denied to them earlier—Colonel Bates mixed the squadrons up without regard to color. Morale skyrocketed along with their proficiency, as their white squadron mates began to show and teach them the tricks and ways of the veteran combat fighter pilot.[8] This strategic move provided just the kind of mentoring and seasoning these fledglings needed and would have received had there been combat wise black veterans ahead of them.

The measure of the respect shared between the two groups is highlighted by an incident in which a member of the 99th damaged his landing gear on takeoff for a mission. With his gear partially retracted and partially hanging down, the pilot went on to complete the assigned mission. He returned and had to crash land his already damaged craft, clearly demonstrating that here was a man ready and willing to fight. Near the end of January 1944, after missions of dive bombing and strafing attacks for five successive days, 99th planes finally engaged enemy planes over the Anzio beachhead. Outnumbered two to one, the 99th zoomed into action and damaged five enemy planes within four minutes. That same afternoon they destroyed three more but this time at a very bitter price. Lieutenant Samuel Bruce became the first member of the 99th to die in aerial combat.[9] Six others had previously lost their lives in nonaerial combative action accidents. On the very day that Charles B. Hall became the first member of the 99th to score an enemy kill—Lieutenants James Mc Cullin and Sherman White lost their lives in a mid-air collision near the coast of Sicily. And, ironically, Bruce himself, in another mid-air mishap, sliced off the tail section of Lieutenant Paul G. Mitchell when the latter's P-40 veered into his path with apparent engine trouble. Bruce managed to bail out from his damaged craft but Mitchell was too close to the water to even have a chance of exiting from his plane.[10]

While Colonel Davis remained in the States testifying and forming the 332nd, Captain George "Spanky" Roberts, the first black man accepted into the Army Air Corps flight training program, became the 99th CO again, having been in that position when the 99th first formed. Although the usual number of missions was 50 before pilots rotated out of combat activity, Roberts rose to the rank of Major and completed 78 missions before ending his tour of duty and returning to the United States.[11] Operations changed for the 99th once more as they moved to Licata, Sicily to continue their dive bombing, strafing, and patrol duties as the full invasion of Sicily began. It took approximately 12 days of bombings and strafing attacks, beginning May 30, 1943, before the stubborn island surrendered, marking the first time in military history that an enemy territory would capitulate from the pounding force of air might alone.[12]

Before the arrival of the 332nd Fighter Group, the 99th would be released from the 79th and assigned to the 324th Fighter Group, an attachment not much better than when they had been with the 33rd under Colonel Momeyer. Their new job, escort duty for a B-25 Medium Bomber Group. Then they were, for a very short time, bounced over to the 86th Fighter Group, before finally joining up with the new all-black 322nd Fighter Group with its three squadrons in Ramitelli, Italy.

The 332nd Fighter Group was activated at Tuskegee Army Air Base in October of 1942, and eventually consisted of the 100th, the 301st, and 302nd fighter squadrons. Starting out with a bare eight men the 100th was first led by Richard Caesar who had been held back from the 99th to form the group. Caesar's entry into the Air Corps had taken a very devious almost tortuous course after he had graduated from Morehouse College in 1940, and worked at the New York World's Fair as he waited to enter Meharry Dental School. Caesar became houseboy to the famous strip tease artist Gypsy Rose Lee until the fair closed. He secured another job in Florida and managed to duck being drafted as he worked his way up to Chicago and eventually back down, in horse shoe style, to birthplace Lake Village, Arkansas. The local draft board called him, but after noting that he was a college graduate he was told that an Air Corps recruiter would be coming to Little Rock and he should take the test. Conferring with and agreeing with a group of white Air Corps recruit candidates to meet the next morning at the train station for the trip to Little Rock, Caesar went home happy and confident. "The next morning when I arrived at the station there wasn't a soul around, there was nobody there at all. I went back home and told my father that I had to

take a test in Little Rock and he drove me there just in time for the test."
In Little Rock, Caesar managed to stay with an aunt so he could take the last
part of the test the next day. At the end of the testing he said, "The white
captain who had conducted the testing told me that I had done very well and
to go home and wait until I heard from Washington." Caesar returned home
and waited and waited for more than a month until finally his draft board
said he would have to go in, his time had run out. This time instead of
ducking, he figured it would only be about six months so he might as well get
it over with and serve his time; dental school would have to wait.

Caesar boarded a train in Little Rock along with a number of other black
draftees. They traveled for days not knowing where they were going or when
they would arrive. Finally the train stopped and the men discovered that they
had arrived where none had ever been before, in Cheyenne, Wyoming. Here
they would all be trained in the Army Quartermaster School. All the other
men in his class would be shipped out after training but they held Caesar
back to teach succeeding classes. "I steadfastly refused to become a teacher
so they promptly shipped me out to Denver, Colorado where I became a
company clerk, my office being a desk in the middle of a huge gymnasium
surrounded by the desks of other white enlisted men." The company
commander took a liking to Caesar and would often take him along for
breakfast; which he recalled consisted of several good jolts of whiskey.

Eventually orders came for Caesar to head for Tuskegee and with those
orders came a set of train tickets longer than both of his arms. Caesar
successfully completed the pilot training program graduating as cadet
captain with Class 42-H and became one of the original members of the
99th. When the 99th finally shipped out for combat Caesar was again
held back to help form the new 100th Fighter Squadron, the first unit of
the 332nd Fighter Group. The buildup of more men began under the
553rd Fighter Squadron designed to be the primary transition mill that
would be the supply source of men for the 332nd. During transition training
in the P-40, Caesar led a nine-plane flight to Selfridge Field, Michigan after
stopping to refuel at a designated civilian airfield in Kentucky. The fledgling
100th landed at Selfridge and Caesar had the misfortune of blowing out a tire
on landing. The commanding officer immediately called him into his headquarters office and summarily told him that he was grounded. From that day
forward Caesar became the Engineering Officer of the 100th Fighter Squadron and, most importantly, his love for flying came to an abrupt and very
bitter end. "After I was grounded, after all the training, after leading the
flight all the way from Tuskegee here I was grounded without a hearing or
even a reasonable inquiry into what had caused the blowout. I was so
angry at the way that I was treated that I really didn't care about flying
after that."[13]

Lieutenant Colonel Charles Gayle commanded the 553rd and he set
the initial racial tones with regard to the Officers Club at Selfridge.

The 477th Bombardment Group had just arrived at Selfridge and three black officers had been refused entrance to the Officers Club, though none of these were from the 477th. Sensing trouble, Gayle told all black officers under his command that he, " ... would court-martial for inciting a riot, the first man who stepped into the Officers Club."[14] This early abuse and denial of rights to which all officers were entitled began to grow, festering beneath the surface like something terribly, terribly dangerous.

Behind the 100th came the 301st and then the 302nd Fighter Squadrons, each swelling to full complement month by month as the classes of pilots graduated. These three groups would form the all-black 332nd Fighter Group, the first fighting unit of its kind, as conceived by Under Secretary of War, Robert Patterson a full year before the idea became fact.[15] The 100th remained at Selfridge for little more than a month and then transferred to Oscoda Army Air Field in Michigan. The other two squadrons soon joined them as transition training continued in the well-worn P-40s, some so old that they still were marked with the original Flying Tigers logo, the open shark's mouth. Gunnery and dive bombing practice took place not only at Oscoda, a sub base 200 miles away from Selfridge, but also at designated practice sites across the border into Canada. For a time the Air Corps brass considered bringing in P-47s which caused delays and more reconsiderations, a disruptive element in the training. Finally, they introduced a new type aircraft to the three squadrons, the Bell P-39 Airacobra. The P-39 was unique because although it sported the Allison engine as did the P-40, the engine, now located behind the pilot, had the propeller shaft running under the cockpit and the pilot's legs. The prop shaft also housed the barrel of its 20 millimeter nose cannon. The P-39 had other firsts, such as a door that opened like a car door instead of a sliding or hatched canopy. This was also the Air Corps' first single-seat fighter with tricycle landing gear. Originally, the British tried out the P-39 while it was equipped with a 37 millimeter nose cannon and 7 mm machine guns, but without turbo charging or supercharging the plane proved useless above 10,000 feet, its rate of climb so slow as to be totally unacceptable. Compared to the old P-40s the brand new P-39s at first were welcomed by the men until they gradually began to see its severe limitations of slow climb rate, low service ceiling, too much armor, and too much weight for its horsepower. They all would have preferred to stay with the old P-40s for combat.

Month after month of training finally ended with Lieutenant Colonel Benjamin Davis, Jr. assuming command of the 332nd replacing Colonel Robert Selway who would go on to stir up less than desirable attention as CO of Freeman Field. With Davis at the helm, the 332nd boarded ship at Hampton Roads, Virginia in what would become a month long odyssey at sea. Caesar recalled that after they had been at sea for about three days it seemed that the whole convoy turned around and headed back toward the port from which they had earlier departed. He also remembered that there was an "awful amount of sea sickness from the landlubbers spending so much time at sea." They finally landed at Taranto, Italy almost a full month later without being the target of any of the infamous German submarine wolf packs. After disembarking in a very heavy rainstorm the group ended up in a muddy and wet tent city complex before the 100th moved on to the Montecorvino Air Base to begin actual combat operations. A week later, the 301st and 302nd arrived at Montecorvino to be gradually absorbed into the fringes of combat. All three squadrons were assigned to do coastal patrol and harbor protection. The few times any German aircraft were encountered, the P-39s were not able to climb fast enough or high enough to offer any real threat even to those relatively slow observation planes. The pilots could see the P-39s operational inferiority up close and personal.

In time, the 332nd made another move to a permanent base site at Capodichino Air Base near Naples. Mt. Vesuvius was in the midst of showing off its might with spectacular pyrotechnics at night but also continuously showering everything for miles and miles around with gritty volcanic ash that seemed to permeate everything, covered and uncovered. Caesar clearly remembered that in addition to being victims of the persistent ash, at one point, the Germans began to saturate the area with bombs every night for a week. One night, in particular, stands out in his memory. Because the bombing and firing was so heavy and continuous he was unable to sleep. He got out of bed and went to the entrance to open the tent flap. "The whole sky was aglow with the antiaircraft guns and the tracer shells firing at the German bombers, it was almost like daytime. I closed the tent flap and went back to my bed. There exactly where my head had been was a big chunk of hot smoking metal, shrapnel or bomb fragment, I guess. If I had stayed in that bed just a couple minutes longer I wouldn't have made it out of there alive! Man, I was more than just a little lucky that night!"

It did not take very long for the Air Force brass to recognize that with its poor performance, the P-39 had no place in that theater of operations and the decision came to bring in the P-47 Thunderbolt. The very first of those planes brought in were some well-used D models commonly called "Razorbacks" that had been used by the 325th Fighter Group. Although now flying the more powerful P-47s, the assignments of the three squadrons remained the same—patrol, ground support, dive bombing, and strafing. These assignments still offered no opportunities to engage the enemy at the higher altitudes where the attacks on allied bombers took place. Even though more than 9,000 models of the P-39 were built, more than half of that number were sold to the Russians who proceeded to strip off the heavy armor and successfully used the Airacobra below 10,000 feet for ground assault duties.[16]

The three squadrons of the 322nd gradually began to acquire more used P-47s, the acquisition occurring because the other units of the Air Force were now being equipped with the new darling of the skies, the P-51 Mustang.

Still, just how quickly the men adjusted to the P-47 is remembered by Lieutenant Wendell Pruitt's crew chief Samuel Jacobs. "We had been flying the Thunderbolts for about a week. ...representatives from Republic Aviation and some Air Corps brass had been scheduled to arrive and teach us how to fly and crew the 47s. ...by the time they arrived our Engineering Officers and Line Chiefs had schooled us on everything we needed to know. ...I remember this Major standing atop a munitions carrier telling us 'boys' all about the 'flying bathtub' and how it should never be slow rolled below a thousand feet due to its excessive weight. No sooner had he finished his statement than, A flight was returning from its victorious mission. Down on the deck, props cutting grass, came Lieutenant Pruitt and his wingman Lee Archer, nearly touching wings. Lieutenant Pruitt pulled up into the prettiest victory roll you'd ever see with Archer right in his pocket as the Major screamed, 'But you can't do that!!!'"[17]

During the slightly more than 30 days the 332nd operated the Thunderbolts, it acquitted itself in a manner unequaled by any other group during the war. On the way back from a mission, a flight of five P-47s spotted a German destroyer or destroyer escort at port in Trieste Harbor taking on either supplies or making repairs. Led by Captain Joseph Elsberry, Lieutenants Charles Dunne, Joe Lewis, Gwynne Pierson, and Wendell Pruitt dived to the attack. Before the era of rockets, their planes had empty bomb racks but on successive passes the five, despite heavy return fire from the ship's gun batteries, first hit the destroyer's magazine then succeeded in exploding and sinking it.[18] Of course, such a damaging operation had never been carried out before using only 50 caliber machineguns and while the Air Force brass was skeptical, the gun cameras from the planes established the proof of the claim.

Up to this point in the fighting, the 99th had still not become part of the 332nd, it remained with the 86th Fighter Group until late June 1943, when the 332nd made its final major move to Ramitelli, Italy. Along with this move came the arrival of the heralded new P-51s that were already beginning to kick the hell out of the Luftwaffe. The first prototype models of the Mustang were not at all extraordinary; in fact, they were just ordinary, more like a better rendition of the P-40. The P-51 remained just ordinary after first being fitted with the Allison engine then the Packard-Merlin engine and finally the Rolls-Royce Merlin. The latter engine gave the P-51 the needed oomph to vault it into the superior class. The first models used by the 332nd were the B and C models with the side opening canopies.

When the 99th joined the other three squadrons of the 332nd Fighter Group making it the only four-squadron Fighter Group in operation, there were apprehensions among the men from all the squadrons because only the 99th had acquired the hard frontline combat experience. There were thoughts that the pilots of the three newer squadrons would merely play second fiddle with the responsibility roles going to the more experienced men of the 99th. Moreover, the 99th men definitely did not want to be relegated to flying as wingmen to the unseasoned newcomers.[19] All of those ill-founded misconceptions came to naught as the men began to mesh and merge together as a unit ready to take on the best the Germans could offer.

As Engineering Officer of the 100th, Caesar became an unyielding task-master, driving the men under him to the limit and perhaps a little beyond, but they all learned to respect and like him because of his fairness and understanding. One incident still sticks in Caesar's craw, one that after the passage of all these years still refuses to go away. On the return from a mission, one of the 100th pilots flipped his P-51 over on its back in landing when he tried to correct running out of runway by slamming down hard on the brakes. That action may have blown a tire causing the craft to flip over. The plane skidded down the metal matting of the runway and when it stopped, the pilot trapped inside and hanging upside down, could not unsnap his harness. Caesar raced out to the damaged plane, and he could smell the high octane fuel leaking as he pried and forced open the canopy. By sheer strength he reached in and unhooked the helpless pilot from his harness then tugged and pulled to get him out of the cockpit. He grabbed the man under the arms dragging him away as the plane began to smoke. No sooner had the dazed pilot been dragged to safety when a small explosion ignited the gas fumes and turned the cockpit into a raging furnace.

Medics carried the semi-conscious pilot off to the medical station and then released him after a thorough examination. The next day, Caesar bumped into the man he had rescued outside of the mess hall. He spoke to him and started to inquire about how he felt after such a close call ordeal. The lucky pilot barely acknowledged Caesar's presence and, in fact, never really spoke to him after the incident. More than a little puzzled, Caesar tried in vain for days to justify the pilot's extremely odd behavior of not thanking him for saving his life. The more he thought about it the more it gnawed at him. Even though the pilot was not apparently ill-tempered he seemed to go out of his way to avoid even speaking to Caesar. "I don't know, maybe he had a death-wish or maybe it was because someone had to help him stay alive and he resented it. He didn't even offer me a coke or a highball in gratitude." The remembrance of that afternoon quickly flooded back because he was still aware that he could just as easily have lost his own life while trying to pull the pilot clear. His eyes took on a distant look. "I didn't understand it then when it happened and I still don't understand it today." I watched as Caesar grew pensive, my own thoughts churning for an answer. Then he said, "How can anyone not thank someone for saving their life?" My own thoughts searched but I found no answer either.

Now ranked as a Captain, Caesar remembered yet another incident at Ramitelli. One afternoon, as he superintended the repair of a damaged P-51, an army jeep pulled up through the base gates and stopped. The vehicle started again, rolling slowly toward him then made a sudden U-turn and sped back out through the gates. Curious, Caesar walked to the gates to question the guards. He was told that there were two white officers in the jeep who had come to thank the pilots who had escorted them to safety after their bomber had been severely damaged. "It came to me that after those white pilots saw that we were all black men they decided to keep their thanks for having their lives saved." Caesar shook his head. "I hope those men survived the war and lived to remember that bullets and bombs don't pick out certain skin colors to hit. Some of our guys had obviously saved their butts so they could have at least said thanks or tipped their caps even if they looked away while doing it."

Apparently because of his recognized teaching abilities Caesar had twice in his military career been held back. One would have kept him in the Quartermaster Corps and the other would have put him in the middle of the 99th Fighter Squadron but it was either fate or fortune that dealt him the cards that he played and he played them with skillful deliberation. Even before rescuing the ungrateful pilot from being cooked in that blazing cockpit, Caesar had resolved to never become personally involved with the loss of men when one or the other in the 100th failed to return from a mission. But he was like a mother hen, with each plane under his care being watched and cared for with maternal concern. Caesar chuckled when he remembered opposing Colonel Davis who had asked him to take some parts from one P-51 that was already undergoing maintenance to repair another that needed those same parts to fly. "I looked at him and said, No, sir! I absolutely cannot do that until some new parts come in. He didn't like it but years later he thanked me for doing what I knew was right."[20]

Without question, Colonel Davis was a stern disciplinarian having spent his four years at West Point under the "silent treatment" from his class-mates. He was only spoken to in the line of duty and forced to room alone while all his classmates had roommates, buddies to talk to and converse with. It must have been this iron will to succeed while surrounded by racially opposing forces that gave Davis his no nonsense attend-to-duty character. It was he who ordered the pilots of the 332nd to stay with the bombers under escort and not be lured off for possible kills that brought the group its fame and unequalled recognition. The 332nd laid claim to an achievement not matched by any other group during WWII, that of not losing a single allied bomber to any enemy fighter.

Early in its existence, the 332nd had adopted a color scheme of having the tail sections of all the planes painted solid red that led to the group being called the "Red Tails" or "Red Tail Angels." To distinguish between the squadrons, the nose sections, propeller spinners, and trim tabs were painted different colors, for example the 100th had black trim tabs, while the 301st had blue. The 100th had a solid red nose section and the 99th had a blue and white checkerboard. Also during this time, the Air Force decided to stop painting its airplanes in olive drab. This accomplished at least two good things, it greatly reduced maintenance and it gave a slight boost to airspeed with the smoother skin surface.

As the war wore on, the C models gradually began being replaced by the newer D model and the joy of the men flying them increased several notches. It should be strongly noted that the act of flying so many different types of aircraft points up the remarkable abilities of the mechanics and technicians who had to service all these changes with such precision. Each airplane had different designs and required different remembered specifications and techniques. Enough can never be said about the skilled performances and dedication contributed by the hundreds of black specialists who kept not only the high performance combat aircraft operating in the heat of battle but also the several types of training craft even before the pilots graduated. They must be applauded because during that time of black denigration the Air Force was not ready to force a white mechanic or technician to service a black pilot's aircraft.

One late afternoon, still operating from Ramitelli, Bill Campbell, who had acquired the nickname of "Wild Bill," was leading a flight of eight P-51s back to the base following a strafing mission. He spotted six aircraft approaching his group heading in the direction they had just come from. The oncoming aircraft were about 100 feet higher than his flight. "I saw these planes coming and they passed, zoom, right over the top of us. As they did I noticed that they all had tail wheels sticking out. The thought suddenly hit me that no American planes had non-retractable tail wheels. That's when I wheeled around bringing the whole flight with me. They were Germans!" Campbell's flight caught up with the Germans in minutes. "That's when all hell broke loose! We had a hell of a dogfight and when it was all over only one of the six bandits got away. I got one and the other men downed the other four." His flight returned to Ramitelli without the loss of a single man from the impromptu aerial battle just ten minutes away from their home base.

In that same week, as Campbell led another group back to the base from a strafing mission he found that they were missing two planes. He frowned as he relived the memory of that afternoon. "We never did know what happened to that guy and his wingman." He did not mention the pilot's name. "That guy had a habit of not keeping up. He had been warned a number of times to keep up and not straggle and to stay with the group but he was always hanging behind. We guessed they must have been picked off while they were straggling behind us." He shook his head. "No one saw them go down. They just sort of disappeared."

One of the later arrivals to the war zone was Leon "Woody" Spears who had graduated in class 44-F. On his fifty-first mission but his very first mission of flying cover escort for squadrons of B-17 bombers over Berlin, Spears relaxed just a bit and became fascinated by the fact that Germany's famed airfield, Tempelhof, was built smack dab in the middle of Berlin. Something he had never seen before, a full airport located in the middle of a city. Spears recalled it as the first of three major mistakes he made that day. "I was circling looking down at that airport like a visiting spectator on an aerial sightseeing tour. That's when I noticed this little speck on the canopy. The speck turned out to be an antiaircraft shell that exploded under my left wing leaving a gaping hole and dripping hydraulic lines." Spears got out of there as fast as his now ailing plane would take him and headed, he hoped, for Poland because there was no way that his plane would last to return to his base. He cleared the German border with his engine beginning to sputter from overheating and he could see a small airfield up ahead. As he approached the "heaven sent landing strip just when he needed it," he made the second mistake. The normal procedure before landing is to lower the landing gear and then the flaps on the base and approach legs. But with an ailing engine and a huge hole in the wing he forgot and did the normal thing at an abnormal time. "I realized what I had done in a hurry because now I could see that I had lost all the airspeed I needed to reach that darn landing strip. By sheer luck I cleared the fence at the edge of the field but I hit hard and bounced in badly injuring my left foot." He painfully pulled himself from the confines of the cockpit to the badly damaged wing and saw a car rapidly coming to help him. As it rolled closer and turned near the side of the wing he could see that it was a staff car filled with German officers getting out with guns in their hands.

Spears said, "I made two more back to back mistakes. First, I had forgotten that Poland was still German occupied and second, I had waved after I climbed out of the cockpit. That was before I saw the swastika painted on the side of the staff car." Spears became a prisoner of war in a boarded up hotel for six days. He was treated with respect as an officer and even became friendly with the enlisted guard of his private room, friendly enough to have the guard show him the correct way to dismantle and reassemble the machinegun that he carried.

Near the end of March 1945, the Russians rescued Spears from his captors when the Russian tanks and ground troops swarmed into Posan, Poland to rout the remaining Germany infantry units. He eventually ended up on a converted freighter in the Black Sea along with hundreds of other repatriated allies including two other Tuskegee Airmen.[21]

There is no question that the introduction of the Merlin-powered P-51 Mustang instrumentally gave the allies, primarily the U.S. Air Force, air superiority over the fading might of the Luftwaffe fighters. Prior to the P-51s entry, the losses to allied bombers had been staggering as they attempted strikes deep into enemy held territory. Estimates of up to sixty percent and higher losses were inflicted as the bombers reached farther into those areas where the concentrations of enemy fighter planes and antiaircraft density increased. To put that on a more understandable basis, for every ten allied bombers flying deep into enemy territory, only three or four would return to safety. There are no statistics available to separate the number of allied bombers downed by German fighter aircraft compared to those destroyed from the ground by antiaircraft fire. At any rate, this makes the record of the Red Tails even more outstanding, and laudable, to have not lost any bombers they escorted to enemy fighters! But that unparalleled and unequalled record had a price and the terrible cost, the loss of 66 men of the 450 black combat pilots who had to fight their own countrymen in order to help fight the enemy!

The squadrons of the 332nd began to excel in all aspects required or asked of them. They compiled a commendable record of enemy aircraft shot down or destroyed on the ground, locomotives, boxcars, boats and barges destroyed, oil and ammunition dumps knocked out, and a host of other destructive missions. As a result of flying 1578 missions and more than 15,500 sorties, the four squadrons amassed numerous awards and medals with clusters, all topped by a total of 150 Distinguished Flying Crosses.[22]

After the devastating losses the Germans suffered in their frigid winter battle at Stalingrad, desperation gripped the once unstoppable German war machine. Hitler had refused to heed the experts, his commanding generals, and leave Russia alone. As a result, long vulnerable supply lines, the bitter cold, and the unyielding resolve of the defenders brought the first crushing defeat to the vaunted Vermacht. The world's first jet aircraft, the Me-262s, were launched by the Luftwaffe as interceptors in an attempt to plug some of the gaping holes in a very leaky dike, the obliteration of all war production items that the relentless and steadily increasing allied bombing was causing. Military experts say had the Me-262 been introduced earlier, air superiority probably would have been given to the Luftwaffe. The 262, calculated to be at least 100 miles an hour faster than any allied fighters, meant if an engaged fighter pilot missed his targeted 262 on the angle, he had no hope of catching or overtaking his opponent. The primary advantage the P-51 had over the Me-262 was its maneuverability, a positive attribute learned earlier by U.S. pilots in tangling with the very maneuverable Japanese Zero. The P-40 could not turn with the Zero and the 262 could not turn with the P-51. Any craft able to turn inside the other had the distinct advantage.

The pilots of the 332nd were not the first to see and have confirmed kills of the super fast Me-262, when they were encountered. Only two had been previously shot down. Of the eight claimed on the day that they did meet, the 332nd bagged three of those confirmed kills. German air power steadily grew weaker and weaker, reeling from the heavy pounding and devastation of oil and fuel supplies—the vital ingredients necessary to feed the hungry—and constant demands of its aircraft that were now no longer on the offensive.

Despite the early disbelief and utter rejection by white bomber pilots that skilled black fighter pilots manned those red-tailed planes they saw sticking to the bombers and nursing many sick and damaged ones home, the truth finally emerged. Word must have soon spread that the red tails were not losing bombers to enemy fighters and that word became reality. As a bomber pilot your best chance of surviving your sitting-duck bombing runs and returning, even in crippled condition from ground fire, would be in having the red tails as your escort. This led the former skeptics—those who had ridiculed the idea of there being black fighter pilots—to request that the red tails be their escorts whenever the opportunity arose. It would be a logical and more than reasonable conclusion to go with the odds even if they happened to be blue polka dot colored pilots in those red tailed P-51s.

# CHAPTER 10

# Bomber Pilots

Without question, the fighter pilots of the 99<sup>th</sup> Fighter Squadron and the 332<sup>nd</sup> Fighter Group have received the lion's share of the publicity and attention directed toward and about the Tuskegee Airmen. And this homage is certainly not without great merit, but to neglect the efforts and tribulations of the 477<sup>th</sup> Bombardment Group would be an abominable omission and a subversion of fact. The first class of fighter pilots graduated in March 1942, but the first scheduled class of bomber pilots did not receive their wings until November 1943, a year and eight months later, because no planned class had been trained before class 43-J. Leslie A. Williams trained in that first class.

In 1942, all the battle lines had already been drawn, all of the major participants and players had cast their lots and picked sides. It was then that Williams decided to beat the draft and enlist in order to make his contribution to the war effort. But he did not want to be a foot soldier, he wanted to fly. He had grown up in San Mateo, California where life for him had been completely free of segregation and discrimination. At the recruiting office in San Francisco he told the recruiter that he wanted to fly to do his fighting. After filling out the necessary papers the recruiter told him to return home and wait for the call from Washington. Confident that all was well, Williams returned home to anxiously await his call to enter pilot training. With only a breath of bitterness he said, "Like many of the other young black men I waited and waited and waited for the call that never came."

Williams had become an accomplished dancer and by jumping around the country he stayed just ahead of the pursuing federal officers who were after him for draft dodging. For a while he eluded being caught by staying at military bases with the black enlisted men. That worked exceedingly well because only rarely would white officers visit the enlisted men's quarters. But months of ducking and dodging finally ended when Williams decided to get it over with. However, rather than place an able bodied draft dodger in prison the draft board decided to stick him in the Quartermaster Corps. As a result he ended up in Seattle, Washington helping to load and unload ships as well as to do other nonskilled tasks. During that time he formed a group to entertain ranking officers at their various social functions. As luck would have it, at one of these functions a general became so impressed with the performance of the group that he later asked each one his military goal. Williams informed the general about his goal. "I told him that I wanted to fly and that was all it took."[1] He had finally two-stepped his way into the Air Corps as he had wanted to do from the beginning. However, when he began basic training he quickly realized that he decidedly did not feel really suited for all the aerobatics. Flying, yes, but he wanted something with a lot less loops and rolls. More of the straight and level stuff would do just fine. Fortune continued to beam down on Williams because just at that time the Air Force finally decided to begin training black multi-engine pilots, the straight and level guys. This first class became part of the nucleus of the 477th Medium Bombardment Group that would eventually consist of the 616th, 617th, 618th, and 619th squadrons. The men of these squadrons would eventually be denied the opportunity of ever seeing the combat that they had trained so diligently for, but they would successfully battle and defeat the base indignities and insults thrown at them. By their resolve and resolute determination to be recognized as men without regard to skin color by their own countrymen, the men of the 477th defied the "separate but equal" practice of segregation and defended with honor their given rights.

In today's U.S. military services, respect abounds for an individual's ability to do something and for the degree of excellence he or she attains in performing that something. The old dogma which, in America, withheld respect for African-Americans regardless of proven ability has been replaced by individual judgment and evaluation that does not have race or skin color in any part of the equation. If there must be an official stamp or date to this monumental change and a place or locale to be recognized, then perhaps it should be July 26, 1948, in Washington, DC, when President Harry Truman signed Executive Order 9981 ending segregation in the armed services. This document stated: "It is essential that there be maintained in the Armed Services of the United States the highest standards of democracy, with equality of treatment and opportunity for all those who serve. ... It is hereby declared to be the policy of the President that there shall be equality of treatment and opportunity for all persons in the Armed Services without regard to race. ... There shall be created in the national Military Establishment an advisory committee to be known as the President's Committee on

Equality of Treatment and Opportunity in the Armed Services...the committee is authorized...to examine into the rules, procedures and practices may be altered or improved with a view to carrying out the policy of this order."[2]

Even though that order was in place and uncontested, almost two more years passed before the services, led first by the Air Force, began cutting through the deep roots of color prejudice and discrimination that had been thriving for centuries. Still, it was the military, not a city or town in the North or West or East that slowly, reluctantly showed the way by example, an example that is as highly profiled and proud today as its racially sullied post antebellum past. A direct and exclusive indictment of the military cannot be made because the military merely carried forward and continued the mores and practices of America. Now with the armed services showing the way, the rest of America is slowly, reluctantly beginning to follow suit with more than a little room left for more positive changes and equality for all minorities.

When WWII ended and demobilization of the services began, dozens of pilots with hundreds of flying hours, both fighters and bombers, started thinking of continuing their skills out of the military, namely within the budding airline industry. But the roots of racism and bigotry still held strong and long lasting. These expectant prospects were whip-sawed by the high profile of skin color. It was "yes" over the telephone but "no" in the face to face meetings. The airline pilot's union had its doors tightly shut in refusing to admit any African-Americans, and unless you currently belonged to the union the airlines steadfastly pointed to their outlet, there was no union membership or hiring. Of course blacks could be "skycaps" and "porters" or operate the shoeshine stand in the airport terminal and maybe graduate to baggage handlers but that was the upper limit. The old catch 22 game held until the mid-1950s, following WWII. Perry Young had earlier been among the cadre of black civilian flight instructors at Tuskegee before becoming a licensed helicopter pilot. New York Airways hired him. A scheduled helicopter line New York ferried passengers and cargo from suburban airports to a Manhattan heliport.[3] James Plinton, another of those dedicated civilian instructors at Tuskegee, hit the same airlines brick wall; so he and a partner, Maurice De Young, formed their own airline, Quisqueya, Ltd., a small interisland service with its main operation in Haiti. Their business prospered and thrived until the 1956, revolution in Haiti. This persuaded Plinton to contact a childhood friend who at the time was a captain for TWA. The friend, Robert Buck, introduced Plinton to TWA's bigwigs and thus began his career making him the first black to hold an executive position with a major airline. He remained at TWA for 15 years leaving only because a vice presidency spot always seemed to escape from his grasp when it should not have. Eastern Airlines quickly snapped up Plinton and there he rose to become the first black vice president of a major U.S. airline, a position he held until his retirement in 1979. Plinton recalled that at Eastern, "It wasn't a cake walk. I had to prove myself again and again." He said, "By some, I was resented because of my race. Some didn't know how to accept me as an equal, and some didn't want to accept me."[4]

What really began tearing down the racial barriers for black airline pilots was the long and protracted lawsuit filed in 1957, and won by Marlon Green in 1965, against Continental Airlines. Green, who had spent nine years in the Air Force, is credited with being the first black pilot hired by a major U.S. airline. Another of the early major airline hires, David Harris, would become captain for American Airlines as did Jack Noel. William Norwood was hired by United Airlines. Otis Young copiloted when Pan American made its inaugural flight in 1970, from London to Los Angeles with the biggest, most complicated plane of the time, the jumbo Boeing 747. By 1979, the Flying Tigers Airline boasted of ten black pilots in its ranks, the highest number in any company in the industry at the time.[5] Innovative Ed Daly of charter airline, World Airways, hired Bailey Pendergrass, Jr., as a first officer aboard a Boeing 707 in May 1967.

Black women also began taking to the air in increasingly responsible roles above flight attendants. Jill Brown, the U.S. Navy's first black female pilot, grabbed another distinction by becoming the first black woman pilot for a major commercial airlines company, Texas International Airlines. Marcella A. Hayes, the Army's first black woman pilot graduated in 1979 from Ft. Rucker, Alabama receiving her wings as a helicopter pilot. Hayes became the first black woman pilot in armed forces history.[6]

Shirley Tyus, a native of Spartanburg, South Carolina, became the first black female to fly for United Airlines. She began as a United Flight Attendant in 1972, with the overpowering urge to become a pilot. Working and taking pilot training, Tyus earned a commercial pilot's license in August 1979. With that license Tyus began flying cargo at night for the black-owned Wheeler Airlines in Raleigh, North Carolina while keeping her flight attendant's job. In 1985, she received the sought after Air Transport Pilot Rating that led to being hired as a pilot for advanced training by United Airlines in 1987.[7] Following Tyus, came Theresa Claiborne to United Airlines. Claiborne became the U.S. Air Force's first black female pilot graduating in 1983, at Laughlin AFB, Texas.[8] United hired her in February 1990, just months ahead of Stayce D. Harris. Born in June 1959, in Los Angeles, Harris was given an Air Force Reserve Officer Training Corps scholarship from the ROTC program at the University of Southern California. Upon completing the officer training program at the University of North Carolina, she was accepted by the Air Force for a pilot training scholarship. All was going well for Harris; she received her commission, then went on active duty to be trained as a pilot but suddenly her visual acuity fell below the 20/20 minimum.

Harris spent the next year and a half as a line officer. Then just as suddenly her eye sight, after another physical, returned to 20/20. Into the pilot training program she went, getting her training at Williams Air Force Base, Arizona. At the time no women were being allowed into fighter aircraft so she chose the C-141s at Norton AFB, in California. Norton closed in 1991, so Harris again became a reservist and the civilian part of her joined United Airlines about six months following Claiborne's hiring. Harris credits her success to the attitude of never giving up. She said, "I wake up every day as a black woman. That's my reality." Currently first officer of a Boeing 747 for United Airlines, Harris became the first black woman to command an active Air Force Flying Squadron when she was promoted to full Colonel and took command of the 729th Airlift Squadron in April 2002. As of this writing Harris made another giant step in becoming the first woman to take command of an Air Force Wing. On May 15, 2005, Colonel Harris took command of the 459th Air Refueling Wing at Andrews Air Force Base.[9] This step put her in direct line for a possible promotion to General. Not too shabby for having failing eye sight at one point of her career.

In existence since 1790, the U.S. Coast Guard admitted its first African-American in 1939, when renowned author Alex Haley enlisted in its ranks. Four years later in 1943, Joseph C. Jenkins became the Coast Guard's first African-American commissioned officer. In 1967, after 24 had years passed, Bobby C. Wilks emerged as the first black pilot for the Coast Guard. Although women were performing ground duties with the Coast Guard, it was not until 1977, that Janna Lambine became its very first female pilot. Lambine was a helicopter pilot stationed at Air Station, Astoria, Oregon where she participated in search and rescue missions as well as pollution and fisheries surveillance operations. Almost three decades later, Jeanine McIntosh, born in Jamaica, became the Guard's first African-American female pilot in 2005. McIntosh graduated from Florida International University and urgently wanted to join the Coast Guard after seeing its operations of rescue, law enforcement, and humanitarian flights. But she had two major hurdles to leap. Her eyesight was far below normal and she was deathly afraid of water. Taking a chance, she successfully underwent an eye operation that corrected her vision. The next step was the most difficult, overcoming her fear of the water in learning how to swim but McIntosh pushed herself hard enough to pass the Guard's tough swim test. At 26-years-old, Lieutenant J.G. McIntosh put her name in the record books by becoming the first female in the Coast Guard to fly the Hercules HC-130 search and rescue craft from Air Station Barbers Point, Hawaii. Commenting on her achievements Jeanine said she was aware that there are still barriers that need to be broken for African-Americans as well as for women in general.[10]

The Organization of Black Airline Pilots (OBAP), established in 1976, listed as of the end of 2003, some 1,800 black pilots, including 22 women, among the 87,000 pilots in the airline industry. In the early 1960s, this number totaled less than three. Progress has been made and is still being made as airlines now generally reach out to encourage minorities to come into the fold through various programs sponsored by individual airlines. Despite the progress there still remain hurdles or barriers that black aspirants must clear to get into and stay within the industry. OBAP president, Robert Brown, stated that OBAP had been directly responsible for the hiring of some 600 of the total number but the financial troubles of the industry had caused the furlough of approximately 300 black airline pilots. Brown said, "Black pilots are still the last hired and the first fired or the first to be furloughed off. It's the same old story."[11]

The direct flow of pilots from the military services has been heavily stemmed by the military, increasing the commitment times pilots must make in exchange for the millions of dollars it costs to train them. Earlier, there were two-year commitments but now, to protect their investments those terms have been increased by the military services to eight and ten years. The result has created a shortage as veteran captains reach the mandatory retirement age of 60.

In order to do justice to the exploits and accomplishments of the 477th Bombardment Group, that all-black group of bomber pilots who were denied the opportunity to prove their merits in combat as did the fighter pilots, we must mention some of the trials they had to face—trials that had nothing to do with flying skills or intelligence.

Numerous disparaging remarks came from the upper brass of the Air Force on the abilities and capabilities of black bomber pilots, the same kinds of resentful comments made of the innate deficiencies and genetic shortcomings of the black fighter pilots. Seemingly, each step from flight training to combat readiness had to be proved from day to day and week to week. Class 43-J graduated at Tuskegee on November 11, 1943, with 9 of the total class of 27 men receiving the multi-engine rating. As with the naming of the very first class of fighter pilots to graduate from Tuskegee, it should be equally as important to name the first scheduled class of bomber pilots and their listed home towns. Alphabetically they were; Herman R, Campbell, Jr., New York; Henri F. Fletcher, San Antonio, Texas; Perry E. Hudson, Jr., Atlanta, Georgia; Haldane King, Jamaica, New York; Vincent J. Mason, Orange, New Jersey; Harvey N. Pinkney, Baltimore, Maryland; Jerome D. Spurlin, Chicago, Illinois; William D. Tompkins, Fall River, Maryland, and Leslie A. Williams, San Mateo, California. There was an unscheduled training element subsequent to this group which will be clarified later.

Two weeks after graduation, these men, the nucleus of the first squadron of the four-squadron 477th Bombardment Group, were sent to Mather Field, California for their transition training in the B-25 medium bomber. Les Williams remembered that when the men arrived at Mather they were just newly graduated pilots taking transition training—no segregation—everything was open. Ironically, everyone got along just fine for a couple of weeks until a certain General Ralph Cousins came on a scheduled inspection tour. During the inspection, as the men passed in parade review General Cousins spotted some black faces among the officers. Seeing integration taking place he ordered the immediate institution of segregation in the officer's club where the men had previously taken all of their meals. That evening, at mealtime, Williams revealed the manner in which the segregation order took. "When we entered the officer's club for dinner they had placed a big round table off to one side with nine chairs around it. We immediately understood what had happened and refused to have our meals in a separate but equal fashion." Williams explained what he and the other men did in response to this racial snub. "We leaned those chair backs against the table in protest and drove in to town for our dinners. We left those chairs leaning against that table until the day we transferred from Mather." For their breakfast and snacks the men bought candy and peanuts from the PX for the two and a half weeks that remained in their transition training.[12] At completion of their transition it literally took months before there were full crews for any of the four squadrons. Typically a full crew would be from five to seven men, pilot, copilot, navigator, bombardier, radio operator, and gunners.

The significance here is that prior to this first scheduled class of nine multi-engine graduates there were none, zip! You either became a fighter pilot or nothing. It did not matter if a black pilot had thousands of civilian flying hours if he happened to be not suited as a fighter jock or he failed to graduate in his fighter class; he would be returned to his original unit. An example of not being suited would be a prospective pilot who was too tall, over six feet or one too heavy. Fighter plane cockpits did not favor those with large physical statures. This fact of physical size played a direct role on a group of graduated cadets who had already finished their transition training in the P-40 fighter and were preparing to leave Selfridge Field for their port of embarkation in New York.

Here another consequential shift from the normal course of practice was created by picking this special group. Nine officers from six different classes, because of their statures of six feet or over, were given the option of entering multi-engine transition in the B-25 medium bomber without any prior twin-engine training. Once that option was exercised, no vacillation or change was allowed. Several of the men, after seeing the B-25s up close had second thoughts and wanted to change their minds and stick with the fighters. Change was disallowed, this was a one-way street. These men would become the very first black pilots to actually transition in a medium bomber without following the normal course of multi-engine training. Alphabetically they were James Carter, 43-D; Bill Ellis and Daniel "Chappie"James, 43-G; Hubert Jones, 43-H; George Knox, 42-E; Jim Mason, 43-G; Charles Stanton, 43-A; Peter Verwayne, 42-K; and Charles Williams, 43-D. These nine later joined the earlier elements that had begun to form the nucleus of the long-time forming 477th Bombardment

Group even though these individuals had already been classified as fighter pilots.

This group also took its training at Mather Air Base under Air Corp instructors but without the advance training normally given to those in multi-engine. According to Bill Ellis, "Oh, we had fun going from a single engine fighter to a twin engine bomber. You know such things as sitting side by side in a two-seated airplane with a control wheel instead of a stick and having the darn throttle on the right side instead of on the left." Ellis mentioned other things like learning to land on two wheels with a nose wheel instead of the customary three-point landing with the P-40.[13] By the time 43-J had completed approximately more than half of its 100-hour transition time, two other classes totaling 30 multi-engine graduates had pinned on their wings at Tuskegee. The buildup of pilots for the bomber unit was finally underway. On the other hand the buildup would be drawn out over such an elongated period in swelling to four squadrons that the delay and protraction would try and test men beyond patience. Certainly without the multi-engine pilot there would be no need for copilots, navigators, bombardiers, or radiomen. No mixing of the races was allowed.

Like the 99th Fighter Squadron that preceded it, the 477th was not supposed to happen. The Air Force was forced to create the 477th solely to relieve the intense pressure constantly coming from the black press, the NAACP, the National Urban League, and others who followed the line of remarks and questions posed by Judge Hastie. Although sorely needed why no bomber pilots? The 477th became the pressure relief valve that the Air Force could point to and say, "see, we're training black bomber pilots." Unlike the fighter pilot's status of having one man in one airplane the bomber crews featured men working together in a larger confined space as a team. Their designed operation was to deliver a load of bombs on the enemy and return home in a condition that would allow the repetition of that sequence. The bombers were slower, less maneuverable, and more vulnerable to attack from the ground and air, therefore gun crews were needed at critical positions within the craft.

Many months passed after the activation of the 477th before it filled out enough to have approximately 12 to 16 planes in each of the four squadrons, the 616th, 617th, 618th, and 619th. Filled out means having a full crew for each airplane in every squadron. The first of many, many bases for the 477th began with Selfridge Field, Michigan, where, then base commander, Colonel William I. Boyd made it blatantly clear that black officers were not welcome at the base officer's club. This racial prohibition was enforced despite the governing Army regulation AR 210-10 stating that officer's clubs were open to all officers at a base.[14] Ultimately this enforced violation of the Army's own regulation led to the direct cause of the mutiny that later took place at Freeman Field. It seems as if Colonel Boyd, and later Colonel Robert Selway, one of the first two commanding officers of the 332nd Fighter

Group, forgot or neglected to consider the fact that they were dealing with intelligent men, men whose astuteness equaled or perhaps ranked superior to their own. These two commanding officers, with the full backing of their own superiors spent an enormous amount of time trying to devise ways and schemes to maintain the segregation patterns of the South on their bases. Somehow it mysteriously eluded these two commanding officers that the men of the 477th could also figure out ways to counteract and cerebrally deal with the various attempts to second-rate them as they fought to contribute their skills to the war effort.

It would be unfair to point out only Boyd and Selway, they were only two of the many in the horizontal grades and in the several vertical grades above them who fought to keep the War Department's doctrine of segregation in the armed services intact. It was easier to control the black enlisted man not because of a disparity in acumen but rather due to the wide gap in military rank. And as it turned out, the higher the rank the more difficult it became to enforce humility and denigration on the black officer. The Army Air Force hierarchy tried to play checkers in a game of chess where the opponents were not the typically thought of "hands on the plow handle" unlettered adversaries. The low esteem and spiteful hatred of blacks at that time had been so deeply ingrained that the power structure could only act as its individuals had grown up to believe, black skin, without doubt, had to be inferior to white skin.

Although the concept of the all-black bomber group had been on the drawing boards since June of 1943, it was not until January of 1944, that the 477th Bombardment Group became activated. Even then its political expediency was designed to give the War Department and the Army Air Force a tiny bit of breathing space from the relentless hounding coming from the NAACP and the black press. From the beginning no real intent of actually using the 477th existed; it served merely as an adjunct of appeasement to quiet that rumbling, annoying noise coming from the balcony. That is only one of the reasons the 477th remained horribly out of synchronization with the training of the vital crew members needed to make it truly operational for more than a year. There were constant delays, hitches, shortages, and duplication of training efforts, not to mention the pinball-machine-like transfers from base to base. Even after the group could have tested combat ready the Air Force brass kept scratching their heads over what to do with them. This was a medium bombardment group, not the type of weapon really needed in the European Theatre of Operations (ETO) although it could have been sent there to help bridge the gap created by the high casualty rate of the heavy bombers. The 332nd had already escorted medium bombers on their runs over the enemy so the 477th could have also been shipped out.

As stated earlier the bouncing pinball first stopped at Selfridge Field, Michigan outside Detroit. The setting was good for the crews but the commanding officers treated them as less than unwanted stepchildren.

There had already been troubles of a racial nature at Selfridge and on the arrival of the 477th, three black officers, not attached to the 477th, had made an unsuccessful attempt to enter the segregated officers' club. Sensing a larger potential problem the CO, now aware that the presence of the 477th might just aggravate the situation, decided to close the club.[15] Closure of the club removed all questions of who could enter and who would be refused entry on the basis of any distinction. But this presented another disagreeable quandary because now the white officers were also prevented from using the club. Instead of accurately trying to determine and understand the nature of the problems the base command staff and Air Force investigator immediately began pointing fingers at the outside. They blamed agitators from the Detroit area and "communist" sympathizers for fomenting all the troubles on the base. The commanding officer and his staff decided that the best solution lay in shipping the 477th out of there as soon as possible to break the connection of that off-base influence. The best place for these potential troublemakers would be back to the South, Godman Field, Kentucky, to be specific.

Godman Army Air Field was a rundown poorly maintained base, too small for the bombers; the runways sorely needed repair, they were too short, there was a shortage of hangar space, there was no range for air-to-ground gunnery, and on top of that the weather soon became so bad that flying training was cut by an estimated sixty percent. The official stated explanation for the move was that the weather at Godman would be better.[16] Godman did offer full use of all base facilities without restriction, but all the white officers were quartered at Fort Knox and used those facilities which could not be used by the men at Godman since they were not stationed there. Again, a classic example of defacto segregation that just by chance happened to align itself with the designed intent of racial separation by location.

The 477th had been moved to Godman in early May 1944, and by the following mid-January, with crew strength increasing, the group had amassed more than 17,000 flying hours with only two minor mishaps,[17] a very creditable record considering the far less than optimal conditions with which it had to contend. Still, because of the terrible conditions at Godman, the Training Command decided on yet another move to Freeman Field near the town of Seymour in southern Indiana in March 1945. By this time, the 477th had been pinballed from Walterboro to Selfridge to Sturgis to Atterbury and to Godman Fields thus making some 38 disruptive moves in training, with the major changes being from Selfridge to Godman to Freeman Fields. And each time the flipper whacked the pinball morale decreased and the discontent and resentment increased. All these unwarranted moves created just the opposite effect of what they were intended to achieve. Instead of keeping the men calm and in an honestly busy training mode to enter combat, a festering wound was being severely aggravated.

If the commanding officers had been observant and sensitive enough in understanding that the core of their troubles had not been created by the influence of "outside agitators" but rather by the deliberate maltreatment on the various bases, the nasty ordeal of Freeman Field would never have occurred. It did not take too many of those moves from base to base and pillar to post before the men realized that they were being "jerked" around and they, as quickly, reasoned why.

Despite having hundreds of flying hours behind them none of the black officers of the 477th ranked above major while, at the same time, the 477th was seen as a promotion generator for the white supervisors and trainers. One example given is that one white supervisor who had recently been promoted to captain managed to jump to major about a month after he had been assigned to the 477th.[18] Moreover, it was discovered that some of the men in the 477th had more flying time in the B-25 than some of the supervisors who were there to teach them all about handling the B-25.[19]

To get bad race relations off to a very good start, none other than Major General Frank O'D. Hunter, commanding officer of the First Air Force, which was over the 477th and Selfridge Field, stated to one of the black newspapers that, "Negroes can't expect to obtain equality in 200 years, and probably won't except in some distant future."[20] Hunter made certain that his appraisal and opinion of blacks was fully understood as the 477th settled in at Godman, " . . . I will not tolerate any mixing of the races and anyone who protests will be classed as an agitator, sought out, and dealt with accordingly."[21] With such demeaning and humiliating racial statements being made by top Air Force officers and those attitudes being carried out by the chain of command officers under them, the big blowout at Freeman Field had "guaranteed to take place" stamped all over it.

At Freeman, Colonel Selway, who had not learned from previous mistakes, concocted an elaborate scheme to keep the black officers from using the white officers' club. He designated Club Number 1 for trainee officers, who were all-black, and Club Number 2 for supervisors, all of whom were white. Actually, Club Number 1 had previously been a noncommissioned officers' club and was dubbed "Uncle Tom's Cabin" by the men of the 477th.[22] Thus, Selway thought that he had the perfect solution to keep the black officers, who were classified as trainees, from entering the white officers' club that was meant for supervisors and permanent base personnel only. After all the plotting and scheming he neglected to consider or complacently ignored the large flaw in this latest order. Among the base personnel were several other black officers, including a chaplain and a flight surgeon who were certainly not trainees, but they too were assigned to "Uncle Tom's Cabin."

Although Selway later became the scapegoat and narrowly skirted a reprimand for his actions at Freeman he always consulted with and was fully supported and encouraged by General Hunter as he sought to control the black surge for social equality. From the time the 477th had returned to Freeman, small groups of black officers continually tested the unwritten segregation policy of Club Number 2. They would arrive unannounced in groups of five, ten, or more, always polite, always courteous, always disciplined, and always properly dressed. Selway became increasingly agitated and made numerous phone calls to General Hunter for advice and support. On March 15, Selway addressed all of the 477th officers and informed them of General Hunter's order to maintain separate facilities, namely, Club Number 1 and Club Number 2. Announcement of that order became the tiny, one straw too many on the camel's back, the spark that would soon cause the explosion. Exactly three weeks later, Selway was tipped off by a phone call that there would be an attempt by more black officers, who had arrived from Godman that very afternoon, to enter the white club. He immediately ordered all doors except the main entrance locked and posted a guard from the Provost Marshall's office with orders to arrest any who tried to enter.[23] By early evening, the simmering cauldron had heated up to a full boil over. All the days, the weeks, and the month and months of taking it, the turning of the other cheek ended.

The date was April 5, 1945, and the time approximately 8:30 pm, and the place, the entrance to Club Number 2. Four properly dressed black officers approached that entrance and sought admission. Admission was denied and the four left without creating a ruckus. But a few minutes later a larger group of black officers brushed past the guard and gained entry. All of these men were ordered back to their quarters by the club officer and placed under house arrest. A short time later another group of officers pushed into the forbidden club and were similarly arrested. Within minutes a group of three more officers forced their way in and joined the others, arrested in quarters.[24] There was more to come. The next day another group of twenty-four officers entered the club. The Provost Marshall had forgotten to post a guard, but they were also arrested by the club officer. Colonel Selway, by now, was in a real dither. He anxiously, and with good reason, consulted with General Hunter about the course of action he should follow now that he had arrested so many black officers. He had given the soda bottle a good shaking, had his thumb over the opening, and he could feel the building pressure. What should he do now, remove his thumb and allow the pent up fluid to geyser out or try to keep that tiring thumb in place as a cap. His first act was to immediately close the club until the plan of action he should take had been fully clarified. With advice from First Air Force headquarters, Selway prepared a new base regulation, Base Regulation 85-2. That regulation specifically forbade any "trainees" from using Club Number 2. In addition, General Hunter ordered all officers to sign the new regulation indicating that they understood and agreed to it.[25]

But what came next was a totally unexpected negative blow to the schemes of First Air Force headquarters and General Hunter. The judge advocate general advised Colonel Selway that he had to release all of the arrested officers except the three who had allegedly used force to enter the club.[26] All the arrested men were released except for Lieutenants Shirley Clinton, Roger Terry, and Marsden Thompson who were charged with pushing a superior officer as they entered the club. In a written opinion to General Hunter, the air judge advocate stated that although segregation of buildings by base commanders was severely limited, individual officers would have no legal grounds of complaint. On the surface this appeared to be a safe and logical position, for it would allow base CO Selway to say that both clubs, in question, were essentially the same with one being just, perhaps, a temporary extension of the other.[27]

Each and every officer on the base was asked to sign Base Regulation 85-2. All of the white officers signed it and all but 101 black officers signed. A number of black officers signed some altered version of this order. These 101 determined men were then each read the 64th Article of War and individually ordered to sign the regulation in the presence of witnesses. The willful disobedience of a direct order under the 64th Article during a time of war carried the maximum penalty of death. All 101 men still refused to sign and were individually placed under house arrest. The next day (it was now near mid-April), the 101 renegades, which did not include the 3 who allegedly brushed a superior officer, were loaded aboard C-47s and flown back to Godman Field. While these men remained under arrest and under armed guards they could observe German prisoners of war moving about without restrictions. The German POWs laughed at the black officer arrestees.[28] After all, the POWs with big white letter "Ps" on their backs, had more freedom of movement than the black American officers. Besides spotlights, it had been originally planned to encircle the arrest area with barbed wire. Apparently someone forgot to put up the wire. Indeed, a very bitter pill presented itself to be swallowed by those who volunteered to serve their country against a common enemy, the same enemy who now on the other side of the imaginary barbed wire, had greater freedom than they. But that bilious pill defied swallowing absolutely and positively refused to go down.

What had begun as a craftily conceived subterfuge to keep the races separated at Freeman Field, by order of the commanding general, began to cave in on itself from the sheer numbers of men. They no longer were dealing with five or six men, officers who could be court-martialed for disobeying a direct order of a superior. Now there were more than one hundred awaiting their fate under quarters arrest for the same charge—refusing to sign a base regulation that seemed in conflict with Army Regulation 210-10. To make an unglamorous situation even more publicly shocking, the War Department then released statements regarding the arrests and completely ignored any input from First Air Force Commander General Hunter under whose command all these events had taken place.[29]

One of the first groups to spring into action was the McCloy Committee, a special advisory committee created within the War Department to formulate Negro Troop Policies. Headed by Assistant Secretary of War, John J. McCloy, the committee began an immediate investigation into the matter that also drew torrents of inquiries to the War Department, many from concerned senators and representatives. The committee gave due consideration to a report made by the Inspector General. After his investigation they deliberated the question that had sparked the mutiny, the segregation of base facilities. In its own report and recommendations the Air Force maintained that since blacks and whites throughout the nation did not normally socialize and fraternize they should not be forced on any base to do what they did not do in public life. In other words the Air Force wanted it clearly mandated that certain base facilities should remain segregated to maintain the norm of the country's standard.

The committee took the opposite stand to having segregated base facilities. But what the War Department finally issued was a tempered but clear cut position to be followed by all base commanding officers. The War Department stated that it was allowable and reasonable to have some separate facilities but such separations should not be based on race.[30]

That determination settled one part of the explosive question of segregation on bases but another enormous part remained unanswered, what to do with the 104 arrested black officers. The missing solution came forth quickly. Chief of the Air Staff, Major General Barney Giles recommended, and General George C. Marshall, Chief of Staff, agreed that the 101 officers should be released, all charges against them to be dismissed and they should all be given an administrative reprimand.[31] All the black officers were released except the three charged with touching the Assistant Provost Marshall in pushing their way into the club. The three Lieutenants were court-martialed but the outcome did not make either General Hunter or Colonel Selway happy in any way. Shirley Clinton and Marsden Thompson were members of base officers' personnel so they were found not guilty of any of the charges. Only Roger Terry was found guilty and fined $50 a month for three months. Yet, those administrative reprimands remained for years on the records of all those who had been under quarters arrest. It came only from the persistent and diligent efforts of James C. Warren, one of the 101, who doggedly pointed out the wrongness that had been perpetrated in the futile efforts to perpetuate segregation in the military. After his retirement from the Air Force as a Lieutenant, Colonel Warren dug and delved through piles of classified documents to come up with the proper evidence in order to file for the correction of his military record and have the letter of reprimand removed by expungement. In fact, it took years before the Air Force would agree that it was wrong. Not until August 1995, did the Air Force agree to expunge the letters of reprimand from the records of the 101 men by allowing them, or their families to submit a form DD149 requesting a correction of records.[32] At the time of this writing only an estimated 26 requests, approximately 25 percent, had been filed and granted. And it now seems more than likely that the others will never file for a correction. In fact some have absolutely refused to submit a request saying they would rather see that eternal embarrassment to the Air Force remain as a matter of record.

At the time of the so-called mutiny there were some 425 black officers at Freeman and it was not until days later that those who had refused to sign realized that three quarters of their number had, in some manner, signed the infamous order. Asked about the general attitude of the nonsigners toward those who had signed, Jim Warren said, "We were not at all happy with the guys who knuckled under and signed that damned illegal document. We had hoped for a unified front in opposing the segregated practices being carried out in defiance to AR 210-10. We didn't think they were afraid, they were just more interested in protecting their individual behinds." Warren, in filing for his correction request, also filed to have the records of the other 100 expunged as well as having the court martial conviction of Bill Terry reversed.

Lest it be overlooked or slighted, the serious troubles leading up to the rebellious refusal of 101 black officers to sign a document under direct orders from a superior officer did not begin at Freeman Field, Indiana. The actual seeds of resentment had been sown much earlier in 1943, at Selfridge Field when General Hunter had ordered that the only officers club on the base be reserved for white officers. He said the black officers would just have to wait until one was constructed for their use.[33] Hunter's order mushroomed, it became more than a mere flap and eventually caused the then base commanding officer, Colonel William Boyd, to be officially repri-manded. Hunter's order was repudiated by a large number of black officers who entered the restricted club to be arrested. That is when the cauldron really began boiling, or perhaps, seething more accurately describes the vicious battle between command's attempted control and the black officers' demand of social justice. General Hunter tried unsuccessfully to have the blame for issuing that order shifted to him but Air Force Headquarters in Washington adamantly pressed forward. It had been extremely vexed and embarrassed by all the unwanted publicity surrounding the Selfridge Field uproar.

Hunter's order, which Colonel Boyd had carried out, fully ignored and subverted AR 210-10 which stated in part "[N]o officers club, mess, or similar social organization of officers will be permitted by the post commander to occupy any part of any public building, other than the private quarters of an officer, unless such club, mess, or other organization extends to all officers on duty at the post the right to full membership."[34]

Unwittingly, Boyd became the sacrificial scapegoat for carrying out his superior's orders, and his punishment could not be turned aside or softened by his boss. The gist of the reprimand stated in part "...racial discrimination against colored officers...was due to your conduct in denying to colored officers the right to use the Officer's Club...Such action is in violation of Army Regulations and explicit War Department instructions. ...You are hereby formally reprimanded and admonished that any future action on your part will result in your being subjected to the severe penalties prescribed."[35]

This would be the burr under the saddle of the horse that the Air Force hierarchy desperately tried and wanted to ride. The regulation stated "all officers" without restriction as to color or grade but the Air Force Commanders wanted to sidestep the intent of the regulation without actually amending it as had been done with the 14th and 15th amendments to the constitution in order to specifically include Negroes as part of America's citizenry.

General Hunter, a two-star general, the commanding officer of the First Air Force, headed thousands of men but his cast-in-concrete attitude and contempt of black troops only served to place him in a hopelessly embarrassing position. It must be remembered that his subordinate ranking officers followed his directions not under duress or with objection, but willingly because they too agreed with the ill-founded concept of segregation as well. At both Selfridge and Freeman Fields, blacks were squelched and blocked from promotions. No black was allowed to outrank a white even if the black had acquired combat experience and his white counterpart had not. Blacks were allowed to be mechanics but none could become a crew chief. It did not matter how skilled or how much competence a black exhibited he was not considered as good as a less competent white. If a white received a promotion and moved up to another job position, another white replacement would be given his former position.[36]

For following the leader, Colonel Boyd received a stern official reprimand. Next, in almost an identical scenario, Colonel Selway somehow dodged the ricocheting projectile that had felled Colonel Boyd. The McCloy Committee report determined that Selway had acted properly in arresting the 101 officers but it found that his action of segregating the two clubs was wrong. It further requested that the Air Force Inspector General's report, which was favorable to Selway, be returned so that its nonconformity with AR 210-10 and policies established by the War Department itself be pointed out to the commanding general of the Air Forces.[37] As it turned out, Selway came dangerously close to a reprimand but instead he was replaced as commander of the 477th by none other than Colonel Benjamin Davis, Jr. Not only was Selway replaced, the entire command structure at Freeman was staffed with blacks by order of General Arnold. What came next was containment and the whole unit shipped out to Godman once more. It was a case of segregation again but this time it became concentrated to the highest degree possible. It was a fully segregated base but for the very first time in U.S. history, a black man became commander of a military base, and all of the subordinate command officers of the base were black.

It is difficult to look at the two incidents of Seflridge and Freeman as they happened, and in chronological order, and not wonder how or why General Hunter anticipated seeing a different outcome stemming from the same reasons at Freeman. There was and is an order of command and although Hunter was near the top, we see the operational word "near," as he was not at the top. Ahead of him were the Air Staff Chief, General Giles, Air Force Chief, General Arnold, Army Chief of Staff, General George Marshall, the War Department and of course, President Franklin D. Roosevelt. Hunter remained bitter for years later because he had been boxed in, unable to fully exercise his considerable powers by the likes of his own superiors that led him to imply that his orders ultimately came from, "...orders from...Mrs. Roosevelt."[38]

This less than full description of some of the humiliation that the members of the 477th had to endure attempts to balance the contributions they were attempting to give in a time of war with those of the black fighter pilot units. Obviously that cannot be done using the same rule of measurement but a kind of equivalence can be readily seen in the skirmishes and battles that both fought just for the privilege of preparing to fight. Of the 450 black fighter pilots who entered combat, 66 were killed in action. There is no balancing type of measure that can equal that kind of tragedy but then consider that 101 black officers refused to sign a document under direct order by a superior officer in a time of war. They fully understood that the maximum penalty for that refusal could be death.

The denigration continued right up to the very end of the war. After years of protracted delays and moves, the 477th was close to combat ready at Godman Field and General Ira Eaker, at the change of command ceremonies, told the men that they would soon be able to do what they had trained so hard to do, in the Pacific Theater of action. If the war had not ended as it ultimately did, the action Eaker promised would surely have taken place. But it would have come over the objections of Air Force Chief General Arnold and General George C. Kenney, Air Force commander in the Pacific. General Douglas Mac Arthur, commander in chief in the Pacific, was willing to have the all-black 477th there but General Kenney balked because he would have to formulate plans to segregate it from any white units. Kenney had already seen what critical storms segregation attempts had produced in the states and probably envisioned the squalls that would be generated by having black and white bomber groups operating from one of his segregated bases. It would certainly seem more than a little odd and unique to have black and white bomber groups fighting the same enemy, operating the same planes from the same bases, but flying, fighting, and dying on a segregated basis. So, although the 477th Bombardment Group was never allowed to enter combat, its members fought at a different level for dignity and equality, and paradoxically the enemy came not from one of the Axis Nations but from within the very heart of the country they called home. The enemy was not in front of their guns or below their bomb racks, the enemy stood alongside of and in front of them in positions of authority and command.

It must be said that the Tuskegee Airmen led such a forceful and successful assault against the bastions and pillars of segregation and racism in the military services, that the entire system for perpetuating and keeping those demeaning twins intact was ripped asunder and destroyed.

With the crumbling of the color walls at the end of WWII, black men and women have since made gigantic strides in all areas of their endeavors and these strides have been based on individual abilities. Looking only at segments of the space programs, I would mention some of those pioneers who have participated, such as Dr. Guion Stewart Bluford, Jr., who was the first African-American into space. Holding a doctorate in aerospace engineering, Bluford was selected as an astronaut after accumulating 144 fighter pilot missions in Vietnam. There is a prelude to Bluford's historic achievement. Edward Dwight had been picked in 1962, as the first African-American to enter the space program. Amid rumors, allegations, and accusations of racism, Air Force veteran pilot Dwight was put on hold and then dropped from the program. He resigned from the Air Force four years later. With a doctorate in nuclear chemistry, Robert Lawrence had been picked as an astronaut in 1967, while he was an Air Force Major but Lawrence tragically lost his life in an aircraft accident before he could enter the space program. Isaac T. Gillam, IV, a Special Assistant for Space Transportation Systems at the National Aeronautics and Space Administration (NASA) became Director of the Dryden Flight Research Center at Edwards Air Force Base where he also served as Director of Shuttle Operations. Dr. Ronald E. McNair, with a doctorate in physics from MIT, was tragically killed along with six of his crewmates in the January 1986 explosion of Challenger on its tenth mission. Frederick D. Gregory, a 1964 graduate of the Air Force Academy, was the first African-American to command a space shuttle mission, Discovery, on its August 1989 flight. Gregory also became Director of Contingency Operations at Edwards Air Force Base when the space shuttle Columbia was launched.[39] Charles F. Bolden, Jr., a 1968 graduate of the U.S. Naval Academy, a Major General in the Marine Corps, became the fourth black astronaut in 1981. He officially retired with that rank in August of 2004. Bolden flew four space missions and was the pilot of the Space Shuttle Discovery that successfully deployed the Hubble Space Telescope while setting an orbiting altitude record of 400 miles. On his third mission he was commander of the Space Shuttle Atlantis. He became the Commanding General of the 3$^{rd}$ Marine Aircraft Wing in August 2000, while stationed in Southern California.

The African-American distaff side could not be kept out of the space programs any more than the earlier releases from earthbound activities.

Mae C. Jemison, the youngest of three siblings, was born in 1956 to Charlie and Dorothy Jemison, a maintenance worker and teacher in Decatur, Alabama. Jemison received a degree in chemical engineering from Stanford University in 1977. She was turned down on her first application to NASA but proceeded to earn a medical degree from Cornell University in 1981. Jemison applied to NASA a second time and was accepted for the program in 1987, as one of only 15 successful candidates out of some 2,000. She completed her astronaut training in August 1988, and became the first black woman to travel into space taking her place in history with the four black males who preceded her. After leaving NASA, Jemison spent time teaching at Dartmouth University and eventually formed her own technology company.[40]

There were other black civilians, such as Neal Loving and John Greene, Jr., who were strongly and determinedly involved in flying and in aviation during WWII. Loving tragically lost both legs below the knee in a glider accident but went on to fly planes and design them as well. In his autobiography, Loving points out that he and Charles Lindbergh, the first man to make a solo flight across the Atlantic, had the same birth dates. Loving, after earning a degree in engineering from Wayne State University at the age of 45, continued to design planes and have a distinguished career as an aerospace research engineer. He designed the several models of gliders and planes which he flew and also, historically, became the first black double amputee to qualify as a racing pilot by the National Aeronautic Association and the Professional Racing Pilots Association. Loving not only designed and raced one of his own airplanes, he created an airplane that was convertible and roadable for highway use.[41] Lest it be criticized as oversight, Loving was not the only black to design and pilot his own aircraft. The very same Lewis Jackson who came to Tuskegee as an instructor under Chief Anderson also designed a number of experimental aircraft including a number that were operable on the highway as well as in the air. Jackson, with a doctorate in education, became President of Central State University in Ohio after the war.[42]

It can be said with absolute assurance that the contributions, the exploits, and the sacrifices, some of them the ultimate, made by the Tuskegee Airmen ripped the massive door of segregation from its hinges so that all who wished could enter. They also proved that "their place" was alongside fellow Americans of whatever color and of whatever endeavor.

The historical fact of blacks flying and learning to fly despite opposition is well recorded. These early efforts had little weight or impetus primarily because of the comparatively small numbers. Only after approximately a 1000 black military pilots were trained along with the thousands of aeronautical technicians did the battering ram become meaningful. Although during a time of war, this blunt increase in numbers lends full and admiral support to the old but credible expression of there being strength in numbers.

The term Tuskegee Airmen includes all, the men and the women, who helped in the valiant effort of winning a bare knuckles battle for human justice in America. It was not just the pilots, the technicians, the officers, the office typists, or the many civilians who contributed to the war effort, the total combination must be credited. That battered and battle-scarred door has remained open. The way, however, is still not smooth. Complex and subtle difficulties still arise seeking alternate negative routes leading to reversals of progress. Concealed dangers continue to bristle along this still narrow pathway, but opportunities do arise for those determined to go through it.

It should be pointed out that a work of this size could not possibly include all of the events and names of those black men and women whose achievements and accomplishments aided in the broad advancements that have led to the spreading of black wings in the blue skies. While an earnest attempt has been made to present as many of the stories and events involving the people ignored or forgotten by reason of perceived stature of importance, here too, much more will forever remain untold. There are so many who have contributed and so many who continue to contribute to the once isolated realm of flying as to present an impossible task to name all. And the inexorable advance and passage of time cannot be held or even slowed to allow the thousands of unnamed individuals to recall and relate their exciting personal histories. Sadly this means that, literally, many thousands of pieces of this total picture will never be filled in, never mentioned, or preserved for future reference, forever lost to the generations that follow.

# Notes

**Chapter 1: The Early Days**

1. Merriam-Webster's Collegiate Encyclopedia, q.v. "Daedalus."

2. Ibid. q.v. "Montgolfier."

3. Nancy Winters, *Man Flies:Master of the Balloon* (New Jersey: Ecco Press, 1997) 46–50. Like Da Vinci, Santos-Dumont appears to have been far ahead of his time with designs of airplanes that came to be built many years later.

4. William H. Longyard, *Who's Who in Aviation History* (Novato, CA: Presidio Press, 1994) 115. An alphabetical rendering of some of the most prominent names in aviation, but some such as Bessie Coleman and less prominent Charles Wesley Peters, the first black pilot, are not included.

5. James H. Jones, *Bad Blood: The Tuskegee Syphilis Experiment* (New York: Free Press, 1993) Horrifying exposure of illiterate Alabama blacks infected with a life threatening disease and being studied, without treatment or their knowledge of the progressive seriousness of nontreatment by the U.S. Public Health Service.

6. David A. Price, *Love and Hate in Jamestown* (New York: Alfred A. Knoph, 2003) 194–199. Brings out the recording of the first Africans purchased for slavery in the new American colonies. Reveals that some freed slaves themselves were slave owners.

7. Ibid.

8. Esmond A. Wright, et al., *History of the World: The Last Five Hundred Years* (UK: Bonanza Books, 1984) 456. Southern states fought to preserve slavery as a way of life and as a profitable venture after the northern states stopped. Scores of issues surfaced for thousands of blacks with the end of slavery and the Civil War. Freedom was precarious and unstable.

9. Gunnar Myrdal, *An American Dilemma* (New York: McGraw-Hill, 1964) Vol 1., 100. Explains why so many deliberate falsehoods debasing Negroes were perpetuated as extensions of White superiority.

10. Ibid. 91. nb. Relates how a medical student's false test results on Negro cadavers were uncovered and exposed by his own professor.

11. Noel F. Parrish, *The Segregation of Negroes in the Army Air Forces* (Dissertation for Air Command and Staff School, May 1947) Points out some of the myths of racism dealing with Negro athletes and how scientific analysis revealed the truth. Physical attributes of black sprinter Jesse Owens are compared to that of the white sprinter Frank Wycoff.

12. Army War College, Office of the Commandant (Memorandum for Chief of Staff) *The Use of Negro Manpower in War:* Washington, DC, October 30, 1925. An insightful look into how the AWC regarded black soldiers and black officers using biased approaches which essentially concluded that blacks were subhuman.

13. Ibid.

14. Otto Klineberg, *Characteristics of the American Negro* (New York: Harper and Bros, 1944) 36. Comments on the factors left out that could make major differences in test scores, a different picture of blacks being at the bottom of the intellectual scale as put forward by the AWC.

15. Parrish, *Segregation of Negroes,* 10–11. Recites the confused efforts to keep test results of black and white soldiers under wraps because the results were contrary to those wanted.

16. Alan M. Osur, *Blacks in the Army Air Forces During World War II: The Problem of Race Relations* (Office of Air Force History, September 1975) 8. The Army refused to make any attempt at curing the social ills afflicting this country's posture on race relations.

17. Alan L. Gropman, *The Air Force Integrates,1945–1964* (Special Studies, Office of Air Force History, November 1976) 5. War Department policy was clearly stated–keep the races separate because that is the way it had always been.

18. Le General Robineau, "Biographies taken from the military records of two black men who fought for the French," Armee de L' Air, Service Historique; Chateau de Vincennes (1994) The biographies of Sosthene Mortenol and Eugene Bullard indicate that black men were fighting in leadership roles prior to and successfully flying during WWI. Mortenol was a French subject while Bullard was an American.

19. Ibid.

20. James Wakefield Burke, "The Black Eagle," *The Retired Officer* (May 1984) The world's first black pursuit pilot flew with great success for the French but was racially shunned by the United States Army Air Corps. In August 1994, 77 years after that rejection and racial snub and 33 years after his death the U.S. Air Force posthumously commissioned Bullard as a second lieutenant.

21. Robineau, French military's official comment on the value and valor of Bullard and his complete rejection by the U.S. Army Air Corps.

22. Doris L. Rich, *Queen Bess: Daredevil Aviator* (Washington, DC: Smithsonian Institution Press, 1993). The moving story of a black manicurist who successfully defied the twin barriers of color and sex in becoming the first black woman in the world to be licensed to fly with gusto and bravado.

23. Betty Kaplan Gubert, *Invisible Wings* (Connecticut: Greenwood Press, 1994) Bibliographical compilations of a number of black Americans who became aviators between 1916–1963.

24. William R. Scott, "Days of the Brown Condor," *Pan-African Journal* (April 1988) Details part of the life of John Robinson who flew in the war between Ethiopia and Italy after another black pilot had earlier soured the Ethiopian emperor.

25. George Edward Barbour, "Early Black Fliers of Western Pennsylvania; 1906–1945," *Western Pennsylvania Historical Magazine* (April 1986) Lists a host of African-Americans who learned to fly in Pennsylvania marking that state as the primary American cradle for would-be black fliers.

26. James L. H. Peck, Interviewed by author, June 1994. Peck verified flying for the Loyalists during the Spanish Civil War and becoming an ace. He was not wanted by the U.S. Army Air Corp or the U.S. Naval Air Service because of his race despite being a combat veteran.

## Chapter 2: Breaking the Barrier

1. Barbour, "Early Black Fliers," Details about the first black man to build and fly his own airplane not long after the Wright Brothers historic flight.

2. Ibid.

3. Gubert, "Invisible Wings," Names the first black pilot licensed by the US and the two black men who made the first transcontinental jaunt from Los Angeles to New York in 1932.

4. Von Hardesty and Dominick Pisano, *Black Wings: The American Black* in *Aviation* (Washington, DC: National Air and Space Museum, 1983) Strong pictorial presentation of blacks moving into the field of aviation despite the overall efforts to keep them out.

5. Stanley Sandler, *Segregated Skies* (Washington, DC: Smithsonian Institution, 1992) First black to earn a commercial license after buying his own airplane and paying for flying lessons in United States. Here again the state of "Brotherly Love" led all others in offering training to blacks.

6. Hardesty, *Black Wings*. Pictures the first black man ready to fly a US airmail route in 1938 yet the elitism would keep blacks from flying for the military until the Air Corps was so harried and pressured to accept them.

7. Gubert, *Invisible Wings*, 46–51. First US black female to become a commercial pilot and her pilot husband, the first black licensed airplane mechanic, opened a flight school with the thought of training more blacks.

8. Ibid.

9. Robert A. Rose, *Lonely Eagles*, (Los Angeles, 1976) 10 Cites flight of Chauncey Spencer and Dale White from Los Angeles to Washington, DC and their chance meeting with then senator Harry Truman who promised to help their efforts. This flight and meeting were important aspects of blacks entering a government financed training program.

10. Osur, *Blacks in the Army Air Forces*, 15. President Roosevelt made appointments just before election day to strengthen his chances of a third term reelection and it paid off with the first three term presidential election in history.

11. Gropman, *Air Force Integrates*, 7. Chief of Air Corps was dead set against having black officers over white enlisted men while at the same time the Secretary of War predicted that Negroes would fail in their attempt at pilot training.

12. AWC, conclusions gave all possible negative attributes possible to Negroes such as unmorality, lying, having weak character and most damning, they were cowards.

13. Osur, *Blacks in the Army Air Forces*, 8–9. The U.S. Supreme Court ruling of 1896, the separate but equal doctrine, was a further stanchion supporting the pillars of segregation.

14. Wright, *History of World*, 283. Indicates population growth of colonies over span of 27 years with both black and white almost doubling by the time of first official census.

15. Sandler, *Segregated Skies*, 4–7. Blacks fighting in the civil war and the Spanish-American War between 1863–1898 indicate that black and white military personnel fought and lived alongside of each other.

16. Myrdal, *American Dilemma*, 8–9. Relates how American Creed developed with the central threads being equality, liberty, and Christianity but for convenience Negroes were not allowed into that circle to be accorded the precepts of the Creed.

17. Ibid. Introduction, lxxiii.

18. Wright, *History of World*, 672. The United States was eventually actively and officially forced into WWII.

19. Osur, *Blacks in the Army Air Forces*, 21–22. The Air Corps continued its stalling to keep Blacks out of its ranks even though PL 18 had designated one school to train them.

20. George L. Washington, "Unpublished papers, History of Military and Civilian Pilot Training of Negroes at Tuskegee, Alabama, 1939–45," Although Tuskegee became the aviation giant among the other black colleges, its application for the CPT program was initially turned down. At least two major concessions were made to allow Tuskegee into the program.

21. Ibid. His words indicate the custom of currying a favor request from a black to a southern white man.

22. Chattanooga News-Free Press, (April 21, 1940) White reporter marvels at the test scores and the apparent exceptional flying abilities of Tuskegee's students.

23. Washington, Concessions given to Tuskegee began to backfire because the maximum travel distance was being exceeded by four times the limit. The school was starting to come out of pocket to pay for the program.

24. Ibid. Tuskegee had to enlist the help of all-white Alabama Polytechnical Institute in order to conduct its secondary flight classes.

25. Edward C. Ambler, *History of Tuskegee Army Air Field, Tuskegee, Alabama, From Conception to 6 December 1941*, 26. TAAF base historian Ambler suggests that a large amount of politicking (unwritten and unrecorded actions) took place that governed the founding of the all-black military flying center for the Air Corps.

26. Ibid.

27. Washington, Unannounced visits by one of the CAA's heads signaled definite leanings in the battle to secure secondary flight training for Tuskegee rather than Chicago.

28. Robert J. Jakeman, *The Divided Skies, Establishing Segregated Flight Training at Tuskegee, Alabama, 1934–1942* (Tuscaloosa, Alabama; University of Alabama Press, 1992) 246–248. Shows that without the considerable influential help of First Lady Eleanor Roosevelt, Tuskegee's role in securing secondary CPTP would have ended.

29. Osur, *Blacks in the Army Air Forces*, 25–26. The Aviation Battalions, as they were called, were Air Corps' way, sort of repositories, in absorbing its required allotment of blacks without allowing any technical training.

30. Ambler, *History of Tuskegee*, 1–2. Original intent for Tuskegee was to have all white supervisors in leading training programs until blacks could be trained to replace them.

31. Washington, 102–103. The search for land to build TAAF in Tuskegee was stymied by aggressive and strong opposition from Tuskegee town officials. There was apprehension to having heavily armed blacks in their midst.

32. Ambler, *History of Tuskegee*, 5–6. Announcement of segregated training for Negroes divided black community into two bitter camps; one side wanted only full integration while the other side saw segregated training as the proverbial foot in the door.

33. Ibid. The site board's recommendations indicate the heavy guiding influence Tuskegee Institute was expected to have in the training and conditioning of blacks on

how they should conduct themselves in the Deep South. This was the posture of being accommodating.

34. Ibid. With pressure so great on the White House and the War Dept. there was great urgency to find a suitable site for TAAF immediately.

35. Washington, 166. With the Washington, DC Headquarters decision to let Tuskegee have the secondary training program, the president of Tuskegee Institute turned thumbs down on letting Chicago in on any of the proposed expansions in training by the Air Corps. President Patterson was solidly in the camp of segregated training as an acceptable beginning

36. Ibid. 238–240.One black construction firm refused to cooperate with another, preferring instead to subcontract with a white firm. No printed evidence indicates why McKissack and his company refused to join forces with the Alexander and Repass firm.

## Chapter 3: Training Begins

1. Robert Wilson, Interview by author, Berkeley, CA, May, 1994.

2. Fred McLaurin, Interview by author, Berkeley, CA, May, 1994.

3. George Porter, Interview by author, Berkeley, CA, June, 1994. Printed biography supplied by interviewee.

4. Luther Pugh, Interview by author, Berkeley, CA, June, 1994.

5. Rose, *Lonely Eagles*, 16–17. Some of the personal traits and expectations of the men in the first class of black cadets at Tuskegee ends with some totally unexpected outcomes.

6. Ambler, *History of Tuskegee*, 30–34. The first men to graduate and the raw conditions that faced both the cadets and the instructors during the first months of TAAF's existence gave proof of the determination and perseverance leading to success.

7. Ibid. 5. Appendix I. Comments on the ribbing the first base commander took from fellow officers because he wanted Tuskegee to be first class and the reaffirmation of Tuskegee's president not allowing Chicago to have or participate in any part of the training.

8. Sandler, *Segregated Skies*, 19. The NAACP took a very firm stand against segregation and maintained it without waffling or accepting the concept of a segregated military.

9. Gropman, *Air Force Integrates*, 9–10. Judge Hastie was kept in the dark like an unwanted figurehead and decisions in matters that he had been selected to participate in, were made without his knowledge and collaboration. This exclusion led to his ire and resignation.

10. Osur, *Blacks in the Army Air Forces*, 36. Chief of the Air Staff began to make major changes in the way blacks were to be treated in the Air Corps by removing some previous barriers and changing earlier practices.

11. Washington, 217. Biographical sketch of Colonel Parrish compared to Colonel Von Kimble. Kimble was born in Oregon and Parrish in Kentucky and their attitudes toward Negroes were virtually diametrically opposed.

12. Parrish, *Segregation of Negroes*, 2. In his dissertation Parrish focused on the dangers a prejudiced officer presents to troops under his command.

13. Ibid. 8. Relates some of the questions asked by those who should have been more knowledgeable in the upper echelons of government and in the military about Negroes and flying. Humorous today, the questions at the time reflected the thinking of white Americans, in general, in their views of blacks.

## Chapter 5: Learning to Fly

1. Wendell Lipscomb, Interview by author, Berkeley, CA. May 1996.

2. Another source, Charles F. Frances, "The Tuskegee Airmen," (Branden Publishing, 1993) 301. Indicates that Captain Pruitt may have been killed because the passenger in the rear cockpit may have panicked and grabbed the control stick when Pruitt tried a victory roll near the ground. Captain Pruitt had performed that maneuver many times previously although flying a more powerful plane.

3. Adolph Moret, Interview by author, Santa Rosa, CA. August 1994.

## Chapter 6: Making Changes

1. LeRoy F. Gillead, Interview by author, Berkeley, CA, June 1994. Gillead was in the first class of navigators to be trained after the Air Corps decided to train bomber pilots in mid-1943.

2. Harold J. Hoskins, Interview by author, Danville, CA, May 2004. Hoskins was a member of the Air Force's second integrated class following WWII. He also had trained at Tuskegee as the war ended but left the service before completing his training there.

3. Hardesty, *Black Wings*, 62–63. The Air Force and the Navy removed all doubt that black and white military personnel could train, work, live, and die side by side in perfect harmony.

4. Gubert, *Invisible Wings*, 134–135. Mentions both Jesse Brown and Earl L. Carter, the latter becoming the first black jet pilot for the Navy.

5. Frank E. Petersen, Jr., http:www.au.af.mil/au/goe/eaglebios/96bio/peters.htm, 2005. Accessed on October 1, 2006.

6. Gubert, *Invisible Wings*, 222. Gives partial biography of U.S. Army's first black female helicopter pilot.

## Chapter 7: Fighter Training

1. Sandler, *Segregated Skies*, 125–126. The beginning of serious racial troubles at Freeman Field amplify with the base commanding officer attempting to keep black officers from using the base officers club.

## Chapter 8: Changing Cockpits

1. Sandler, *Segregated Skies*, 123. One of the early 99th pilots got into a fisticuffs fight with the Walterboro mayor that caused quite a ruckus with strong after ripples.

2. Gropman, *Air Force Integrates*, 29–30. The 477th group is purposely kept out of combat because of the racism still affecting and distorting the thinking of commanding officers.

3. John W. Kitchens, *They Also Flew; Pioneer Black Army Aviators* (U.S. Army Aviation Digest, September/October 1994) A two part series on black liaison pilots of WWII. Dr. Kitchens was Aviation Branch Command Historian at the Fort Rucker, Alabama Army Aviation Center. Describes training of the little known and rarely mentioned black pilots who flew with the infantry as artillery observers.

4. Sherman Smith, Interview by author, Seaside, CA, October 2003. Smith was one of the group of men who flew dangerously for the infantry.

5. Kitchens, *They Also Flew*, States how Charles Brown, the first black liaison pilot was recalled to active duty after WWII to Korea and while recommended for the

Distinguished Flying Cross his commanding officer refused to sign the recommendation saying that as a black officer Brown already had enough medals.

6. William Moulden, Interview by author, Palo Alto, CA, May 1994.

7. Oliver Lanaux, Interview by author, Oakland, CA, October 2000.

8. Ira O'Neal, Interview by author, Berkeley, CA, October 1998.

9. Florence Murray, *The Negro Handbook*, (Current Reference Publications, New York, 1944) 10. A Tuskegee U.S. Army Air Corps nurse was, after allegedly being beaten and jailed by Montgomery city police, given no recourse because the U.S. Justice Deptartment investigated and reported it found no grounds for prosecution. This shameful incident occurred about a decade before Rosa Parks made headlines.

10. Osur, *Blacks in the Army Air Forces*, 54. A CO, inebriated, acted just as he might have during slavery days toward a black soldier under his command.

## Chapter 9: Combat

1. William A. Campbell, Interview by author, Seaside, CA, October 2003.

2. Rose, *Lonely Eagles*, 56. The 99th squadron intensified its training in North Africa with brand new airplanes. This training along with the previous hours accumulated as the Air Corps stalled in sending the unit into combat pushed the total number of flying hours for each of the men far above what they would have normally entered combat with.

3. Campbell, See note 1.

4. Sandler, *Segregated Skies*, 48. Commander of fighter group gave negative grades to the 99th in their initial engagements with the enemy. He made no effort to help or offer the means to correct any deficiencies in his unwarranted criticisms.

5. Osur, *Blacks in the Army Air Forces*, 49. Colonel Momyer's negative quote of the abilities of the 99th under combat conditions completely ignores the unit's lack of having seasoned mentors pointing out the tricks and tactics they should or could have used.

6. Ibid. Gen. House Made more negative remarks and recommended assigning the 99th to coastal patrol duties out of the combat areas.

7. Sandler, *Segregated Skies*, 50–51. A command staff officer revised Gen. Hap Arnold's negative letter to President Roosevelt and then he capped that change with a warning and his own positive recommendations.

8. Ibid. 53–54. The 99th was assigned to a group whose commander gave the men the first experienced mentoring they needed for combat by having them fly together with his men. That was exactly what Colonel Momeyer should have done earlier rather than post negative remarks.

9. Rose, *Lonely Eagles*, 64. The first 99th member to be killed in combat action.

10. Charles E. Francis, *Tuskegee Airmen*, (Boston, 1993) 67. More casualties struck the 99th as their combat involvement increased.

11. Rose, *Lonely Eagles*, 65. Leadership changes were made for the 99th when Col. Davis was called back to stateside to testify in rebuttal of the negative evaluations given to the 99th.

12. Francis, *Tuskegee Airmen,* 59. Cites the historical first of air power alone causing an enemy to capitulate during a war.

13. Richard Caesar, Interview by author, San Francisco, October 2003.

14. Osur, *Blacks in the Army Air Forces,* 55. A commanding officer threatened his subordinate black officers from entering the base officers club. More of the designed policy to keep the wall of segregation intact.

15. Sandler, *Segregated Skies*, 89. Three more all-black squadrons were formed to expand into the first all-black fighter group. The 332nd Fighter Group had four squadrons instead of the normal three.

16. Enzo Angelucci, et al., *World War II Combat Aircraft* (Rome: Barnes & Noble, 2001) 276. The P-39 probably could have been competitive with the German fighters with less heavy armor and more horsepower.

17. Rose, *Lonely Eagles*, 68. Black pilots showed some firsthand aerial abilities they weren't supposed to have.

18. Francis, *Tuskegee Airmen*,123. An unbelievable but indisputable big first for black fighter pilots. That feat was not recorded by any other flying group during WWII. Despite the disbelief by Air Force hierarchy gun cameras gave proof of the claim.

19. Rose, *Lonely Eagles*, 69. The 99th finally joined the 332nd but there were unsettling questions about inexperience that are gradually answered. 99th members were not about to play a secondary role in the 332nd since its three squadrons had less combat experience.

20. Caesar, Interview by author, San Francisco, CA, October 2003.

21. Leon "Woody" Spears, Interview by author, Alameda, CA, October 2002.

22. Rose, *Lonely Eagles*, 156. The honor, medals, number of missions and destruction caused by 332nd showed without a doubt that this fighting group did not take a back seat to any other. Its number one claim which no other fighter group could claim was not having lost a single allied bomber to enemy fighters. A second was having sunk a German destroyer by machinegun fire alone.

**Chapter 10: Bomber Pilots**

1. Leslie A. Williams, Interview by author, Richmond, CA, 2005.

2. Gropman, *Air Force Integrates*, 109. Excerpt of Executive Order ending segregation in the military, signed by President Harry Truman. That order was signed but none of the services actually implemented it until some two years later.

3. Hardesty, *Black wings*, 73. Photos and story of Blacks beginning to break into commercial aviation.

4. Ebony, November, 1976, From Eastern Airlines reprint of Ebony article on James Plinton a former Tuskegee primary flight instructor who became the first black executive for a major airline.

5. Gubert, *Invisible Wings*, 182–183. Numerous references to blacks beginning to fly for commercial airline companies.

6. Ibid. 222.

7. Shirley Tyus, http://www.scafam-hist.org/currenthonoree_print.asp?month=71999. Accessed on October 1, 2006.

8. Theresa Claiborne, http://www.aetc.randolph.af.mil/pa/AETCNS/Sep2002/02-257.htm. Accessed on October 1, 2006.

9. Stayce Harris, http://www.afmc.wpafb.af.mil/HQ-AFMC/PA/news/archive/2003/Mar/0314-03.htm. Accessed on October 1, 2006.

10. Jeanine McIntosh, http://info.mgnetwork.com. Accessed on October 1, 2006.

11. Robert Brown, Interview by author, Richmond, CA, 2003.

12. Leslie A. Williams, Interview by author, Richmond, CA, 2005.

13. William B. Ellis, Interview by author, Richmond, CA, 2005.

14. Osur, *Blacks in the Army Air Forces*, 55. Army Regulation 210-10 stated that officer's clubs on all bases were open to all officers but that regulation was purposely ignored in the futile attempt to keep segregation in place.

15. Sandler, *Segregated Skies*, 122. CO of Selfridge Field closed the officer's club rather than admit black officers.

16. Gropman, *Air Force Integrates*,16. The 477th was sent to an inferior field to train in order to remove the men from so-called outside "agitator" influence and also to preclude their entering the officer's club.

17. Ibid. The 447th compiled an excellent flying record despite the obstacles created by adverse training conditions and the surreptitious attempts to close the unit down.

18. Osur, *Blacks in the Army Air Forces*,110. The 477th was put on a merry-go-round of base changes that played havoc with morale and scheduling of training.

19. Sandler, *Segregated Skies*,123. The white supervisors of the 477th were considered as being in a promotion mill while the black officers were pretty much held in grade with none having a rank above major.

20. Ibid. 124. Gen. Hunter typified the superior attitude held towards blacks in general with a degrading statement he made to one of the several black newspapers.

21. Ibid. Hunter drew a rigid line between the races in addressing an assembly of black officers in the form of a threat to keep them in "their place." But he failed to consider their sensitivity or their intelligence in opposing that threat.

22. Rose, *Lonely Eagles*, 126. The CO of Freeman Field designated two separate clubs for so-called trainees and for base personnel. This was more of the same attempt to keep black officers out of the club they wanted to be used exclusively by white officers.

23. Sandler, *Segregated Skies*, 126. The kettle began to boil over when the CO decided to arrest any and all black officers who attempted to frequent the club set aside for white officers. Unwittingly the CO and his superior Gen. Hunter made one bad move after another and of course those moves came back to bite them.

24. James C. Warren, *The Tuskegee Airmen Mutiny at Freeman Field* (Conyers Publishing, 1995) 7–9. Group arrests began when black officers began to resist the segregation orders by base CO Selway.

25. Ibid. 53–55. General Hunter and Colonel Selway collaborated in trying to find a specific way to exclude black officers from the club they wanted for white officers. They created Base Regulation 85-2 which was supposed to work. Instead that regulation marked the beginning of the end of segregation in the military. The regulation was poorly contrived and contrary to Army Regulation 210-10.

26. Gropman, *Air Force Integrates*, 22–23. A ruling by the Air Judge Advocate on the arrest of the more than 100 black officers severely blunted the plans of General Hunter and Colonel Selway to maintain segregation.

27. Sandler, *Segregated Skies*, 127. Air Judge's office in support of Hunter and Selway tried to devise a safe and sustainable position in keeping the clubs separate, but AR 210-10 precluded any attempt to go around its meaning and intent.

28. Warren, *The Tuskegee Airmen Mutiny*, 94. While under arrest and bearing up under the humility of seeing German and Italian prisoners of war with more freedom than they, the black officers used their time to formulate future plans of unified action. They also leaked to the black press what was happening on their side of the fence.

29. Osur, *Blacks in the Army Air Forces*, 118. The War Department bypassed Gen. Hunter in making public announcements about the mutiny which obviously undermined his authority and severely damaged his self esteem.

30. Ibid. 120. The Air Force tried hard to support its stand of racial separation based on national practices but the Assistant Sec. of War, who was also chair of the McCloy Committee, patently disagreed in a letter to the Secretary of War.

31. Osur, *Blacks in the Army Air Forces*, 118. The Air Force Chief of Staff fortuitously formulated a solution to stop the ticking bomb of having 100 officers arrested for disobeying a direct order to sign the highly questionable base regulation at Freeman.

32. Warren, *The Tuskegee Airmen Mutiny*, 207–211. The Air Force agreed to remove the reprimands from the records of the arrested men some 50 years later and this came after months of extensive research by Warren.

33. Gropman, *Air Force Integrates*, 18. The early mistreatment of black officers was not forgotten or ignored but was carried forward leading to the acts of retribution by the insulted men.

34. Posts, Camps, and Stations Administration, Army Regulation AR 210-10, paragraph 19.

35. Gropman, *Air Force Integrates*, 18–19. Air Force Headquarters in Washington refused to soften its reprimand of Col. Boyd or let Gen. Hunter take the brunt of the castigation. A reprimand becomes part of an officer's record and essentially puts a massive wall up for further promotions.

36. Ibid. 20. Blacks were summarily blocked from advancement and none was allowed a superior position to a white counterpart.

37. Ibid. 28. The McCloy Committee came down hard on Col. Selway for his actions but stopped just short of a reprimand. Selway acted under the orders and encouragement of Gen. Hunter.

38. Sandler, *Segregated Skies*,130. Apparently Gen. Hunter never fully recovered from his defeats relative to segregated bases under his command that led to the so-called mutiny of Freeman Field.

39. Hardesty, *Black Wings*, 76–77. Lists other leading blacks in the U.S. space programs.

40. Mae C. Jemison, http://www.nwhp.org/tlp/biographies/jemison. Accessed on October 1, 2006.

41. Neal V. Loving, *Loving's Love* (Smithsonian Institution, 1994) The autobiographical story of the unstoppable drive urge of a man to fly after losing both legs in an air accident.

42. Hardesty, *Black Wings*, 71–72. Highlights two of an unknown number of blacks who designed, built, and flew their creations; includes the successes of Loving. See note 41.

# Bibliography

Ambler, Edward C. *History of Tuskegee Army Air Field, Tuskegee, Alabama: From Conception to 6 December 1941.* Air Force Historical Research Agency, Maxwell Air Force Base, Alabama, October 10, 1943.

Angelucci, Enzo and Matricardi Paolo. *World War II Combat Aircraft.* New York: Barnes and Noble, 2001.

Army War College. *The Use of Negro Manpower in War.* Memorandum for the Chief of Staff: Office of the Commandant, Washington DC, October 30, 1925.

Barbour, George E. *Early Black Flyers of Western Pennsylvania.* Western Pennsylvania Historical Magazine, April 1986, Vol. 69.

Burke, James W. *The Black Eagle.* The Retired Officer. May 1984.

Claiborne, Theresa. http://www.aetc.randolph.af.mil/pa. Accessed January 2006.

Ebony, *Airline Pioneer.* November 1976.

Francis, Charles F. *The Tuskegee Airmen: The Men Who Changed a Nation.* Boston: Branden, 1993.

Gropman, Alan L. *The Air Force Integrates, 1945–1964.* Washington, DC: Office of Air Force History, 1985.

Gubert, Betty Kaplan. *Invisible Wings.* Westport, CT: Greenwood, 1994.

Hardesty, Von and Dominick Pisano. *Black Wings: The American Black in Aviation.* Washington, DC: Smithsonian Institution Press, 1983.

Harris, Stayce. http://www.afmc.wpafb.af.mil. Accessed January 2006.

Hastie, William H. *On Clipped Wings: The Story of Jim Crow in the Army Air Corps.* Washington, DC: Crisis, 1943.

Jakeman, Robert J. *The Divided Skies: Establishing Segregated Flight Training at Tuskegee, Alabama, 1932–1942.* Tuscaloosa, AL: University of Alabama Press, 1992.

Jemison, Mae C. http://www.nwhp.org/tlp/biographies/jemison. Accessed January 2006.

Jones, James H. *Bad Blood: The Tuskegee Syphilis Experiment.* New York: Free Press, 1993.

Kitchens, John W. *They Also Flew: Pioneer Black Army Aviators.* U.S. Army Aviation Digest. September/October 1994.

Klineberg, Otto. *Characteristics of the American Negro.* New York: Harper and Brothers, 1944.

Longyard, William H. *Who's Who in Aviation History.* Novato, CA: Presidio Press, 1994.

Loving, Neal V. *Loving's Love.* Washington, DC: Smithsonian Institution, 1994.

McIntosh, Jeanine. http://ap.tbo.com/ap/florida. Accessed February 2006.

Murray, Florence. *The Negro Handbook.* New York: Current Reference Publications, 1944.

Myrdal, Gunnar. *An American Dilemma:The Negro in a White Nation.* New York: McGraw-Hill, 1964.

"Negro Youth Proficient in Groundwork," *Chattanooga News-Free Press,* April 21, 1940, Sunday edition.

Osur, Alan M. *Blacks in the Army Air Forces During World War II.* Washington, DC: Office of Air Force History, 1975.

Parrish, Noel F. *The Segregation of Negroes in the Army Air Forces.* Dissertation for Air Command and Staff school. Maxwell Air Force Base, Alabama, 1947.

Petersen, Frank E. http://www.au.af.mil/au/goe/eaglebios. Accessed January 2006.

Price, David A. *Love and Hate in Jamestown.* New York: Alfred A. Knopf, 2003.

Rich, Doris L. *Queen Bess: Daredevil Aviator.* Washington, DC: Smithsonian Institution Press, 1993.

Rose, Robert A. *Lonely Eagle: The Story of America's Black Air Force in World War II.* Los Angeles, 1988.

Sandler, Stanley. *Segregated Skies: All-Black Combat Squadrons of WW II.* Washington, DC: Smithsonian Institution Press, 1992.

Scott, William R. *Days of the Brown Condor.* Pan-African Journal, August 1988.

Tyus, Shirley. http://www.scafam-hist.org. Accessed January 2006.

Warren, James C. *The Tuskegee Airmen Mutiny at Freeman Field.* Vacaville, CA: Conyers Publishing, 2001.

Washington, George L. *The History of Military and Civilian Pilot Training of Negroes at Tuskegee Alabama 1939–45.* Washington, DC: n.d.

Winters, Nancy. *Man Flies: Master of the Balloon; The Story of Alberto Santos-Dumont.* New Jersey: Ecco Press, 1997.

Wright, Esmond, Geoffrey Barraclough, G. R. Elton, William McNeill, et al. *History of the World: The Last Five Hundred Years.* UK: Bonanza, 1984.

Yerkes, R. M. *Psychological Examining in the US Army.* Washington, DC: National Academy of Science, 1921.

# Index

**About the Author**

SAMUEL L. BROADNAX enlisted in the Army Air Corps at age 17 and graduated from Tuskegee Army Air Base with Class-45A in March 1945 as a fighter pilot, after which he was assigned to the 332nd Replacement Training Unit. He attended Yuba college, Howard University, and UC Berkeley, and has worked as a newscaster and journalist.